Modern English Series

ONE-ACT PLAYS OF TO-DAY

SECOND SERIES

SELECTED BY

J. W. MARRIOTT

EDITOR OF "ONE-ACT PLAYS OF TO-DAY" FIRST THIRD
AND FOURTH SERIES "SHORT STORIES OF TO-DAY" ETC.
AUTHOR OF "MATRICULATION ENGLISH"
"A YEAR'S WORK IN ENGLISH" "EXERCISES IN
THINKING AND EXPRESSING" ETC.

GEORGE G. Harrap & CO. LTD.
LONDON   BOMBAY   SYDNEY

Uniform with this Volume

ONE-ACT PLAYS OF TO-DAY
FIRST SERIES

THE BOY COMES HOME, *A. A. Milne.* FOL-
LOWERS, *Harold Brighouse.* THE STEPMOTHER,
Arnold Bennett. THE MAKER OF DREAMS, *Oliphant
Down.* THE LITTLE MAN, *John Galsworthy.* A
NIGHT AT AN INN, *Lord Dunsany.* CAMPBELL OF
KILMHOR, *J. A. Ferguson.* THE GRAND CHAM'S
DIAMOND, *Allan Monkhouse.* THREAD O' SCARLET,
J. J. Bell. BECKY SHARP, *Olive Conway.* X=0:
A NIGHT OF THE TROJAN WAR, *John Drinkwater.*

ONE-ACT PLAYS OF TO-DAY
THIRD SERIES

THE DUMB AND THE BLIND, *Harold Chapin.*
HOW THE WEATHER IS MADE, *Harold Brighouse.*
THE GOLDEN DOOM, *Lord Dunsany.* RORY
AFORESAID, *John Brandane.* THE MASTER OF
THE HOUSE, *Stanley Houghton.* FRIENDS, *Herbert
Farjeon.* MIMI, *Olive Conway.* THE BISHOP'S
CANDLESTICKS, *Norman McKinnel.* BETWEEN
THE SOUP AND THE SAVOURY, *Gertrude Jennings.*
MASTER WAYFARER, *J. E. Harold Terry.* THE
POT OF BROTH, *W. B. Yeats.* A KING'S HARD
BARGAIN, *Lt.-Col. W. P. Drury.*

ONE-ACT PLAYS OF TO-DAY
FOURTH SERIES

THE PRINCE WHO WAS A PIPER, *Harold Brig-
house.* SQUARE PEGS, *Clifford Bax.* THE MAN IN
THE BOWLER HAT, *A. A. Milne.* THE BETRAYAL,
Padraic Colum. THE FLIGHT OF THE QUEEN, *Lord
Dunsany.* ST SIMEON STYLITES, *F. Sladen-Smith.*
THE PATCHWORK QUILT, *Rachel Lyman Field.*
FIVE BIRDS IN A CAGE, *Gertrude Jennings.* PADDLY
POOLS, *Miles Malleson.* THE POACHER, *J. O.
Francis.* THE CONSTANT LOVER, *St John Hankin.*

First published September 1925
by GEORGE G. HARRAP & CO. LTD.
39-41 Parker Street, Kingsway, London, W.C.2
Reprinted: January 1926; February 1927; September 1927;
May 1928; May 1929; January 1930; January 1931

Printed in Great Britain by Turnbull & Spears, Edinburgh

FOREWORD

THE First Series of *One-Act Plays of To-day*—the forerunner of the present volume—was frankly an experiment. No such collection had ever appeared in England, and no one could predict the sort of reception it would be likely to have. It happened, however, that the book was welcomed from the day of its publication, and there can no longer be any doubt that the one-act play appeals to a much larger circle than any but the most sanguine had expected.

One of the most hopeful auguries of the present day is the fact that modern drama is being recognized and appreciated in so many of our schools and colleges. Until quite recently the teachers of drama began with Shakespeare—which is rather like beginning the study of landscape-painting by an analysis of the pictures of Turner, or like starting juvenile musicians on their career with an inquiry into the nature of a Beethoven symphony or a Wagner opera.

The newer method of teaching English by means of drama is to study good one-act plays written in contemporary idiom, for the two reasons that the one-act play is, in itself, an art-form as significant as the short story, and that, being brief, it exerts upon the reader's interest a hold which could, in the case of a five-act play, be only perfunctory. The one-act play is not necessarily less in quality than the five-act play, but it is less in quantity. Wherefore, it may be fairly argued, a taste for drama should be cultivated by means of one-act plays of first-rate quality rather than inhibited by premature attempts to force interest in plays of greater length.

The present volume consists of twelve plays by modern authors, nine of whom were not represented in the former collection, while the remaining three are revealed in new moods. An attempt has been made to give examples of as many different types of work as possible. There are, for instance, specimens of Irish comedy and tragedy, Lancashire comedy, ironical plays, war plays, studies in fantasy and horror, a costume play, and a Nativity play. The only omission is the pure farce, but farce by its very nature is inevitably less readable than ' actable.'

On glancing through the dozen plays that make up the volume, one cannot help observing how frequently the dramatist finds inspiration among the middle and lower classes. Drama is a democratic art, dealing as it does with flesh and blood, and the emotions which are common to all humanity irrespective of social elevation. Like poetry and music, it does not teach or prove anything. As J. M. Synge so unanswerably put it on one occasion : "The drama is made serious—in the French sense of the word—not by the degree in which it is taken up with problems that are serious in themselves, but by the degree in which it gives the nourishment, not very easy to define, on which our imaginations live."

J. W. M.

CONTENTS

ACKNOWLEDGMENTS

THE compiler desires to express his thanks to the following authors and publishers for the permission given to print the plays in this volume :

The representatives of the late J. M. Synge and Messrs George Allen and Unwin, Ltd., for "Riders to the Sea," from *Plays of J. M. Synge* ; Mr Harold Brighouse for " Lonesome-like " ; Lady Gregory and Messrs G. P. Putnam's Sons, for " The Rising of the Moon," from *Seven Short Plays* ; Miss Olive Conway for " The King's Waistcoat " ; Mr Allan Monkhouse and Messrs Constable and Co., Ltd., for " Night Watches," from *War Plays* ; and the authors or their representatives and Messrs Samuel French, Ltd., for " Waterloo," " It's the Poor that 'Elps the Poor," " A Marriage has been Arranged," " The Dear Departed," " 'Op-o'-me-Thumb," " The Monkey's Paw," and " The Child in Flanders."

RIDERS TO THE SEA

BY J. M. SYNGE

CHARACTERS

MAURYA, *an old woman*
BARTLEY, *her son*
CATHLEEN, *her daughter*
NORA, *a younger daughter*
MEN AND WOMEN

This play was first performed in the Molesworth Hall, Dublin, on February 25, 1904, with the following cast:

Maurya	HONOR LAVELLE
Bartley	W. G. FAY
Cathleen	SARA ALLGOOD
Nora	EMMA VERNON

THE late J. M. Synge was born in Ireland in 1871. His plays are masterly both in conception and technique, and " Riders to the Sea " has been described as the greatest one-act play of modern times.

It is on record that Synge wandered about Europe with a violin, and that the credit of discovering his genius must be given to Senator W. B. Yeats, the well-known Irish poet, who wrote of him : " He loves all that has edge, all that is salt in the mouth, all that is rough to the hand, all that heightens the emotions by contrast, all that stings into life the sense of tragedy. . . . The food of the spiritual-minded is sweet, an Indian scripture says, but passionate minds love bitter food."

Synge wrote in a language which had a music of its own, even before his genius took hold of it. He has proved to the world that the poetry of drama is not necessarily written in verse.

RIDERS TO THE SEA [1]

SCENE : *An island off the west of Ireland.*

*Cottage kitchen, with nets, oilskins, spinning-wheel, some new
boards standing by the wall, etc.* CATHLEEN, *a girl of
about twenty, finishes kneading cake, and puts it down in
the pot-oven by the fire ; then wipes her hands, and begins
to spin at the wheel.* NORA, *a young girl, puts her head
in at the door.*

NORA [*in a low voice*]. Where is she ?

CATHLEEN. She's lying down, God help her, and maybe
sleeping, if she's able.

[NORA *comes in softly and takes a bundle from under
her shawl.*

CATHLEEN [*spinning the wheel rapidly*]. What is it you
have ?

NORA. The young priest is after bringing them. It's a
shirt and a plain stocking were got off a drowned man in
Donegal.

[CATHLEEN *stops her wheel with a sudden movement,
and leans out to listen.*

We're to find out if it's Michael's they are, some time herself
will be down looking by the sea.

CATHLEEN. How would they be Michael's, Nora ? How
would he go the length of that way to the far north ?

---

[1] Applications regarding amateur performances of this play should
be addressed to Messrs Samuel French, Ltd., 26 Southampton Street,
Strand, London, W.C.2, or 25 West 45th Street, New York.

NORA. The young priest says he's known the like of it. "If it's Michael's they are," says he, "you can tell herself he's got a clean burial, by the grace of God; and if they're not his, let no one say a word about them, for she'll be getting her death," says he, "with crying and lamenting."

[*The door which* NORA *half closed is blown open by a gust of wind.*

CATHLEEN [*looking out anxiously*]. Did you ask him would he stop Bartley going this day with the horses to the Galway fair?

NORA. "I won't stop him," says he; "but let you not be afraid. Herself does be saying prayers half through the night, and the Almighty God won't leave her destitute," says he, "with no son living."

CATHLEEN. Is the sea bad by the white rocks, Nora?

NORA. Middling bad, God help us. There's a great roaring in the west, and it's worse it'll be getting when the tide's turned to the wind. [*She goes over to the table with the bundle.*] Shall I open it now?

CATHLEEN. Maybe she'd wake up on us, and come in before we'd done [*coming to the table*]. It's a long time we'll be, and the two of us crying.

NORA [*goes to the inner door and listens*]. She's moving about on the bed. She'll be coming in a minute.

CATHLEEN. Give me the ladder, and I'll put them up in the turf-loft, the way she won't know of them at all, and maybe when the tide turns she'll be going down to see would he be floating from the east.

[*They put the ladder against the gable of the chimney;* CATHLEEN *goes up a few steps and hides the bundle in the turf-loft.* MAURYA *comes from the inner room.*

MAURYA [*looking up at* CATHLEEN *and speaking querulously*]. Isn't it turf enough you have for this day and evening?

14

CATHLEEN. There's a cake baking at the fire for a short space [*throwing down the turf*], and Bartley will want it when the tide turns if he goes to Connemara.

[NORA *picks up the turf and puts it round the pot-oven.*

MAURYA [*sitting down on a stool at the fire*]. He won't go this day with the wind rising from the south and west. He won't go this day, for the young priest will stop him surely.

NORA. He'll not stop him, Mother; and I heard Eamon Simon and Stephen Pheety and Colum Shawn saying he would go.

MAURYA. Where is he itself?

NORA. He went down to see would there be another boat sailing in the week, and I'm thinking it won't be long till he's here now, for the tide's turning at the green head, and the hooker's tacking from the east.

CATHLEEN. I hear some one passing the big stones.

NORA [*looking out*]. He's coming now, and he in a hurry.

BARTLEY [*comes in and looks round the room. Speaking sadly and quietly*]. Where is the bit of new rope, Cathleen, was bought in Connemara?

CATHLEEN [*coming down*]. Give it to him, Nora; it's on a nail by the white boards. I hung it up this morning, for the pig with the black feet was eating it.

NORA [*giving him a rope*]. Is that it, Bartley?

MAURYA. You'd do right to leave that rope, Bartley, hanging by the boards. [BARTLEY *takes the rope.*] It will be wanting in this place, I'm telling you, if Michael is washed up to-morrow morning, or the next morning, or any morning in the week; for it's a deep grave we'll make him, by the grace of God.

BARTLEY [*beginning to work with the rope*]. I've no halter the way I can ride down on the mare, and I must go now quickly. This is the one boat going for two weeks or beyond it, and the fair will be a good fair for horses, I heard them saying below.

MAURYA. It's a hard thing they'll be saying below if the body is washed up and there's no man in it to make the coffin, and I after giving a big price for the finest white boards you'd find in Connemara. [*She looks round at the boards.*]

BARTLEY. How would it be washed up, and we after looking each day for nine days, and a strong wind blowing a while back from the west and south ?

MAURYA. If it isn't found itself, that wind is raising the sea, and there was a star up against the moon, and it rising in the night. If it was a hundred horses, or a thousand horses, you had itself, what is the price of a thousand horses against a son where there is one son only ?

BARTLEY [*working at the halter, to* CATHLEEN]. Let you go down each day, and see the sheep aren't jumping in on the rye, and if the jobber comes you can sell the pig with the black feet if there is a good price going.

MAURYA. How would the like of her get a good price for a pig ?

BARTLEY [*to* CATHLEEN]. If the west wind holds with the last bit of the moon let you and Nora get up weed enough for another cock for the kelp. It's hard set we'll be from this day with no one in it but one man to work.

MAURYA. It's hard set we'll be surely the day you're drowned with the rest. What way will I live and the girls with me, and I an old woman looking for the grave ?

[BARTLEY *lays down the halter, takes off his old coat, and puts on a newer one of the same flannel.*

BARTLEY [*to* NORA]. Is she coming to the pier ?

NORA [*looking out*]. She's passing the green head and letting fall her sails.

BARTLEY [*getting his purse and tobacco*]. I'll have half an hour to go down, and you'll see me coming again in two

a better thing to raise your voice and tell what you seen, than to be making lamentation for a thing that's done? Did you see Bartley, I'm saying to you?

MAURYA [*with a weak voice*]. My heart's broken from this day.

CATHLEEN [*as before*]. Did you see Bartley?

MAURYA. I seen the fearfullest thing.

CATHLEEN [*leaves her wheel and looks out*]. God forgive you; he's riding the mare now over the green head, and the grey pony behind him.

MAURYA [*starts, so that her shawl falls back from her head and shows her white tossed hair. With a frightened voice*]. The grey pony behind him . . .

CATHLEEN [*coming to the fire*]. What is it ails you at all?

MAURYA [*speaking very slowly*]. I've seen the fearfullest thing any person has seen since the day Bride Dara seen the dead man with the child in his arms.

CATHLEEN *and* NORA. Uah.

[*They crouch down in front of the old woman at the fire.*

NORA. Tell us what it is you seen.

MAURYA. I went down to the spring well, and I stood there saying a prayer to myself. Then Bartley came along, and he riding on the red mare with the grey pony behind him [*she puts up her hands as if to hide something from her eyes*]. The Son of God spare us, Nora!

CATHLEEN. What is it you seen.

MAURYA. I seen Michael himself.

CATHLEEN [*speaking softly*]. You did not, Mother. It wasn't Michael you seen, for his body is after being found in the far north, and he's got a clean burial, by the grace of God.

MAURYA [*a little defiantly*]. I'm after seeing him this day, and he riding and galloping. Bartley came first on the red mare, and I tried to say " God speed you," but something choked the words in my throat. He went by quickly; and "The blessing of God on you," says he, and I could say nothing. I looked up then, and I crying, at the grey pony, and there was Michael upon it—with fine clothes on him, and new shoes on his feet.

CATHLEEN [*begins to keen*]. It's destroyed we are from this day. It's destroyed, surely.

NORA. Didn't the young priest say the Almighty God won't leave her destitute with no son living?

MAURYA [*in a low voice, but clearly*]. It's little the like of him knows of the sea. . . . Bartley will be lost now, and let you call in Eamon and make me a good coffin out of the white boards, for I won't live after them. I've had a husband, and a husband's father, and six sons in this house—six fine men, though it was a hard birth I had with every one of them and they coming to the world—and some of them were found and some of them were not found, but they're gone now the lot of them. . . . There were Stephen and Shawn were lost in the great wind, and found after in the Bay of Gregory of the Golden Mouth, and carried up the two of them on one plank, and in by that door.

[*She pauses for a moment, the girls start as if they heard something through the door that is half open behind them.*

NORA [*in a whisper*]. Did you hear that, Cathleen? Did you hear a noise in the north-east?

CATHLEEN [*in a whisper*]. There's some one after crying out by the seashore.

MAURYA [*continues without hearing anything*]. There was Sheamus and his father, and his own father again, were lost in a dark night, and not a stick or sign was seen of them when the sun went up. There was Patch after was drowned out of a curragh that was turned over. I was sitting here with

Bartley, and he a baby lying on my two knees, and I seen two women, and three women, and four women coming in, and they crossing themselves and not saying a word. I looked out then, and there were men coming after them, and they holding a thing in the half of a red sail, and water dripping out of it—it was a dry day, Nora—and leaving a track to the door.

> [*She pauses again with her hand stretched out towards the door. It opens softly and old women begin to come in, crossing themselves on the threshold, and kneeling down in front of the stage with red petticoats over their heads.*

MAURYA [*half in a dream, to* CATHLEEN]. Is it Patch, or Michael, or what is it at all?

CATHLEEN. Michael is after being found in the far north, and when he is found there how could he be here in this place?

MAURYA. There does be a power of young men floating round in the sea, and what way would they know if it was Michael they had, or another man like him, for when a man is nine days in the sea, and the wind blowing, it's hard set his own mother would be to say what man was in it.

CATHLEEN. It's Michael, God spare him, for they're after sending us a bit of his clothes from the far north.

> [*She reaches out and hands* MAURYA *the clothes that belonged to* MICHAEL. MAURYA *stands up slowly and takes them in her hands.* NORA *looks out.*

NORA. They're carrying a thing among them, and there's water dripping out of it and leaving a track by the big stones.

CATHLEEN [*in a whisper to the women who have come in*]. Is it Bartley it is?

ONE OF THE WOMEN. It is, surely, God rest his soul.

> [*Two younger women come in and pull out the table. Then men carry in the body of* BARTLEY, *laid on a*

*plank, with a bit of a sail over it, and lay it on the
table.*

CATHLEEN [*to the women as they are doing so*]. What way was
he drowned ?

ONE OF THE WOMEN. The grey pony knocked him over into
the sea, and he was washed out where there is a great surf on
the white rocks.

[MAURYA *has gone over and knelt down at the head of
the table. The women are keening softly and swaying themselves with a slow movement.* CATHLEEN
and NORA *kneel at the other end of the table. The
men kneel near the door.*

MAURYA [*raising her head and speaking as if she did not see
the people around her*]. They're all gone now, and there isn't
anything more the sea can do to me. . . . I'll have no call
now to be up crying and praying when the wind breaks from
the south, and you can hear the surf is in the east, and the surf
is in the west, making a great stir with the two noises, and
they hitting one on the other. I'll have no call now to
be going down and getting Holy Water in the dark nights
after Samhain, and I won't care what way the sea is when
the other women will be keening. [*To* NORA] Give me the
Holy Water, Nora ; there's a small sup still on the dresser.
[NORA *gives it to her.*]

MAURYA [*drops* MICHAEL's *clothes across* BARTLEY's *feet, and
sprinkles the Holy Water over him*]. It isn't that I haven't
prayed for you, Bartley, to the Almighty God. It isn't that
I haven't said prayers in the dark night till you wouldn't know
what I'd be saying; but it's a great rest I'll have now, and it's
time, surely. It's a great rest I'll have now, and great sleeping
in the long nights after Samhain, if it's only a bit of wet flour
we do have to eat, and maybe a fish that would be stinking.

[*She kneels down again, crossing herself, and saying
prayers under her breath.*

CATHLEEN [*to an old man*]. Maybe yourself and Eamon would make a coffin when the sun rises. We have fine white boards herself bought, God help her, thinking Michael would be found, and I have a new cake you can eat while you'll be working.

THE OLD MAN [*looking at the boards*]. Are there nails with them ?

CATHLEEN. There are not, Colum ; we didn't think of the nails.

ANOTHER MAN. It's a great wonder she wouldn't think of the nails, and all the coffins she's seen made already.

CATHLEEN. It's getting old she is, and broken.

[MAURYA *stands up again very slowly, and spreads out the pieces of* MICHAEL's *clothes beside the body, sprinkling them with the last of the Holy Water.*

NORA [*in a whisper to* CATHLEEN]. She's quiet now and easy; but the day Michael was drowned you could hear her crying out from this to the spring well. It's fonder she was of Michael, and would anyone have thought that ?

CATHLEEN [*slowly and clearly*]. An old woman will be soon tired with anything she will do, and isn't it nine days herself is after crying and keening, and making great sorrow in the house ?

MAURYA [*puts the empty cup mouth downwards on the table, and lays her hands together on* BARTLEY's *feet*]. They're all together this time, and the end is come. May the Almighty God have mercy on Bartley's soul, and on Michael's soul, and on the souls of Sheamus and Patch, and Stephen and Shawn [*bending her head*] ; and may He have mercy on my soul, Nora, and on the soul of every one is left living in the world.

[*She pauses, and the keen rises a little more loudly from the women, then sinks away.*

MAURYA [*continuing*]. Michael has a clean burial in the far north, by the grace of the Almighty God. Bartley will have a fine coffin out of the white boards, and a deep grave surely. What more can we want than that ? No man at all can be living for ever, and we must be satisfied.

[She kneels down again, and the curtain falls slowly.

WATERLOO

A DRAMA IN ONE ACT

By Sir Arthur Conan Doyle

CHARACTERS

Corporal Gregory Brewster, *aged ninety-six*
Sergeant Archie McDonald, *R.A.*
Colonel James Midwinter, *Royal Scots Guards*
Norah Brewster, *the Corporal's grandniece*

This play was first produced at the Prince's Theatre, Bristol, on September 21, 1894, with the following cast, and at the Lyceum Theatre, London, on May 4, 1895:

Corporal Gregory Brewster . . .	Henry Irving
Sergeant Archie McDonald, R.A. .	Fuller Mellish
Colonel James Midwinter . . .	W. Haviland
Norah Brewster	Annie Hughes

SIR ARTHUR CONAN DOYLE is known to everybody for his excellent novels and short stories. His *The White Company*, *Rodney Stone*, and *Micah Clarke* make delightful reading, and his Sherlock Holmes stories are immensely popular. Several of the latter have been adapted for the stage by other hands, and one (*The Speckled Band*) by himself. Most of Sir Arthur Conan Doyle's stories, being full of action and healthy excitement, lend themselves to dramatization, and already the Brigadier Gerard stories and others have been adapted in this way.

Waterloo is endeared to the memory of playgoers by its association with the late Sir Henry Irving. It is a characteristic work, having humour and pathos and a spirit of courage which stirs the blood like a bugle-call.

WATERLOO[1]

SCENE : *A front room in a small house in Woolwich. Cooking range at fire. Above the fire a rude painting of an impossible military man in a red coat with a bearskin. On one side a cutting from a newspaper framed. On the other a medal, also within a frame. Bright fire-irons, centre table, Bible on small table in window, wooden armchair with cushion, rack holding plates, etc.*

June 1881

Curtain rising discovers the empty room ; door opens, and enter NORAH BREWSTER, *a country girl, with a bundle of her effects. She looks timidly about her, and then closes the door. Basket on bandbox. During dialogue takes hat and cloak off and puts them on sideboard L., takes apron out of basket, chair R. of door, and puts it on.*

NORAH. And this is Uncle Gregory's [*crosses to fireplace*]. Why, there's his portrait just above the fireplace, the very same as we have it at home—and there is his medal by his portrait. Oh, how strange that I should have a house all to myself. Why, it's next door to being married. I suppose Uncle isn't up yet, they said that he was never up before ten. Well, thank goodness that housekeeper has lit the fire before she went away. She seems to have been a nice sort of a party, she does. Poor old Uncle ! he does seem to have been

[1] Applications regarding amateur performances of this play should be addressed to Messrs Samuel French, Ltd., 26 Southampton Street, Strand, London, W.C.2, or 25 West 45th Street, New York.

neglected. Never mind! I've come to look after him now. Let me see if everything is ready for Uncle when he does come. Won't he be surprised to see me! Of course he would have had Mother's letter to say I was coming, but he wouldn't think I'd be here so early. [*At table R. C.*] I wonder what makes the milk look so blue. [*At drawer at back R. C.*] Oh my! what nasty butter. I'm so glad I brought some other butter with me. [*Takes pat of butter off plate, puts it in basket. Takes pat out of basket and puts it on plate.*] Now for the bacon. Oh, what a cruel piece! Why, our Essex pigs would blush to own bacon like that! [*Puts rasher in frying-pan and puts pan on hob.*] Now I'll make the tea if the kettle boils. Kettle doesn't boil. Never mind, I'll warm the pot. [*Puts water out of kettle on fire in pot and pot on table.*] Dear old Uncle [*looking at portrait*], don't he look grand! They must have been awful brave folk to dare to fight against him. I do hope I'll be able to make him happy. [*Knock down in flat, L. C.*] Oh, dear! A knock! I wonder who it is! [*Knock again.*] I suppose I must see who it is. [*Up to door in flat R. C. opens it.*]

Enter SERGEANT MCDONALD

SERGEANT [*saluting*]. Beg your pardon, miss, but does Corporal Gregory Brewster live here?

NORAH [*timidly*]. Yes, sir.

SERGEANT. The same who was in the Scots Guards?

NORAH. Yes, sir.

SERGEANT. And fought in the battle of Waterloo?

NORAH. Yes, the same, sir.

SERGEANT. Could I have a word with him, miss?

NORAH. He's not down yet.

SERGEANT. Ah, then, maybe I'd best look in on my way back. I'm going down to the butts, and will pass again in an hour or two.

NORAH. Very well, sir. [*Going out.*] Who shall I say came for him? [SERGEANT *returns and places carbine L. of sideboard L.*]

SERGEANT. McDonald's my name—Sergeant McDonald of the Artillery. But you'll excuse my mentioning it, miss: there was some talk down at the Gunners' barracks that the old gentleman was not looked after quite as well as he might be. But I can see now that it's only foolish talk, for what more could he want than this?

NORAH. Oh, I've only just come. We heard that his housekeeper was not very good to him, and that was why my father wished me to go and do what I could.

SERGEANT. Ah! he'll find the difference now.

NORAH [*bustling about putting tea in pot*]. Two for Uncle and one for the pot. We were all very proud of Uncle Gregory down Leyton way. [*Takes teapot to fire and fills it from kettle.*]

SERGEANT. Aye, he's been a fine man in his day. There's not many living now who can say that they fought against Napoleon Boneypart.

NORAH. Ah, see, there's his medal hung up by his portrait.

SERGEANT [*after her*]. But what's that beside the medal?

NORAH [*standing on tiptoe, and craning her neck*]. Oh, it is a piece of print, and all about Uncle. [*Brings frame.*]

SERGEANT. Aye, it's a slip of an old paper. There's the date, August 1815, writ in yellow ink on the corner.

NORAH [*takes down medal*]. It's such small print.

SERGEANT [*front of table*]. I'll read it to you.

NORAH. Thank ye, sir!

SERGEANT [*clears his throat impressively*]. "A heroic deed." That's what's on the top. "On Tuesday an interesting ceremony was performed at the barracks of the third regiment of Guards, when in the presence of the Prince

Regent, a special medal was presented to Corporal **Gregory Brewster**——"

NORAH [*R. of* SERGEANT]. That's him! That's Uncle!

SERGEANT. "To Corporal Gregory Brewster of Captain Haldane's flank company, in recog—recognition of his valour in the recent great battle. It appears that on the ever memorable 18th of June, four companies of the third Guards and of the Coldstreams, held the important farmhouse of Hugymount at the right of the British position. At a critical period of the action these troops found themselves short of powder, and Corporal Brewster was dispatched to the rear to hasten up the reserve am—ammunition. The corporal returned with two tumbrils of the Nassau division, but he found that in his absence the how—howitzer fire of the French had ignited the hedge around the farm, and that the passage of the carts filled with powder had become almost an impossibility. The first tumbril exploded, blowing the driver to pieces, and his comrade, daunted by the sight, turned his horses; but Corporal Brewster, springing into his seat, hurled the man down, and urging the cart through the flames, succeeded in rejoining his comrades. Long may the heroic Brewster——"

NORAH. Think of that, the heroic Brewster!

SERGEANT. "Live to treasure the medal which he has so bravely won, and to look back with pride to the day when, in the presence of his comrades, he received this tribute to his valour from the hands of the first gentleman of the realm." [*Replaces the paper.*] Well, that is worth being proud of. [*Hands back frame, she puts it on mantel.*]

NORAH. And we are proud of it, too.

SERGEANT. Well, miss, I'm due at the butts, or I would [*taking carbine*] stay to see the old gentleman now. [*Up to door.*]

NORAH [*following*]. I don't think he can be long.

32

SERGEANT. Well, he'll have turned out before I pass this way again, good day, miss, and my respects to you, miss.

[*Exit* SERGEANT MCDONALD, *door in flat L.C.*

NORAH [*looking through door after him*]. Oh, isn't he a fine man! I never saw such a man as that down Leyton way. And how kind he was! Think of him reading all that to me about Uncle! [*Coming L.*] It was as much as to say that Uncle won that battle. Well, I think the tea is made [*over to fire*] now, and——

CORPORAL [*without entering*]. Mary, Mary—I wants my rations.

NORAH [*aside*]. Lord, 'a mercy!

[*Enter* CORPORAL GREGORY BREWSTER, *tottering in, gaunt, bent, and doddering, with white hair and wizened face. He taps his way across the room, while* NORAH, *with her hands clasped, stares aghast first at the man, and then at his picture on the wall.*

CORPORAL [*querulously*]. I wants my rations! The cold nips me without 'em. See to my hands. [*Holds out his gnarled knuckles.*]

NORAH [*gets round behind table*]. Don't you know me, Grand-uncle? I'm Norah Brewster, from down Essex way.

CORPORAL. Rum is warm, and schnapps is warm, and there's 'eat in soup, but gimme a dish of tea for choice. Eh? [*Peers at the girl.*] What did you say your name was, young woman? [*Sits R. of table.*]

NORAH [*L. of table*]. Norah Brewster.

CORPORAL. You can speak out, lass. Seems to me folks' voices ain't as strong as they was.

NORAH [*back of chair*]. I'm Norah Brewster, Uncle. I'm your [*takes up bacon*] grand-niece, come from Essex way to live with you. [*Takes bacon out of pan on fire, puts on plate.*]

33

CORPORAL [*chuckling*]. You're Norah, hey! Then you'll be brother Jarge's gal, likely? Lor, to think o' little Jarge havin' a gal!

NORAH [*putting bacon on table*]. Nay, Uncle. My father was the son of your brother George. [*Pouring out tea.*]

CORPORAL [*mumbles and chuckles, picking at his sleeves with his trembling hands*]. Lor, but little Jarge was a rare un! [*Draws up to the table while* NORAH *pours out the tea.*] Eh, by Jimini, there was no chousing Jarge! He's got a bull-pup o' mine that I lent him when I took the shillin'. Likely it's dead now. He didn't give it ye to bring, maybe?

NORAH [*R. of table, and glancing ever wonderingly at her companion*]. Why, Grandpa Jarge has been dead this twenty years.

CORPORAL [*mumbling*]. Eh, but it were a bootiful pup— bootiful! [*Drinks his tea with a loud supping.* NORAH *pours out second cup.*] I am cold for the lack o' my rations. Rum is good and schnapps, but I'd as lief have a dish o' tea as either.

NORAH. I've brought you some butter and some eggs in the basket. Mother said as I was to give you her respec's and love, and that she'd ha' sent a tin o' cream, but it might ha' turned on the way. [*R., sets chair L. of fireplace.*]

CORPORAL [*still eating voraciously*]. Eh, it's a middlin' goodish way. Likely the stage left yesterday.

NORAH. The what, Uncle?

CORPORAL. The coach that brought ye.

NORAH. Nay, I came by the mornin' train.

CORPORAL. Lor' now, think o' that. The railway train, heh? You ain't afeard o' them new-fangled things! By Jimini! to think of your comin' by railway like that. Why, it's more than twenty mile. [*Chuckling*] What's the world a-comin' to? [*Puffs out his chest and tries to square his shoulders.*] Eh, but I get a power o' good from my rations!

NORAH. Indeed, Uncle, you seem a deal stronger for them. [*Up to the table and begins to clear things away.*]

CORPORAL. Aye, the food is like coals to that fire. But I'm nigh burned out, lass, I'm nigh burned out.

NORAH [*clearing the table*]. You must ha' seen a deal o' life, Uncle. It must seem a long time to you.

CORPORAL. Not so very long, neither. I'm well over ninety, but it might ha' been yesterday that I took the bounty. And that battle, why, by Jimini, I've not got the smell of the burned powder out o' my nose yet. Have you read that? [*nodding to the cutting*].

NORAH. Yes, Uncle, and I'm sure that you must be very proud of it.

CORPORAL [*stands looking at it*]. Ah, it was a great day for me—a great day! The Regent he was there, and a fine body of a man too. [*Tries to stuff some tobacco into his pipe.*] He up to me and he says, "The Ridgement is proud of ye," says he. "And I'm proud o' the Ridgement," says I. "And a damned good answer, too," says he to Lord Hill, and they both bust out a-laughin'. [*Coughs and chuckles, and points up at the mantelpiece.*]

NORAH. What can I hand you, Uncle? [*Gets bottle and spoon from mantelpiece.*]

CORPORAL. A spoonful from that bottle by the brass candlestick, my girl! [*Drinks it.*] It's paregoric, [*music*] and rare stuff to cut the phlegm. [NORAH *looks out of the window.*] But what be you a peepin' out o' the window for? [NORAH *pushes window up, music louder.*]

NORAH [*excitedly*]. Oh, Uncle, here's a regiment o' soldiers comin' down the street.

CORPORAL [*rising and clawing his way towards the window*]. A ridgement! Heh! Where be my glasses? Lordy, I can hear the band as plain as plain. Bands don't seem to play as loud nowadays though as they used. [*Gets to the window.*]

Here they come, pioneers, drum-major, band! What be their number, lass? [*His eyes shine, and his feet and stick tap to the music.*]

NORAH. They don't seem to have no number, Uncle. They've something wrote on their shoulders. Oxfordshire, I think it be.

CORPORAL. Ah, yes. I heard as they had dropped the numbers, and given them new-fangled names. [*Shakes his head*]. That wouldn't ha' done for the Dook. The Dook would ha' had a word there. [*Band up to ff.*] There they go, by Jimini! They're young, but they hain't forgot how to march. Blessed if I can see the light bobs though! [*Band dim. to pp.*] Well, they've got the swing, aye, they have the swing [*gazes after them until the last files have disappeared*].

NORAH [*helping him*]. Come back to your chair, Uncle.

CORPORAL. Where be that bottle again. It cuts the phlegm. It's the toobes that's wrong with me. Joyce says so, and he is a clever man. I'm in his club. There's the card, paid up, under yon flatiron. [*Band stops. Suddenly slapping his thigh.*] Why, darn my skin, I knew as something was amiss.

NORAH. Where, Uncle?

CORPORAL. In them soldiers. I've got it now. They'd forgot their stocks. Not one of them had his stock on [*chuckles and croaks*]. It wouldn't ha' done for the Dook. No, by Jimini, the Dook would ha' had a word there. [*Door opens and* SERGEANT *appears beckoning comrade.*]

NORAH [*peeping towards the door*]. Why, Uncle, this is the soldier who came this morning—one of them with the blue coats and gold braid.

CORPORAL. Eh, and what do he want? Don't stand and stare, lass, but go to the door and ask him what he wants.

[*She approaches the door, which is half open.* SERGEANT

36

MCDONALD *of Artillery, his carbine in his hand, steps over the threshold and salutes.*

SERGEANT. Good day again to you, miss. Is the old gentleman to be seen now ?

NORAH. Yes, sir. That's him. I'm sure he'll be very glad to see you. Uncle, here is a gentleman who wants to speak with you.

SERGEANT. Proud to see you, sir—proud and glad, sir !

[*Steps forward, grounds his carbine, and salutes.* NORAH, *half frightened, half attracted, keeps her eyes on the visitor.*

CORPORAL [*blinking at the* SERGEANT]. Sit ye down, Sergeant, sit ye down ! [*Shakes his head.*] You are full young for the stripes. Lordy, it's easier to get three now, than one in my day. Gunners were old soldiers then, and the grey hairs came quicker than the three stripes.

[SERGEANT *puts carbine by window,* NORAH *takes off apron, folds it up, puts it in basket.*

SERGEANT. I am eight years' service, sir. McDonald is my name, Sergeant McDonald of H Battery, Southern Artillery Division. I have called as the spokesman of my mates to say that we are proud to have you in the town, sir.

[NORAH *finishes clearing table, table-cloth folded in drawer of dresser.*

CORPORAL [*chuckling and rubbing his hands*]. That was what the Regent said, " The Ridgement is proud of you," says he. " And I am proud of the Ridgement," says I. "A damned good answer, too," says he, and he and Lord Hill bust out a-laughin'.

SERGEANT. The non-commissioned mess would be proud and honoured to see you, sir. If you could step as far you will always find a pipe o' baccy and a glass of grog awaitin' you.

CORPORAL [*laughing until he coughs*]. Like to see me,

would they, the dogs ! Well, well, if this warm weather holds I'll drop in—it's likely that I'll drop in. My toobes is bad to-day, and I feel queer here [*slapping his chest*]. But you will see me one of these days at the barracks.

SERGEANT. Mind you ask for the non-com. mess.

CORPORAL. Eh ?

SERGEANT. The non-com. mess.

CORPORAL. Oh, lordy ! Got a mess of your own, heh, just the same as the officers. Too grand for a canteen now. It wouldn't have done for the Dook. The Dook would have had a word there.

SERGEANT [*respectfully*]. You was in the Guards, sir, wasn't you ?

CORPORAL. Yes, I am a Guardsman, I am. Served in the 3rd Guards, the same they call now the Scots Guards. Lordy, Sergeant, but they have all marched away, from Colonel Byng right down to the drummer boys, and here am I, a straggler—that's what I call myself, a straggler. But it ain't my fault neither, for I've never had my call, and I can't leave my post without it.

SERGEANT [*shaking his head*]. Ah, well, we all have to muster up there. Won't you try my baccy, sir ? [*Hands over pouch.*]

CORPORAL. Eh ?

SERGEANT. Try my baccy, sir ?

> [CORPORAL BREWSTER *tries to fill his clay pipe, but drops it. It breaks, and he bursts into tears with the long helpless sobs of a child.*

CORPORAL. I've broke my pipe ! my pipe !

NORAH [*running to him and soothing him*]. Don't, Uncle, oh, don't ! We can easy get another.

SERGEANT. Don't you fret yourself, sir, if you—you'll do me the honour to accept it. 'Ere's a wooden pipe with an amber mouth.

CORPORAL [*his smiles instantly bursting through his tears,* SERGEANT *gets carbine*]. Jimini! It's a fine pipe! See to my new pipe, gal! I lay that Jarge never had a pipe like this. Eh, and an amber mouth too! [*Mumbles with it in his mouth.*] You've got your firelock there, Sergeant.

SERGEANT. Yes, sir, I was on my way back from the butts when I looked in.

CORPORAL. Let me have the feel of it!

SERGEANT. Certainly. [*Gives carbine.*]

CORPORAL. Lordy, but it seems like old times to have one's hand on a musket. What's the manual, Sergeant? Eh? Cock your firelock! Present your firelock! Look to your priming! Heh, Sergeant! [*The breech on being pressed flies open.* NORAH *is now top of table looking on.*] Oh, Jimini! I've broke your musket in halves.

SERGEANT [*laughing*]. That's all right, sir! You pressed on the lever and opened the breech-piece. That's where we load 'em, you know.

CORPORAL. Load 'em at the wrong end! Well, well, to think of it! and no ramrod neither. I've heard tell of it, but I never believed it afore. Ah! it won't come up to Brown Bess. When there's work to be done you mark my words, and see if they don't come back to Brown Bess.

SERGEANT [*rising*]. But I've wearied you enough for one sitting. I'll look in again, and I'll bring a comrade or two with me, if I may, for there isn't one but would be proud to have speech with you. [*Salutes. Exit.*] My very best respects to you, miss.

NORAH. Oh, Uncle, isn't he noble and fine? [*Up to door, looks after him.*]

CORPORAL [*mumbling*]. Too young for the stripes, gal. A sergeant of Gunners should be a growed man. I don't know what we are comin' to in these days. [*Chuckling*] But he gave me a pipe, Norah! A fine pipe with an amber

39

mouth. I'll lay that brother Jarge never had a pipe like that.

NORAH [*aside nodding towards the door*]. To think that he will be like Uncle in sixty years, and that Uncle was once like him. [*Forward to window L.*] He seems a very kind young man, I think. He calls me " miss " and Uncle " sir," so polite and proper. I never saw as nice a man down Essex way.

CORPORAL. What are you moonin' about, gal! I want you to help me move my chair to the door, or maybe yon fancy chair will do. It's warm, and the air would hearten me if I can keep back the flies. They get owdacious in this weather and they plague me cruel.

NORAH. The flies, Uncle ?

[*He moves feebly across to where the sunshine comes in at the door, and he sits in it.* NORAH *helps him.*

CORPORAL. Eh, but it's fine ! It always makes me think of the glory to come. Was it to-day that parson was here ?

NORAH. No, Uncle. [*Kneels on his L.*]

CORPORAL. Then it was yesterday. I get the days kind o' mixed. He reads to me, the parson does.

NORAH. But I could do that, Uncle.

CORPORAL. You can read too, can you ? By Jimini, I never seed such a gal. You can travel by railroad and you can read. Whatever is the world comin' to ? It's the Bible he reads to me. [NORAH *runs, gets Bible, and kneels again.*]

NORAH [*opening the Bible*]. What part would you like to hear ?

CORPORAL. Eh ? [NORAH *repeats.*]

CORPORAL. Oh, them wars.

NORAH. The wars !

CORPORAL. Aye, keep to the wars ; " Give me the Old Testament, Parson," says I, " there's more taste to it," says I. Parson, he wants to get off to something else, but it's

Joshua or nothing with me. Them Israelites was good
soldiers, good growed soldiers, all of 'em.

NORAH. But, Uncle, it's all peace in the next world.

CORPORAL. No, it ain't, gal.

NORAH. Oh, yes, Uncle, surely.

CORPORAL [*irritably knocking his stick on the ground*]. I
tell ye it ain't, gal. I asked Parson.

NORAH. Well, what did he say?

CORPORAL. He said there was to be a last final fight.

NORAH. Fight?

CORPORAL. Why, he even gave it a name, he did. The
battle of Arm—Arm—the battle of Arm——

NORAH. Armageddon.

CORPORAL. Aye, that was the name. [*Pauses thoughtfully.*]
I 'spec's the 3rd Guards will be there. And the Dook—the
Dook'll have a word to say. [*Sinks back a little in his chair.*
NORAH *shuts window, puts Bible back.*]

NORAH. What is it, Uncle? You look tired.

CORPORAL [*faintly*]. Maybe I have had air enough. And
I ain't strong enough to fight agin the flies.

NORAH. Oh, but I will keep them off, Uncle.

CORPORAL. They get owdacious in this weather. I'll get
back to the corner. But you'll need to help me with the
chair. [*Knock.*] Chairs are made heavier than they used
to be.

[*Is in the act of rising when there comes a tap at the
door, and* COLONEL MIDWINTER (*civilian costume*)
puts in his head.

COLONEL. Is this Gregory Brewster's?

CORPORAL. Yes, sir. That's my name.

COLONEL. Then you are the man I came to see.

CORPORAL. Who was that, sir?

COLONEL. Gregory Brewster was his name.

CORPORAL. I am the man, sir.

COLONEL. And you are the same Brewster, as I understand, whose name is on the roll of the Scots Guards as having been present at the battle of Waterloo ?

CORPORAL. The same Brewster, sir, though they used to call it the 3rd Guards in my day. It was a fine ridgement, sir, and they only want me now to make up a full muster.

COLONEL [*cheerily*]. Tut ! tut ! they'll have to wait years for that. But I thought I should like to have a word with you, for I am the Colonel of the Scots Guards.

[CORPORAL *springing to his feet and saluting, staggers about to fall. The* COLONEL *and* NORAH *prevent it.* NORAH *on his L.*

COLONEL. Steady, steady. [*Leads* BREWSTER *to other chair.*] Easy and steady . . .

CORPORAL [*sitting down and panting*]. Thank ye, sir. I was near gone that time. But, Lordy, why I can scarce believe it. To think of me a corporal of the flank company, and you the colonel of the battalion ! Lordy, how things do come round to be sure.

[NORAH *helps him into chair R. of table.* COLONEL *gets by fireplace.*

COLONEL. Why, we are very proud of you in London——

CORPORAL. That's what the Regent said. " The Regiment is proud of you," said he.

COLONEL. And so you are actually one of the men who held Hougoumont ?

[NORAH *sits L. of table with needlework, taken from her basket.*

CORPORAL. Yes, Colonel, I was at Hougoumont.

COLONEL. Well, I hope that you are pretty comfortable and happy.

CORPORAL. Thank ye, sir, I am pretty bobbish when the weather holds, and the flies are not too owdacious. I have a good deal of trouble with my toobes. You wouldn't

42

think the job it is to cut the phlegm. And I need my rations, I get cold without 'em. And my jints, they are not what they used to be.

COLONEL. How's the memory?

CORPORAL. Oh, there ain't anything amiss there. Why, sir, I could give you the name of every man in Captain Haldane's flank company.

COLONEL. And the battle—you remember that?

CORPORAL. Why I sees it afore me, every time I shuts my eyes. Lordy, sir, you wouldn't hardly believe how clear it is to me. There's our line right along from the paregoric bottle to the inhaler, d'ye see! Well then, the pill box is for Hougoumont on the right, where we was, and the thimble for Le Hay Saint. That's all right, sir. [*Cocks his head and looks at it with satisfaction.*] And here are the reserves, and here were our guns and our Belgians, then here's the French, where I put my new pipe, and over here, where the cough drops are, was the Proosians a comin' up on our left flank. Jimini, but it was a glad sight to see the smoke of their guns. [NORAH *helps him into chair.*]

COLONEL. And what was it that struck you most, now, in connection with the whole affair?

CORPORAL. I lost three half-crowns over it, I did. I shouldn't wonder if I were never to get the money now. I lent them to Jabez Smith, my rear-rank man, at Brussels. " Grig ! " says he, " I'll pay you true, only wait till pay-day." By Jimini, he was struck by a lancer at Quarter Brass, and me without a line to prove the debt. Them three half-crowns is as good as lost to me.

COLONEL [*laughing*]. The officers—of the Guards—want you to buy—yourself—some little trifle, some little present which may add to your comfort. It is not from me, so you need not thank me. [*Slips a note into the old man's baccy pouch. Crosses to leave.*]

43

CORPORAL. Thank you kindly, sir. But there's one favour I'd ask you, Colonel.

COLONEL. Yes, Corporal, what is it ?

CORPORAL. If I'm called, Colonel, you won't grudge me a flag and a firing party. I'm not a civilian, I'm a Guardsman, and I should like to think as two lines of the bearskins would be walkin' after my coffin.

COLONEL. All right, Corporal, I'll see to it. [CORPORAL *sinks back in his chair.*] I fear that I have tired him. He is asleep, I think. Good-bye, my girl ; and I hope that we may have nothing but good news from you.

[*Exit* COLONEL.

NORAH. Thank you, sir, I'm sure I hope so too. Uncle, Uncle ! Yes, I suppose he is asleep. But he is so grey and thin that he frightens me. Oh, I wish I had some one to advise me, for I don't know when he is ill and when he is not.

Enter SERGEANT MCDONALD *abruptly.*

SERGEANT. Good day, miss. How is the old gentleman ?

NORAH. Sh ! He's asleep, I think. But I feel quite frightened about him.

SERGEANT [*going over to him*]. Yes, he don't look as if he were long for this life, do he ? Maybe a sleep like this brings strength to him.

NORAH. Oh, I do hope so.

SERGEANT. I'll tell you why I came back so quick. I told them up at the barracks that I'd given him a pipe, and the others they wanted to be in it too, so they passed round, you understand, and made up a pound of baccy. It's long cavendish, with plenty o' bite to it.

NORAH. How kind of you to think of him !

SERGEANT. Do you always live with him ?

NORAH. No, I only came this morning.

SERGEANT. Well, you haven't taken long to get straight.

NORAH. Oh, but I found everything in such a mess. When I have time to myself I'll soon get it nice.

SERGEANT. That sounds like marching orders to me.

NORAH. Oh, how could you think so !

SERGEANT. Tell me, miss, have you ever been over a barrack ?

NORAH. No, I've been on a farm all my life.

SERGEANT. Well, maybe, when he comes up you would come with him ? I'd like to show you over.

NORAH. I'm sure I'd like to come.

SERGEANT. Well, will you promise to come ?

NORAH [*laughing*]. You seem quite earnest about it.

SERGEANT. Well, maybe I am.

NORAH. Very well, I'll promise to come.

SERGEANT. You'll find us rough and ready.

NORAH. I'm sure it will be very nice.

SERGEANT. Not quite what young ladies are accustomed to.

NORAH. But I am no young lady. I've worked with my hands every day that I can remember.

CORPORAL [*in a loud voice*]. The Guards need powder. [*Louder*] The Guards need powder ! [*Struggles to rise.*]

NORAH. Oh, I am so frightened.

CORPORAL [*staggering to his feet, and suddenly flashing out into his old soldierly figure*]. The Guards need powder, and, by God, they shall have it ! [*Falls back into chair.* NORAH *and the* SERGEANT *rush towards him.*]

NORAH [*sobbing*]. Oh, tell me, sir, tell me, what do you think of him?

SERGEANT [*gravely*]. I think that the 3rd Guards have a full muster now.

CURTAIN. SLOW

IT'S THE POOR THAT 'ELPS THE POOR

By Harold Chapin

CHARACTERS

Mrs Harris	Mrs Manly
Mr Harris	Keity
Charles King	Alfred Wright
Mrs Pipe	Walter Wright
Emily Pipe	Mrs Herberts
Willie Pipe	Ted
Mr Pickard	

This play was first produced at the Court Theatre, London, on March 19, 1913, with the following cast of characters:

Mrs Harris . . .	Blanche Stanley
Mr Harris . . .	Walter Hubert
Charles King. .	Allan Jeayes
Mrs Pipe . . .	Armine Grace
Emily Pipe . .	Kathleen Russell
Willie Pipe . .	R. Grassdorff
Mr Pickard . .	Sebastian Smith
Mrs Manly . .	Florence Harcourt
Keity	Lisa Stecker
Alfred Wright .	Vivian Gilbert
Walter Wright .	Sibley Hicks
Mrs Herberts . .	Calypso Valetta
Ted	Perceval Clark

ALTHOUGH Harold Chapin was technically an American citizen he was an English actor, an English playwright, and died as a British soldier. But indeed, even if there had been any doubt about the propriety of including Chapin's play in a volume devoted to British authors, the sheer merit not only of " It's the Poor that 'Elps the Poor," but of his one-act plays generally, would have stood advocate for making in his case an exception.

Insufficient attention has been paid to the theatre of Harold Chapin : that is the fate of the playwright whose fame rests principally on one-act plays. For, exquisite as is the comedy of " The New Morality " and hardly less striking as is, in a more conventional way, the quality of " Art and Opportunity," it is nevertheless in one-act plays such as " The Dumb and the Blind," " Muddle Annie," " The Philosopher of Butterbiggins," " Augustus in Search of a Father," and the example which follows that Chapin manifested most completely his talent for characterization and dialogue.

He has an uncanny psychological insight into the minds and hearts of the poor, but in " Innocent and Annabel," which is included in *Three One-Act Plays* (French), will be found a charming example of the author's comedy when concerned with sophisticated people. The volume will prove delectable to all who appreciate good dialogue and the fastidiously chosen right word.

IT'S THE POOR THAT 'ELPS THE POOR[1]

Scene: *A living-sleeping room off King Street, Camden Town. The furniture, of the 'Why-don't-you-marry-the-girl' hire-purchase variety, is comparatively new. The walls, covered with cheap but cheerful paper, harmonize with the flowered linoleum, which is only beginning to lose its decorated surface in the more-trodden places. The door is L. of C. The fireplace, with a small gas-stove standing out from it, down R. Against the wall opposite the fireplace is a rough—probably home-made—dresser. Against the back wall is a double bed, covered from end to end with a piece of green art serge. A small deal kitchen-table with a red-and-black cloth on it is L. of C. A cheap painted chest of drawers against wall between door and bed.*

An armchair of early Victorian pattern, and in second-hand condition, is above fire, rather far out into room to avoid the gas-stove. Below the stove is another chair—a kitchen elbow-chair of varnished wood. Two Windsor chairs stand one above the table and one at its L. end with its back to the dresser. An assortment of cheap cups, saucers, etc., are on the dresser. A few pots and pans upon the gas-stove and in the hearth.

The curtain rises on an empty stage, but the heavy footsteps of

[1] Applications regarding amateur performances of this play should be addressed to Messrs Samuel French, Ltd., 26 Southampton Street, Strand, London, W.C.2, or 25 West 45th Street, New York.

49

*a small procession are heard on the stairs. They hesitate
outside, and a voice—a deep male voice—with the gruff-
ness of a street-vendor, says, as the door remains a foot
open:*

THE VOICE [PICKARD] [*off*]. You go in first, Kitty.

[KITTY *enters. She is generally known as* MRS HARRIS.
*She is a fat matron of fifty-five with a red face and
large neck. She is dressed heavily in black, with
nodding plumes in her bonnet and twinkling jet
(imitation) on her cape. She is followed by her
husband,* HARRIS, *the eel-vendor. In weight he is her
equal, but not in depth of mourning. He wears a dark
27s. 6d. suit, a black ready-made tie; he carries
a very hard bowler hat, the red imprint of which
is indelibly marked upon his brow.* MR PICKARD,
who addressed MRS HARRIS *as " Kitty," stands back
while they enter, and remains as door-holder for the
rest of the procession, who are slowly climbing the
stairs.* MR HARRIS *follows his panting wife acros.
to the hearth, and as she sits in the smaller armchair he sinks with a sigh of gratification into the
larger one, and places his hat between his feet.* MRS
HARRIS *leans across and remonstrates with great
solemnity.*

MRS HARRIS. I shouldn't take that chair if I was you,
Father.

MR HARRIS [*surprised*]. W'y not? [*Testing the strength of
the spring by several sitting jumps*] It's all right.

MRS HARRIS [*with reproach*]. It would be only decent to
leave it for Mrs 'Erberts, pore sole!

MR HARRIS [*abashed*]. I wasn't thinkin'! [*Lifts his hat and
retreats to bed, where he sits.*]

MRS HARRIS [*more in sorrow than in anger*]. No, you never
do.

[*The procession has continued, and an awkward young man, wearing large yellow boots, which contrast glaringly with the sombre garments of all the rest of the cortège, has entered. He is a typical coster: thirty years of age, slightly tanned and hardened, grey-eyed, with close-cropped fair hair and a curled fringe almost down to his eyes. He wears a cheap dark suit and a black tie over a dicky and turned-down collar, and a dark cap, which he forbears to take off. He is followed by* MRS PIPE, *of the coal-shed, a little, puffing woman in black, who no sooner gets into the room than she collapses in a flood of tears into the chair above the table. A large, well-developed girl, entering behind her, looks at her impatiently.*]

THE GIRL. Oh, chuck it, Muvver! Wot's the good of startin' again?

HER MOTHER. I can't 'elp it. Straight, I can't. It brings things into me 'ed. I've lost five, an' I knows wot it means.

[*A boy of fifteen enters. He addresses the big girl with the air of one discussing a distant pheno-menon.*]

THE BOY. Muvver started again?

THE GIRL [*expressively*]. Not 'arf!

MRS HARRIS [*kindly but firmly, from her elbow-chair*]. If you can't control yourself, Mrs Pipe, it would be better if you went 'ome. You'll only upset pore dear Mrs 'Erberts, pore sole!

THE GIRL [*shrugging hopelessly and regarding her weeping mother*]. That's wot I tell 'er, Mrs 'Arris, but she's such a one! There ain't no checking 'er.

HER MOTHER [*between sobs*]. It—brings—so much---back to me. [*Loudly*] I've buried five, Mrs Harris.

THE GIRL [*exasperated*]. Lor' love a duck! You've got eight left!

> [MR PICKARD *has meanwhile tired of acting as door-keeper and entered the room. He now observes the empty armchair, and crosses to it. He sits in it as the mother's sobs cease.* MRS HARRIS *leans forward and whispers. He says "*Eh?*" She raises her voice.*

MRS HARRIS. It would be only decent to leave it for pore dear Mrs 'Erberts, pore sole. [MR PICKARD *rises and goes to bed, where he sits next to* MR HARRIS.]

> [*There are now seven people in the room :* MRS HARRIS *in the elbow-chair below fire ;* MR HARRIS *on the bed ; on his L.* MR PICKARD, *grizzly bearded and dressed in a shabby double-breasted blue serge suit, carrying a bowler, and sporting the inevitable black tie. He is a potato salesman.* MR KING *stands in front of the chest of drawers. The* PIPE *family are above the table.* EMILY, *the big daughter, in her large black feathered hat and purple velveteen blouse, standing on the R. of her diminutive mother, and* WILLY, *the son, on her L. They have the un-intentional air of threatening her. Eighth and ninth come* MRS MANLY *and her daughter aged eight, the widow and orphan of a deceased coster volunteer, who gave his life for his country and left his wife to live by doing half-days' charing for the wives of less patriotic mates. They are in magnificent and experienced mourning, especially the child, though hers is very small and short in the skirt for her.* MRS MANLY *escorts her down L. of table, sits, and takes her on her knees.*

MRS MANLY. You've got to be very good, Keity, and never not so much as open your mouth. [KEITY *nods, big-eyed.* MRS MANLY *looks around, anxious to express herself.*] P'r'aps

I hadn't ought to 'a' brought 'er, but it would 'a' been crool 'ard to leave 'er be'ind.

MRS HARRIS. Of course.

MRS MANLY [*encouraged*]. You see, she 'asn't never been to a funeral, properly speaking. 'Er father 'aving lost 'is life in Souf Africa an' 'er gran'farver 'aving been blown up 'an pos'-mortemmed.

HARRIS. Benny Herberts 'ad a pos'-mortem on 'im, if it comes to that. It don't make no difference to the funeral.

MRS MANLY [*with pride*]. Ah, but Dad—'e was pos'-mortemmed proper.

[ALFRED *and* WALTER WRIGHT, *brother costers of twenty-five or thereabouts, wearing the ubiquitous mourning garb, enter.* MRS HARRIS *addresses them, rising.*

MRS HARRIS. Is she comin' up?

WALTER [*nodding*]. She asked us not to wait, but to come on up. [*He moves to L. corner above dresser, standing between* WILLY PIPE *and the* MANLYS.]

MRS HARRIS. You drove slow. [*Crosses to door slowly.*]

ALFRED [*moving towards the large chair*]. There wasn't no 'urry. 'N' we 'ad to stop somewhere to break the luck.

PICKARD [*surprised*]. Wot luck?

MRS HARRIS [*severely*]. No one never goes straight 'ome after a funeral, 'Arry. Surely you knows that much?

PICKARD [*abashed*]. Of course, Kitty. I wasn't thinking.

EMILY PIPE. Take that cap o' yours off, Charlie King. Show some respeck for the living, if you can't show none for the dead with them brown boots o' yours.

KING [*guiltily*]. I 'adn't got no others.

EMILY. Couldn't you 'a' borrowed some?

KING [*mournfully*]. Not to wear.

[MRS HERBERTS *appears outside the door.* MRS HARRIS *bustles out to her and leads her in and across to the large armchair just as* ALFRED WRIGHT *has seated*

53

himself therein. He starts out of it guiltily, and finds refuge from MRS HARRIS'S *glare on the bed to the R. of the others.*

MRS HARRIS [*placing the chief mourner in the sacred chair*]. There, dearie. Now don't you worry about nothing. 'Ow pale you look ! 'Ow do you feel ?

MRS HERBERTS. Not ill. I—— [*She staves off approaching tears by wisely ceasing to speak, and leans back wearily. She is a fairly pretty girl of the coster type, not more than twenty-one or two years of age, wearing a black blouse and skirt and a black hat with black feathers.* MRS HARRIS *removes this and takes it to table.*]

MRS HARRIS [*in a businesslike tone*]. Willy, do you mind running out for a drop of something ?

WILLY PIPE [*neither enthusiastically nor unwillingly*]. No.

MRS HARRIS. That's a good boy ! [*To* WALTER WRIGHT] Reach me them jugs, will you, Walter ? [WALTER *obeys.*] 'Ere. [*She gives* WILLY *the smaller.*] A pint an'n'arf of stout. [*Gives the other.*] A quart of four-ale, and [*here she mysteriously produces a clean flask from her cash-pocket under her dress and hands it over*] 'ere, a quartern of special Scotch. Now, can you manage ?

WILLY [*pocketing the flask*]. Yes.

MRS HARRIS. That's a good boy. 'Ere. [*Gives him money.*] Now look sharp.

[WILLY *departs on his errand.* MRS MANLY *rises from her chair and proffers it.*

MRS MANLY. Sit 'ere, Mrs 'Arris.

MRS HARRIS [*complying*]. Thank you, Mrs Manly. [*To* MRS PIPE] You don't mind me sendin' Willy, I'm sure, Mrs Pipe. 'E's a good boy.

MRS PIPE. I only wishes as every mother 'ad as good a son. Some say girls is more haffectionate, but I'm sure I ain't found them so, an' wot with eight living an' five I've buried——

IT'S THE POOR THAT 'ELPS THE POOR

[*The completion of the sentence is deferred by a sharp blow in the ribs from* EMILY's *elbow. Every one looks anxiously at* MRS HERBERTS, *who seems not to have heard the remark.*]

EMILY [*fiercely under her breath*]. Muvver !

MRS PIPE [*peevishly*]. Wot is it ?

EMILY. Can't you be more tactful ? [*She indicates her meaning by a directive glance.*]

MRS PIPE [*realizing her iniquity and accordingly offended with her daughter*]. You put your elbow right into me corsets, Emily ; I believe you've broke that bone I was a-tellin' you about only last night.

EMILY. Oh, shut up, Muvver !

[MRS HERBERTS *has taken out a handkerchief. The others watch her in silent apprehension. She merely blows her nose, however, and returns it to her bosom, when the silence in the room makes her look up to find all the others watching her. She smiles a little weakly, and speaks.*]

MRS HERBERTS. You're very good to see me 'ome. Ted'll be most grateful to you all for looking after me so kind.

MRS HARRIS [*with some pride*]. That's nothing, dearie. We'd 'a' done the same for anyone.

ALFRED [*from the bed*]. It's the poor wot 'elps the poor.

MRS MANLY [*enthusiastically*]. That's a true word. Ah, you've got a lot to be thankful for, Mrs 'Erberts, dear ! I only wish my poor Will could come 'ome and 'ear 'ow good every one's been to me, same as your Ted can.

MRS HERBERTS. Gawd knows 'ow I'm going to tell 'im ! 'E was that fond of the nipper ; 'e fair idolized 'im !

HARRIS. 'E'll get your letter——

CHARLES KING [*quickly and with some heat*]. Not till 'is sentence is up, they don't——

HARRIS [*angrily*]. I know that, don't I ? I'm saying 'e'll get it as soon as ever 'e comes aht.

PICKARD. That'll be a week from yesterday.

WALTER. Do they let 'em out prompt ?

KING [*with increased warmth*]. They jolly well 'ave to. Nice fing if they kept you after your time was up !

EMILY [*scornfully, as she goes to chair below fire and sits*]. They could if they wanted to.

KING. *They—could—not !* Fourteen days is fourteen days.

MRS MANLY. All for leavin' 'is barrer by the kerb w'ile 'e 'ad a drink with a friend !

ALFRED. 'E shouldn't 'ave 'it the p'liceman.

CHARLES KING. 'E did not 'it the p'liceman. 'E only pushed parst 'im, see ?   'E'd 'a' been summonsed for leavin' 'is barrer, anyway.

MRS PIPE. There's one law for the rich and another for the poor, that's a fact.

EMILY. Oh, shut up, Muvver !

WALTER. 'E oughtn't to 'a' got fourteen days just for shovin' a p'liceman.

MRS HERBERTS [*simply*]. It was the same p'liceman wot 'e'd 'ad trouble with before.

PICKARD [*from the bed*]. T't !   Wot luck !

KING. Ah ! 'E 'ad a down on Ted ; I saw 'im—'e was simply askin' 'im to 'it 'im.   Fourteen days !

HARRIS. 'E 'ad the option.

KING [*furiously*]. Wot's the good o' the option to Ted ? W'ere's a pore bloke wot's just bought a barrer-load o' plums to find forty bob an' costs ?

EMILY. Shut up, Ginger !

MRS HARRIS [*oil on troubled waters*]. Don't get arguing *to-day*, Charlie, there's a good boy.

> [*The door opens and* WILLY PIPE *returns, a jug in each hand.   He deposits them on the table, standing in* EMILY's *old place, R. of* MRS PIPE.   *He then pro-*

> *duces the flask from his pocket, lays it beside them,
> then the change beside the flask. The company
> evince interest, but no enthusiasm.* MRS HARRIS
> *rises and begins transplanting the stock of glasses
> and cups from the dresser to the table.*

MRS HARRIS. That's a good boy. T't! 'Ave I 'ad your chair all this time, Mrs Manly ?

MRS MANLY [*regaining it*]. It don't——

WALTER WRIGHT. There's some chairs just across the landing in Tom Adams' room.

MRS HARRIS. I'm sure—— [*he wouldn't mind us, etc.*]

WILLY PIPE [*with a burst of goodness*]. I'll fetch 'em. [*Goes out.*]

MRS HARRIS. *Wot* a good boy 'e is !

MRS PIPE. They ses boys is more trouble, but if I was to 'ave fifty——

EMILY PIPE. Muvver !

MRS HARRIS [*presiding*]. Now [*to* MRS HERBERTS] what do you fancy, my dear ?   A drop o' stout ?

> [MRS HERBERTS, *taken off her guard, breaks into pitiful
> sobs and attempts to cover her face with her hands.*
> MRS HARRIS, *officious but kindly, hurries round the
> table to her.*

MRS HARRIS. There, there, dearie !   Don't give way like that.   Wot ever is it ?

> [*It is some seconds before* MRS HERBERTS *can control
> herself sufficiently to explain.*

MRS HERBERTS. Baby was that fond o' the smell o' a drop o' stout !   Many's the time me an' Ted's let 'im 'ave a sniff at a glass—an' 'e used to laugh that pretty when the froth got up 'is nose.   It used to make Ted laugh too, an' now—— Ow, Gawd ! [*and she leans against the edge of the chair-back
and weeps unrestrainedly. The men look on in awkward sym-
pathy.* MRS PIPE *weeps silently.* MRS MANLY *sniffs, and the*

child looks on wide-eyed. Only CHARLIE KING *keeps his more human feelings in check by a glow of prejudice.*]

CHARLES KING. I 'ope you never gave 'im none.

MRS HERBERTS. Ted wouldn't let me ; 'e was that faddy about baby.

CHARLES KING [*warmly approving*]. Quite right. Why, it might 'ave started the taste in 'im !

MRS HERBERTS [*hopelessly*]. Wot does it matter wot it might 'ave done ? 'E's dead wiv all our faddin'.

CHARLES KING [*lacking the sense to stop, though realizing his blunder*]. Yes, but—you wouldn't like to fink——

EMILY PIPE [*rising and picking up* MRS HERBERT'S *dropped handkerchief, and thereby interposing between her and* KING, *who is roughly C.*]. Shut up, Charlie King— arguing !

[*The return of* WILLY PIPE *laden with two chairs breaks up the situation.*

MRS HARRIS [*who has returned to her task of pouring out at the table*]. There's a good boy. Now we can all sit down. Charlie—— [*Indicates the two jugs.*]

CHARLES KING. 'Arf-an'-'arf, fanx. [*Takes glass and goes with it to foot of bed, where he sits*].

[WALTER *remains unseated, lounging against the dresser above table, L. of* MRS PIPE. MRS MANLY, *who has resumed her chair, takes her orphan daughter on her lap.* WILLY *places one chair C.—that is, to R. of table—and the other above table R. of his mother. On this chair he himself sits, and produces from his pocket a bottle of ginger-beer.*

MRS HARRIS [*handing him a glass*]. Still Band of 'Ope, Willy ? [WILLY *does not deign to reply.*

MRS HARRIS [*knowing tastes, she only offers what will be accepted*]. Walter !

WALTER WRIGHT. Fanx. [*Receives his drink.*]

MRS HARRIS [*uncorking the flask*]. You'll take whisky, I know, 'Arry.   [PICKARD *nods.*

MRS HARRIS [*pouring out some and adding water from dresser*]. Take Mr Pickard that, will you, Willy ? [*To* HARRIS] Farver ?

MRS HERBERTS. Let me help. [*She rises and meets* WILLY, *C., where she takes his glass on to* MR PICKARD, *and returns to table for* HARRIS'S.]

MRS HARRIS [*protesting*]. No, no, dearie. You set still.

MRS HERBERTS. I'd rather be doing something. [*Takes* HARRIS *his glass.*]

HARRIS [*raising it as he receives it*]. Thank you, my dear. Good luck !   [*The company is horrified.*

MRS HARRIS. Farver, I'm surprised at you !

HARRIS [*surprised*]. I only said, " Good luck ! "

MRS HARRIS [*severely*]. I'd 'a' thought you'd 'a' 'ad more feeling !

HARRIS [*abashed, but defending himself*]. I meant—better luck next time.

MRS HARRIS [*more in sorrow than in anger*]. I suppose it's no use, Farver, for me to ask you to mind wot you're saying of.

MRS HERBERTS [*who has moved through this, quite unheeding it, and is now lifting a glass at the table*]. Is this for Alf ?

MRS HARRIS. Yes ; an' this here is yours, dearie—you really ought to take a drop o' something.

MRS HERBERTS. All right. [*She takes the two glasses, carries one to* ALFRED WRIGHT *on the far end of the bed, and goes with the other to below fire, where she sits. The large armchair is empty, and* EMILY PIPE *is standing up, C.*]

MRS HERBERTS [*touching the armchair*]. Sit 'ere, Emily.

EMILY. It's your chair.

MRS HERBERTS. I'm quite comf'table w'ere I am. Do 'ave it.   [EMILY *obeys.*

CHARLES KING [*rising from the foot of the bed with an*

inspiration]. I know a toast is rarver out of place, but 'ere's one as no one can't take exception to. [*With feeling*] Absent friends !

> [*The company is favourably impressed, and the glasses raised to a discreet chorus of muttered* " 'Ere, 'eres ! " *and repetitions of the toast,* MRS PIPE *trying to add something about* " An' may they soon——" *but giving it up as the glass reaches her lips.*

MRS HERBERTS [*after the others*]. Thank you, Charlie.

MRS HARRIS [*across the room*]. Finished your drop o' whisky, Farver ? [HARRIS *nods.*

MRS HARRIS [*suggestively*]. Then don't you think——

HARRIS [*suddenly understanding*]. Oh, ah ! [*Rises and makes for the door, where he pauses.*] You was coming with me, Pickard, wasn't you ? [PICKARD *rises.*

MRS HERBERTS. You're not going, Mr 'Arris ?

MRS HARRIS. 'E's just got somefing 'e's got to see to. 'E'll come back, won't you, Farver ?

HARRIS [*with surprising emphasis*]. Not 'arf ! [*Goes out, followed by* PICKARD, *who closes door cautiously behind him.*]

> [*The orphan* MANLY *suddenly tunes up.*

KEITY. Wot's Mr 'Arris gone for, Mummy ?

MRS MANLY. 'Ush, Keity ! I told you as 'ow——

KEITY [*still more loudly*]. 'E winked——

MRS MANLY [*shaking her severely*]. I told you to 'ush, miss ! [*The child is subdued.*

MRS PIPE [*making conversation in the pause that follows*]. It's been a lovely day for it.

MRS HARRIS. I never see such weather ! Not a drop o rain since last Tuesday week—an' wot a Bank 'Oliday !

ALFRED. I could 'a' done wiv a drop o' rain, it lays the dust.

MRS HARRIS [*to* MRS HERBERTS]. We missed you, my dear.

IT'S THE POOR THAT 'ELPS THE POOR

It was only just about four o'clock when I ses to Farver, "I wonder 'ow Ted 'Erberts's spending '*is* Bank 'Oliday, pore feller!"

MRS MANLY. Four o'clock?

MRS HARRIS. Yes, an'——

MRS MANLY [*greatly impressed*]. W'y, that was just w'en Benny died, wasn't it—four o'clock?

MRS HERBERTS. No.

MRS MANLY [*checked*]. I fought you said——

MRS HERBERTS. 'E was breaving when I went round to try an' find the doctor. That was nigh on five.

MRS MANLY. Well, 'e must 'a'——

    [*There is a quick clatter of feet outside, and a young coster enters. He is well into the room before he realizes that there are many people round him. Then he stops, vaguely thrown out of his bearings by their presence.* MRS HERBERTS *rises in surprise, as do the others without exception.*

MRS HERBERTS. Ted!

TED [*staring round*]. Wot——

CHARLES KING [*recovering first from the general surprise*]. Ted, ol' man, wot O! Aht before yer time? [*He attempts to seize* TED's *hand.*]

TED. Wot are you all doing 'ere?

MRS HARRIS. We're a-keepin' of 'er company after the funeral.

TED [*understanding*]. He's buried, then?

                      [*A universal nod.*

TED [*more impressed than grief-stricken*]. Buried, Gawd's truth! An' las' week 'e was as 'ealthy——

MRS HARRIS [*consolingly*]. 'E 'ad a cough, Ted.

TED [*furiously*]. 'Ad a cough? 'E died 'ungry! It was in the papers. The bloomin' 'Ome Sekeratery 'ad me let out bekos of it. They came an' told me in me cell—died o'

61

negleck an' starvation ! Coroner's verdick, " lack o' nourishment." Couldn't you do nothing for 'im, Lil ?

MRS HERBERTS. Ted, I did all I could.

TED. 'N' 'e died 'ungry ! Couldn't you feed 'im ?

MRS HERBERTS. Ted, I 'adn't got nothin' in the place.

TED. Couldn't you get nothin' ? Wouldn't nobody give you nothin' ?

MRS HERBERTS. They was all away. It was Bank 'Oliday, Ted. I ran short.

TED. Ran short ! Fine, ain't it ? An' 'e died o' negleck !

MRS HARRIS [*with some asperity*]. No, 'e didn't, Ted Herberts. Death *haxcellerated* by negleck was the——

TED. 'Cellerated be damned ! [*To his wife*] Do you mean to say as you 'adn't nothin'—nothin' ? W'y—'adn't you bought nothin' in ?

MRS HERBERTS. 'Ow could I buy anything in, Ted ? I 'adn't got no money. I'd pawned me bes' blouse 'n'——

TED. Wouldn't nobody lend you nothing?

MRS HERBERTS [*with sweet reasonableness*]. They couldn't be expected to keep on, Ted.

TED. Moi Gawd ! [*To others fiercely*] You let Benny die, you——

MRS HERBERTS. It was all through it being Bank 'Oliday, Ted, an' every one that busy on Saturday. 'E 'ad 'is cough, Ted. I didn't know w'ich way to turn, straight I didn't ! Charlie King, 'e lent me 'arf a crahn, but I got Benny's med'cin' 'n' advice wi' that. I counted on Mrs 'Arris, an' she couldn't oblige me.

TED [*turning on* MRS HARRIS]. You——

MRS HERBERTS. Oh, but she 'ad before, Ted, straight she 'ad ; 'n' she's been that good ever since. So's everybody. I'm sure the funeral must 'a' cost poun's an' poun's, an' Mr 'Arris an' Mr Pickard an' Walter an' Alfred 'ave paid for it, every penny.

TED. Paid for it! That's good! Paid for 'is funeral! You couldn't 'ave lent me the money to keep me out an' workin' for 'im, could you? You couldn't lend Lil 'ere the money to feed 'im while I was in prison? Call yourself pals! I don't.

MRS HARRIS. Thank you.

TED. Ah! "Thank you!" When I come to your 'us-band to arst 'im to lend me a thick 'un t'wards me fine, 'e laughed fit to kill 'isself. Yus! An' ol' Pickard sed as 'ow fines didn't ought to be paid.

CHARLES KING. I lent you ten bob.

TED. So you did, ol' pal, an' I 'ad it put away for me in prison w'ile—— Oh, Gawd! if you'd sent to the Governor, Lil.

MRS HERBERTS. I didn't know w'ich way to turn, Ted, straight I didn't. The plums wot you'd bought went bad wiv keepin', an'—— It took me all of a sudden——

MRS HARRIS [*with some feeling*]. You ain't doin' no good roundin' on the pore young thing like that, Ted 'Erberts. You ought to be a-comfortin' of 'er, not——

TED. You mind your own business.

FEMININE CHORUS. Well!

TED [*generally*]. Yus! "Well!" An' get outside my room, the 'ole blooming lot o' you!

MRS HARRIS [*rather finely*]. I'm sure I've no wish——

MRS PIPE [*rising*]. Thank you for your gratitude, Ted 'Erberts!

EMILY. Shut up, Muvver!

CHARLES KING [*coming down L. of* TED]. Look 'ere, ol' Ted. [*His tone is one of brotherly remonstrance.*] I don't think as you ought to rahnd on them as 'as done all they could for you, an' spent good money on 'avin' the little chap buried, an' all.

TED. I know you've done your best, ol' pal.

MRS PIPE. An' *we* 'aven't ? Thank you !

CHARLES KING [*kindly*]. No one can't blame you for being upset.

> [*The scene is once more interrupted, this time by the entrance of* HARRIS *and* PICKARD, *bearing between them a picture-frame of a couple of feet square, or thereabouts, wrapped in flimsy paper.*

HARRIS [*seeing the master of the house*]. Wot, Ted !

PICKARD [*with similar cordiality*]. Out before your time ?

TED [*not responding*]. Looks like it. Wot do you want ?

HARRIS. We've got something 'ere for you an' Mrs 'Erberts, Ted. We was going to—— [*He plucks off the paper, revealing a cheap enlargement of a photograph of an anæmic-looking infant some six to eight months old.*] There ! Ain't it like 'im ? [*His pride is great.*]

> [MRS HERBERTS *regards the photograph with intense admiration, of which an exclamation of " Ow ! " is the culminating point.* TED *is only mystified by its sudden appearance.*

TED. W'ere d'you get it ?

HARRIS [*proudly*]. We 'ad it done as a little surprise for you. We passed the 'at round among——

TED [*calmly and slowly*]. Moi Gawd ! If this ain't the limit ! You—— [*His rising passion suddenly finds vent in a whirl of the arm, with which he snatches the picture and flings it against the door.*] Take the bloody thing away !

> [*His wife gives a genuine cry of pain and reproach.*

MRS HERBERTS. Oh, Ted ! Benny's photograff ! An' w'en they've all been so kind to us !

> [*The reproach in her voice pulls him up strangely. He stares wildly about him. On every face is the expression of genuine commiseration—though not of appreciation of this outburst. They are all still and uncomfortable. He looks last at his wife ; a*

sob chokes him; he puts out a hand to recover the picture, then changes his mind and flings himself on his knees with his face in his wife's lap, sobbing. There is a chorus of pitying approval from the others, MRS HARRIS *being loud in expressing the general opinion that—*

Anyone might be'ave a bit queer wot's been through all wot 'e 'as.

Which not only proves that it's the poor who help the poor, but that they understand and can make allowances for each other's occasional bursts of ingratitude.

CURTAIN

A MARRIAGE HAS BEEN ARRANGED

A DUOLOGUE

By Alfred Sutro

CHARACTERS

Mr Harrison Crockstead
Lady Aline de Vaux

This play was first produced at the Garrick Theatre, London, on March 27, 1904, with the following cast:

Mr Harrison Crockstead . . Arthur Bourchier
Lady Aline de Vaux . . . Violet Vanbrugh

MR ALFRED SUTRO has written a large number of first-rate plays, both long and short, and has also given us some excellent translations of the early works of Maeterlinck. His finest plays are probably "The Walls of Jericho," "The Two Virtues," "The Choice," and "The Perplexed Husband."

Mr Sutro once confessed that before beginning to write the dialogue he drafted out the whole play in detail, paying special attention to securing plausible entrances and exits. The result is that the 'plot' is neat and satisfying; there are no loose ends; and a Sutro play is technically well-knit.

"A Marriage has been Arranged" is a good example of the dramatist's work. His comedy is flavoured with delicate irony, which is swept away when emotion becomes passionate.

A MARRIAGE HAS BEEN ARRANGED [1]

SCENE: *The conservatory of No. 300 Grosvenor Square. Hour—close on midnight. A ball is in progress and dreamy waltz music is heard in the distance.*

LADY ALINE DE VAUX *enters, leaning on the arm of* MR HARRISON CROCKSTEAD.

CROCKSTEAD [*looking around*]. Ah—this is the place—very quiet, retired, romantic—*et cetera*. Music in the distance —all very appropriate and sentimental. [*He motions her to sit in chair R. of table L. C. She moves to settee R. and sits at L. end.*] You seem perfectly calm, Lady Aline?

ALINE [*sitting*]. Anterooms are not unusual appendages to a ball-room, Mr Crockstead; nor is this anteroom unlike other anterooms.

CROCKSTEAD. I wonder why women are always so evasive?

ALINE. With your permission we will not discuss the sex. You and I are too old to be cynical, and too young to be appreciative. And besides, it is a rule of mine, whenever I sit out a dance, that my partner shall avoid the subjects of women—and war.

CROCKSTEAD. You limit the area of conversation—— But then, in this particular instance, I take it, we have not come here to talk? [*Moving R. at back of settee and sits beside her.*]

---

[1] Applications regarding amateur performances of this play should be addressed to Messrs Samuel French, Ltd., 26 Southampton Street, Strand, London, W.C.2, or 25 West 45th Street, New York.

ALINE [*coldly*]. I beg your pardon !

CROCKSTEAD [*sitting beside her*]. Lady Aline, they are dancing a cotillon in there, so we have half an hour before us. We shall not be disturbed, for the Duchess, your aunt, has considerately stationed her aged companion in the corridor, with instructions to ward off intruders.

ALINE [*very surprised*]. Mr Crockstead !

CROCKSTEAD [*looking hard at her*]. Didn't you know ? [ALINE *turns aside, embarrassed.*] That's right—of course you did. Don't you know why I have brought you here ? That's right ; of course you do. The Duchess, your aunt, and the Marchioness, your mother—observe how fondly my tongue trips out the titles—smiled sweetly on us as we left the ball-room. There will be a notice in the *Morning Post* to-morrow : "A marriage has been arranged between——"

ALINE [*bewildered and offended. Rises*]. Mr Crockstead ! This—this is——

CROCKSTEAD [*always in the same quiet tone*]. Because I have not yet proposed, you mean ? Of course I intend to, Lady Aline. Only as I know that you will accept me——

ALINE [*rising, in icy tones*]. Let us go back to the ball-room.

CROCKSTEAD [*quite undisturbed*]. Oh, please ! That won't help us, you know. Do sit down. I assure you I have never proposed before, so that naturally I am a trifle nervous. [LADY ALINE *moves to fireplace.*] Of course I know that we are only supers really, without much of a speaking part ; but the spirit moves me to gag, in the absence of the stage-manager, who is, let us say, the Duchess——

ALINE. I have heard of the New Humour, Mr Crockstead, though I confess I have never understood it. This may be an exquisite example——

CROCKSTEAD. By no means. I am merely trying to do

the right thing, though perhaps not the conventional one. Before making you the formal offer of my hand and fortune, which amounts to a little over three millions——

ALINE [*fanning herself*]. How people exaggerate! Between six and seven, *I* heard.

CROCKSTEAD. Only three at present, but we must be patient. Before throwing myself at your feet, metaphorically, I am anxious that you should know something of the man whom you are about to marry.

ALINE. That is really most considerate!

CROCKSTEAD. I have the advantage of you, you see, inasmuch as you have many dear friends, who have told me all about you.

ALINE [*with growing exasperation, but keeping very cool*]. Indeed?

CROCKSTEAD. I am aware, for instance, that this is your ninth season——

ALINE [*snapping her fan*]. You are remarkably well-informed.

CROCKSTEAD. I have been told that again to-night, three times, by charming young women who vowed that they loved you. Now, as I have no dearest friends, it is unlikely that you will have heard anything equally definite concerning myself. I propose to enlighten you.

ALINE [*satirically*]. The story of your life—how thrilling!

CROCKSTEAD. I trust you may find it so. [*Sits on R. end of settee.*] Lady Aline, I am a self-made man, as the foolish phrase has it—a man whose early years were spent in savage and desolate places, where the devil had much to say; a man in whom whatever there once had been of natural kindness was very soon kicked out. I was poor, and lonely, for thirty-two years: I have been rich, and lonely, for ten. My millions have been made honestly enough; but poverty and wretchedness had left their mark on me, and you will find very few men with a good word to say for Harrison Crockstead. I have no polish, or culture, or tastes. Art wearies me, literature sends me to sleep——

ALINE. When you come to the chapter of your personal deficiencies, Mr Crockstead, please remember that they are sufficiently evident for me to have already observed them.

CROCKSTEAD [*without a trace of annoyance*]. That is true. I will pass, then, to more intimate matters. In a little township in Australia—a horrible place where there was gold—I met a woman whom I loved. She was what is technically known as a bad woman. She ran away with another man. I tracked them to Texas, and in a mining camp there I shot the man. I wanted to take the woman back, but she refused. That has been my solitary love affair; and I shall never love any woman again as I loved her. I think that is all that I have to tell you. And now—will you marry me, Lady Aline?

ALINE [*very steadily, facing man*]. Not if you were the last man in this world, Mr Crockstead.

CROCKSTEAD [*with a pleasant smile*]. At least that is emphatic.

ALINE. See, I will give you confidence for confidence. This is, as you suggest, my ninth season. Living in an absurd *milieu* where marriage with a wealthy man is regarded as the one aim in life, I have, during the past few weeks, done all that lay in my power to wring a proposal from you.

CROCKSTEAD. I appreciate your sincerity.

ALINE. Perhaps the knowledge that other women were doing the same lent a little zest to the pursuit, which otherwise would have been very dreary; for I confess that your personality did not—especially appeal to me.

CROCKSTEAD [*cheerfully*]. Thank you very much.

ALINE. Not at all. Indeed, this room being the Palace of

Truth, I will admit that it was only by thinking hard of your three millions that I have been able to conceal the weariness I have felt in your society. And now—will you marry me, Mr Crockstead ?

CROCKSTEAD [*serenely*]. I fancy that's what we're here for, isn't it ?

ALINE [*stamping her foot*]. I have, of course, been debarred from the disreputable amours on which you linger so fondly ; but I loved a soldier cousin of mine, and would have run away with him had my mother not packed me off in time. He went to India, and I stayed here ; but he is the only man I have loved, or ever shall love. Further, let me tell you I am twenty-eight ; I have always been poor—I hate poverty, and it has soured me no less than you. Dress is the thing in life I care for most, vulgarity my chief abomination. And, to be frank, I consider you the most vulgar person I have ever met. Will you still marry me, Mr Crockstead ?

CROCKSTEAD [*with undiminished cheerfulness*]. Why not ?

ALINE. This is an outrage. [*Crossing to L.*] Am I a horse, do you think, or a ballet-dancer ? Do you imagine I will sell myself to you for your three millions ?

CROCKSTEAD. Logic, my dear Lady Aline, is evidently not one of your more special possessions. For, had it not been for my—somewhat eccentric preliminaries—you *would* have accepted me, would you not ?

ALINE [*embarrassed*]. I—I——

CROCKSTEAD. If I had said to you, timidly : " Lady Aline, I love you ; I am a simple, unsophisticated person ; will you marry me ? " You would have answered, " Yes, Harrison, I will."

ALINE [*L. C. fanning herself*]. It is a mercy to have escaped marrying a man with such a Christian name as Harrison.

CROCKSTEAD. It has been in the family for generations,

you know ; but it is a strange thing that I am always called Harrison, and that no one ever adopts the diminutive.

ALINE. That does not surprise me : we have no pet name for the east wind.

CROCKSTEAD. The possession of millions, you see, Lady Aline, puts you into eternal quarantine. It is a kind of yellow fever, with the difference that people are perpetually anxious to catch your complaint. But we digress. To return to this question of our marriage——

ALINE. I beg your pardon ?

CROCKSTEAD. I presume that it is—arranged ? [*Moving R. a little.*]

ALINE [*haughtily*]. Mr Crockstead, let me remind you that frankness has its limits : exceeding these, it is apt to degenerate into impertinence. Be good enough to conduct me to the ball-room. [*She moves to C. opening.*]

CROCKSTEAD. You have five sisters, I believe, Lady Aline ? [ALINE *stops short.*] All younger than yourself, all marriageable, and all unmarried ?

[ALINE *hangs her head and is silent.*

CROCKSTEAD. Your father——

ALINE [*fiercely*]. Not a word of my father !

CROCKSTEAD [*R.*]. Your father is a gentleman. The breed is rare, and very fine when you get it. But he is exceedingly poor. People marry for money nowadays ; and your mother will be very unhappy if this marriage of ours falls through.

ALINE [*moving down C.*]. Is it to oblige my mother, then, that you desire to marry me ?

CROCKSTEAD. Well, no. But you see I must marry some one, in mere self-defence ; and honestly, I think you will do at least as well as anyone else. [ALINE *bursts out laughing.*] That strikes you as funny ?

ALINE. If you had the least grain of chivalrous feeling,

you would realize that the man who would speak to a woman as you have spoken to me—— [*She pauses.*]

CROCKSTEAD. Yes ?

ALINE. I leave you to finish the sentence.

CROCKSTEAD. Thank you. I will finish it my own way. I will say that when a woman deliberately tries to wring an offer of marriage from a man whom she does not love, she deserves to be spoken to as I have spoken to you, Lady Aline.

ALINE [*scornfully*]. Love ! What has love to do with marriage ?

CROCKSTEAD. That remark rings hollow. You have been good enough to tell me of your cousin, whom you did love——

ALINE. Well ?

CROCKSTEAD. And with whom you would have eloped, had your mother not prevented you.

ALINE. I most certainly should.

CROCKSTEAD. So you see that at one period of your life you thought differently—— You were very fond of him ?

ALINE. I have told you.

CROCKSTEAD [*meditatively*]. If I had been he, mother or no mother, money or no money, I would have carried you off. I fancy it must be pleasant to be loved by you, Lady Aline.

ALINE [*with mock curtsey. Sitting in chair above table L. C.*]. You do me too much honour.

CROCKSTEAD [*still thoughtful, moving C.*]. Next to being king, it is good to be maker of kings. Where is this cousin now ?

ALINE. In America. But might I suggest that we have exhausted the subject ?

CROCKSTEAD. Do you remember your *Arabian Nights*, Lady Aline ?

ALINE. Vaguely.

CROCKSTEAD. You have at least not forgotten that sublime Caliph, Haroun Al-Raschid ?

ALINE. Oh, no—but why ?

CROCKSTEAD. We millionaires are the Caliphs to-day ; and we command more faithful than ever bowed to them. And, like that old scoundrel Haroun, we may at times permit ourselves a respectable impulse. What is your cousin's address ?

ALINE. Again I ask—why ?

CROCKSTEAD. I will put him in a position to marry you.

ALINE [*in extreme surprise*]. What ! [*Rises.*]

CROCKSTEAD. Oh, don't be alarmed, I'll manage it pleasantly. I'll give him tips, shares, speculate for him, make him a director of one or two of my companies. He shall have an income of four thousand a year. You can live on that.

ALINE. You are not serious ?

CROCKSTEAD. Oh yes ; and though men may not like me, they always trust my word. You may.

ALINE. And why will you do this thing ?

CROCKSTEAD. Call it caprice—call it a mere vulgar desire to let my magnificence dazzle you—call it the less vulgar desire to know that my money has made you happy with the man you love.

ALINE [*moved*]. That is generous. [*Sitting in armchair below table L. C.*]

CROCKSTEAD. I remember an old poem I learnt at school —which told how Frederick the Great coveted a mill that adjoined a favourite estate of his : but the miller refused to sell. Frederick could have turned him out, of course— there was no County Council in those days—but he respected the miller's firmness, and left him in solid possession. And

76

mark that, at that very same time, he annexed—in other words stole—the province of Silesia.

ALINE. Ah——

CROCKSTEAD [*moving to fireplace R.*].

" *Ce sont là jeux de Princes :*
Ils respectent un meunier,
Ils volent une province."

[*Music stops.*

ALINE. You speak French ?

CROCKSTEAD. I am fond of it. It is the true and native language of insincerity.

ALINE. And yet you seem sincere.

CROCKSTEAD. I am permitting myself that luxury to-night. I am uncorking, let us say, the one bottle of '47 port left in my cellar.

ALINE [*rises and moves towards settee R.*]. You are not quite fair to yourself, perhaps.

CROCKSTEAD. Do not let this action of mine cause you too suddenly to alter your opinion. The verdict you pronounced before was, on the whole, just.

ALINE. What verdict ?

CROCKSTEAD. I was the most unpleasant person you ever had met.

ALINE. That—was an exaggeration.

CROCKSTEAD. The most repulsive——

ALINE [*quickly*]. I did not say that. [*Sits at L. end of settee.*]

CROCKSTEAD. And who prided himself on his repulsiveness. Very true, in the main, and yet consider ! [*Sitting on R. arm of settee R.*] My wealth dates back ten years ; till then I had known hunger, and every kind of sorrow and despair. I had stretched out longing arms to the world, but not a heart opened to me. And suddenly, when the taste of men's cruelty was bitter in my mouth, capricious fortune snatched me from abject poverty and gave me delirious wealth. I was ploughing a barren field, and flung up a nugget. From that moment gold dogged my footsteps. I enriched the few friends I had—they turned howlingly from me because I did not give them more. I showered money on whoever sought it of me—they cursed me because it was mine to give. In my poverty there had been the bond of common sorrow between me and my fellows : in my wealth I stand alone, a modern Ishmael, with every man's hand against me.

ALINE [*gently*]. Why do you tell me this ?

CROCKSTEAD. Because I am no longer asking you to marry me. Because you are the first person in all these years who has been truthful and frank with me. And because, perhaps, in the happiness that will, I trust, be yours, I want you to think kindly of me. [*She puts out her hand, he takes it ; they move arm in arm to C. and stop.*] And now, shall we return to the ball-room ? The music has stopped ; they must be going to supper.

ALINE [*archly*]. What shall I say to the Marchioness, my mother, and the Duchess, my aunt ?

CROCKSTEAD. You will acquaint those noble ladies with the fact of your having refused me. [*Moving up C. together.*]

ALINE. I shall be a nine days' wonder. And how do you propose to carry out your little scheme ?

CROCKSTEAD. I will take Saturday's boat—you will give me a line to your cousin. I had better state the case plainly to him, perhaps ?

ALINE. That demands consideration. [*Releasing her arm from his.*]

CROCKSTEAD. And I will tell you what you shall do for me in return. Find me a wife !

ALINE. I ?

CROCKSTEAD. You. I beg it on my knees. I give you *carte blanche*. I undertake to propose, with my eyes shut, to the woman you shall select.

ALINE. And will you treat her to the—little preliminaries —with which you have favoured me ?

CROCKSTEAD. No. I said those things to you because I liked you.

ALINE. And you don't intend to like the other one ?

CROCKSTEAD. I will marry her. I can trust you to find me a loyal and intelligent woman.

ALINE. In Society ?

CROCKSTEAD. For preference. She will be better versed in spending money than a governess, or country parson's daughter.

ALINE. But why this voracity for marriage ? [*Moving down.*]

CROCKSTEAD. Lady Aline, I am hunted, pestered, worried, persecuted. I have settled two breach of promise actions already, though Heaven knows I did no more than remark it was a fine day, or enquire after the lady's health. If you do not help me, some energetic woman will capture me—I feel it—and bully me for the rest of my days. I raise a despairing cry to you—Find me a wife !

ALINE [*R.*]. Do you desire the lady to have any—special qualifications ?

CROCKSTEAD. No—the home-grown article will do. One thing, though—I should like her to be—merciful.

ALINE. I don't understand.

CROCKSTEAD. I have a vague desire to do something with my money : my wife might help me. I should like her to have pity.

ALINE. Pity ?

CROCKSTEAD. In the midst of her wealth I should wish her to be sorry for those who are poor.

79

ALINE [*nods*]. Yes. And, as regards the rest—— [*Moving to below settee.*]

CROCKSTEAD. The rest I leave to you, with absolute confidence. You will help me?

ALINE. I will try. My choice is to be final?

CROCKSTEAD. Absolutely.

ALINE. I have an intimate friend—I wonder whether she would do?

CROCKSTEAD. Tell me about her.

ALINE. She and I made our *début* the same season. Like myself, she has hitherto been her mother's despair.

CROCKSTEAD. Because she has not yet——

ALINE. Married—yes. Oh, if men knew how hard the lot is of the portionless girl, who has to sit, and smile, and wait, with a very desolate heart—they would think less unkindly of her, perhaps [*with a smile*]. But I am digressing too.

CROCKSTEAD. Tell me more of your friend. [*Moving towards her.*]

ALINE. She is outwardly hard, and a trifle bitter, but I fancy sunshine would thaw her. There has not been much happiness in her life.

CROCKSTEAD. Would she marry a man she did not love?

ALINE. If she did, you would not respect her?

CROCKSTEAD. I don't say that. She will be your choice; and therefore deserving of confidence. Is she handsome?

ALINE. Well—no.

CROCKSTEAD [*with a quick glance at her*]. That's a pity. But we can't have everything.

ALINE. No. There is one episode in her life that I feel she would like you to know——

CROCKSTEAD. If you are not betraying a confidence——

ALINE [*looking down*]. No. She loved a man, years ago, very dearly. They were too poor to marry, but they vowed to wait. Within six months she learned that he was engaged.

CROCKSTEAD. Ah!

ALINE. To a fat and wealthy widow——

CROCKSTEAD. The old story.

ALINE. Who was touring through India, and had been made love to by every unmarried officer in the regiment. She chose him.

CROCKSTEAD [*meaningly*]. India ? [*Moving to her.*]

ALINE. Yes.

CROCKSTEAD. I have an idea that I shall like your friend. [*Taking her hand.*]

[*Music starts " God save the King." Till curtain falls.*]

ALINE. I shall be careful to tell her all that you said to me—at the beginning——

CROCKSTEAD. It is quite possible that my remarks may not apply after all——

ALINE. But I believe myself, from what I know of you both, that—if she marries you—it will not be—altogether —for your money.

CROCKSTEAD. Listen—they're playing " God save the King." Will you be my wife, Aline ?

ALINE. Yes—Harry. [*He takes her in his arms and kisses her.*]

CURTAIN

LONESOME-LIKE

A PLAY IN ONE ACT

By Harold Brighouse

CHARACTERS

Sarah Ormerod, *an old woman*
Emma Brierley, *a young woman*
The Rev. Frank Alleyne, *a curate*
Sam Horrocks, *a young man*

The scene is laid in a Lancashire village.

This play was produced for the first time on any stage at the Royalty Theatre, Glasgow, by the Glasgow Repertory Company, under the direction of Mr Alfred Wareing, on Monday, February 6, 1911, with the following cast :

Sarah Ormerod	Gwynneth Galton
Emma Brierley	Margaret Nybloc
The Rev. Frank Alleyne . .	Walter Roy
Sam Horrocks	Edmond Breon

Produced by Mr Harold Chapin.

Subsequently performed by Miss Horniman's company and by the Liverpool Repertory Theatre.

Mr Harold Brighouse, like the late Stanley Houghton, has come to be associated with Lancashire plays and the Repertory Theatre of Miss Horniman. In Mr Frank Vernon's crisp history of *The Twentieth-Century Theatre* [1] he is referred to as "the characteristic representative of the Repertory movement," a description which, since the book was published, he has further justified by producing at the Liverpool Repertory Theatre his comedy of Lancashire in London—"Mary's John." [2]

"Lonesome-like" is a little classic in its way. It is utterly simple in structure, yet it is a work that appeals in a wistful way to the emotions. Mr Brighouse can find drama in the grey setting of industrialism. Tragedy and comedy are the warp and woof of human life: wherever there are human beings the dramatist will find the essential material of drama.

[1] Harrap, 5s.   [2] French, 2s. 6d.

LONESOME-LIKE [1]

The scene represents the interior of a cottage in a Lancashire village. Through the window at the back the grey row of cottages opposite is just visible. The outside door is next to the window. Door left. As regards the furniture the room is very bare. The suggestion is not of an empty room, but a stripped room. For example, there are several square patches where the distemper of the walls is of a darker shade than the rest, indicating the places once occupied by pictures. There is an uncovered deal table and two chairs by it near the fireplace right. Attached to the left wall is a dresser and a plate rack above it containing a few pots. The dresser has also one or two utensils upon it. A blackened kettle rests on the top of the cooking range, but the room contains only the barest necessities. The floor is uncarpeted. There are no window curtains, but a yard of cheap muslin is fastened across the window, not coming, however, high enough to prevent a passer-by from looking in should he wish to do so. On the floor, near the fire, is a battered black tin trunk, the lid of which is raised. On a peg behind the door left is a black silk skirt and bodice and an old-fashioned beaded bonnet. The time is afternoon. As the curtain rises the room is empty.

[1] Published by Messrs Gowans and Gray, Ltd. (1*s.*). Applications regarding amateur performances of this play should be addressed to Messrs Samuel French, Ltd., 26 Southampton Street, Strand, London, W.C.2, or 25 West 45th Street, New York.

85

Immediately, however, the door left opens and SARAH
ORMEROD, *an old woman, enters carrying clumsily in her
arms a couple of pink flannelette nightdresses, folded neatly.
Her black stuff dress is well worn, and her wedding-ring is
her only ornament. She wears elastic-sided boots, and her
rather short skirt shows a pair of grey worsted stockings.
A small plaid shawl covers her shoulders.* SARAH *crosses
and puts the nightdresses on the table, surveying the
trunk ruefully. There is a knock at the outside door and
she looks up.*

SARAH. Who's theer ?

EMMA [*without*]. It's me, Mrs Ormerod, Emma Brierley.

SARAH. Eh, coom in, Emma, lass.

> [*Enter* EMMA BRIERLEY. *She is a young weaver, and,
> having just left her work, she wears a dark skirt,
> a blouse of some indeterminate blue-grey shade made
> of cotton, and a large shawl over her head and
> shoulders in place of a jacket and hat. A coloured
> cotton apron covers her skirt below the waist, and
> the short skirt displays stout stockings similar to*
> SARAH's. *She wears clogs, and the clothes—except
> the shawl—are covered with ends of cotton and
> cotton-wool fluff. Even her hair has not escaped.
> A pair of scissors hangs by a cord from her
> waist.*

SARAH. Tha's kindly welcoom. It's good o' thee to think
o' commin' to see an ould woman like me.

EMMA [*by door*]. Nought o' th' sort, Mrs Ormerod. Th'
mill's just loosed and A thowt A'd step in as A were passin'
and see 'ow tha was feeling like.

SARAH [*crossing to box*]. Oh, nicely, nicely, thankee. It's
only my 'ands as is gone paralytic, tha knaws, an' a weaver's
no manner o' good to nobody without th' use o' 'er 'ands.
A'm all reeght in masel'. That's worst of it.

EMMA. Well, while A'm 'ere, Mrs Ormerod, is theer nought as A can do for thee ?

SARAH. A dunno as theer is, thankee, Emma.

EMMA [*taking her shawl off, looking round and hanging it on a peg in the door*]. Well, A knaws better. What wert doin' when A coom in ? Packin' yon box ?

SARAH. Aye. Tha sees theer's a two three things as A canna bear thowt o' parting from. A don't reeghtly knaw if they'll let me tak' 'em into workus wi' me, but A canna have 'em sold wi' rest of stuff.

EMMA [*crosses below* SARAH *to box, going on her knees*]. Let me help yo.

SARAH. Tha's a good lass, Emma. A'd tak' it kindly of thee.

EMMA. They'd do wi' packin' a bit closer. A dunno as they'd carry safe that road.

SARAH. A know. It's my 'ands tha sees, as mak's it difficult for me. [*Sits on chair L. C.*

EMMA. Aye. A'll soon settle 'em a bit tighter.

[*Lifts all out. Burying her arms in the box and re-arranging its contents.*

SARAH. But what's 'appened to thy looms, lass ? They'll not weave by 'emselves while thee's 'ere, tha knows.

EMMA [*looking round*]. Eh, looms is all reeght. Factory's stopped. It's Saturday afternoon.

SARAH. So 'tis. A'd clean forgot. A do forget time o' th' week sittin' 'ere day arter day wi' nought to do.

EMMA. So that's all reeght. Tha's no need to worry about me. Tha's got trouble enough of thy own.

[*Resuming at the box.*

SARAH. Aye, th'art reeght theer, lass. Theer's none on us likes to think o' going to workus when we're ould.

EMMA. 'Appen it'll be all reeght after all. Parson's coomin' to see thee.

87

SARAH. Aye, A knaw 'e is. A dunno, but A'm in 'opes 'e'll do summat for me. Tha can't never tell what them folks can do.

EMMA [*kneeling up*]. Tha keep thy pecker oop, Mrs Ormerod. That's what my moother says to me when A tould 'er A were coomin' in to thee. Keep 'er pecker oop, she says. It's not as if she'd been lazy or a wastrel, she says ; Sal Ormerod's bin a 'ard worker in 'er day, she says. It's not as if it were thy fault. Tha can't 'elp tha 'ands going paralytic.

[*She continues rummaging in the trunk while speaking.*

SARAH. Naw. It's not my fault. God knaws A'm game enough for work, ould as A am. A allays knawed as A'd 'ave to work for my living all th' days o' my life. A never was a savin' sort.

EMMA. Theer's nowt against thee for that. Theer's some as can be careful o' theer brass an' some as can't. It's not a virtue, it's a gift. That's what my moother allays says.

[*Resumes packing.*

SARAH. She's reeght an' all. We never 'ad the gift o' savin', my man and me. An' when Tom Ormerod took an' died, the club money as A drew all went on 'is funeral an' 'is gravestone. A warn't goin' to 'ave it said as 'e warn't buried proper.

EMMA. It were a beautiful funeral, Mrs Ormerod.

SARAH. Aye.

EMMA. A will say that, beautiful it were. A never seen a better, an' A goes to all as A can. [*Rises.*] A dotes on buryin's. Are these the next ?

[*Crosses C. before table for nightdresses. Takes the
nightdresses, and resumes packing.*

SARAH. Aye.

[EMMA *puts them in and rests on her knees listening to*
SARAH'S *next speech.*

SARAH [*pause*]. A've been a 'ouseproud woman all my life, Emma, an A've took pride in 'aving my bits 'o sticks as good as another's. Even th' manager's missus oop to factory 'ouse theer, she never 'ad a better show o' furniture nor me, though A says it as shouldn't. An' it tak's brass to keep a decent 'ouse over your yead. An' we allays 'ad our full week's 'ollydayin' at Blackpool reglar at Wakes time. Us didn't 'ave no childer o' our own to spend it on, an' us spent it on ourselves. A allays 'ad a plenty o' good food in th' 'ouse an' never stinted nobody, an' Tom 'e liked 'is beer an' 'is baccy. 'E were a pigeon-fancier too in 'is day, were my Tom, an' pigeon-fancying runs away wi' a mint o' money. No. Soom'ow theer never was no brass to put in th' bank. We was allays spent oop coom wages neeght.

EMMA. A knaw, Mrs Ormerod. May be A'm young, but A knaw 'ow 'tis. We works cruel 'ard in th' mill, an', when us plays, us plays as 'ard too [*pause*], an' small blame to us either. It's our *own* we're spendin'.

SARAH. Aye. It's a 'ard life, the factory 'and's. A can mind me many an' many's the time when th' warnin' bell went on th' factory lodge at ha'f-past five of a winter's mornin' as A've craved for another ha'f-hour in my bed, but Tom 'e got me oop an' we was never after six passin' through factory gates all th' years we were wed. There's not many as can say they were never late. " Work or Clem," that were what Tom allays tould me th' ould bell were sayin'. An' 'e were reeght, Emma, " Work or Clem " is God's truth. [EMMA's *head in box*.] An' now th' time's coom when A can't work no more. But Parson's a good man, 'e'll mak' it all reeght. [EMMA's *head appears*.] Eh, it were good o' thee to coom in, lass. A bit o' coompany do mak' a world o' difference. A'm twice as cheerful as A were.

EMMA. A'm glad to 'ear tha say so, Mrs Ormerod. [*Rises from the box*.] Is theer owt else ?

SARAH. A were thinking A'd like to tak' my black silk as A've worn o' Sundays this many a year, but A canna think it's reeght thing for workus.

EMMA. Oh, thee tak' it, Mrs Ormerod.

SARAH. A'd dearly love to. Tha sees A'm noan in debt, nobbut what chairs an' table 'ull pay for, and A doan't like thowt o' leaving owt as A'm greatly fond of.

EMMA. Yo doan't, Mrs Ormerod. Thee tak' it. Wheer is it ? A'll put un in. Theer's lots o' room on top. A'll see un's noan crushed.

SARAH. It's hanging theer behind door. [EMMA *crosses back to door, gets clothes.*] A got un out to show Parson. A thowt A'd ask un if it were proper to tak' it if A've to go. My best bonnet's with it, an' all.

[EMMA *goes below table, takes the frock and bonnet, folds it on the table and packs it.*

EMMA. A'll put un in.

SARAH. A'm being a lot o' trouble to thee, lass.

EMMA. That's nowt, neighbours mun be neighbourly.

[*Gets bonnet from table and packs it.*

SARAH [*pause. Looking round*]. Place doan't look much, an' that's a fact. Th' furniture's bin goin' bit by bit, and theer ain't much left to part wi' now.

EMMA. Never mind, it 'ull be all reeght now Parson's takken thee oop.

SARAH. A'm hopin' so. A *am* hopin' so. A never could abide th' thowt o' th' workus—me as 'as bin an 'ard-workin' woman. A couldn't fancy sleepin' in a strange bed wi' strange folk round me, an' when th' Matron said " Do that " A'd 'ave to do it, an' when she said " Go theer " A'd 'ave to a' gone wheer she tould me—me as 'as allays 'eld my yead 'igh an' gone the way A pleased masel'. Eh, it's a terrible thowt, the workus.

EMMA [*rising*]. Now tha's sure that's all ?

SARAH [*pause. Considers*]. Eh, if A havna forgot my neeghtcaps. [*Rises, moves C. and stops.*] A suppose they'll let me wear un in yonder. A doan't reeghtly think as A'd get my rest proper wi'out my neeghtcaps.

EMMA. Oh, they'll let thee wear un all reeght.

SARAH [*as she goes*]. A'll go an' get un. [*Exit R., returning presently with the white nightcaps.*] That's all now.

[*Giving them to* EMMA, *who meets her C.*

EMMA [*putting them in*]. Yo never 'ad no childer, did yo, Mrs Ormerod?

SARAH. No, Emma, no—may be that's as broad as 's long. [*Sits above fire.*] Yo never knaw 'ow they go. Soom on 'em turn again yo when they're growed or they get wed themselves an' forget all as yo've done for 'em, like a many A could name, and they're allays a worrit to yo when they're young.

EMMA. A'm gettin' wed masel' soon, Mrs Ormerod.

SARAH. Are yo, now, Emma? Well, tha art not one o' them graceless good-for-nowts. Tha'll never forget thy moother, A knaw, nor what she's done for thee. Who's tha keepin' coompany with?

EMMA. It's Joe Hindle as goes wi' me, Mrs Ormerod.

SARAH. 'Indle, 'Indle? What, not son to Robert 'Indle, 'im as used to be overlooker in th' factory till 'e went to foreign parts to learn them Roossians 'ow to weave?

EMMA. Aye, that's 'im.

SARAH. Well, A dunno ought about th' lad. 'Is faither were a fine man. A minds 'im well. But A'll tell thee this, Emma, an' A'll tell it thee to thy faice, 'e 's doin' well for 'isself is young Joe 'Indle.

EMMA. Thankee, Mrs Ormerod.

SARAH. Gettin' wed! Think o' that. What, it seems as t'were only t'other day as tha was running about in short frocks, an' now tha's growed up and gettin' thasel' wed!

Time do run on. Sithee, Emma, tha's a good lass. A've gotten an ould teapot in yonder [*indicating her bedroom*] as my moother give me when A was wed. A weren't for packing it in box because o' risk o' breaking it. A were going to carry it in my 'and. A'd a mind to keep it till A died, but A reckon A'll 'ave no use for it in workus.

EMMA. Tha's not gone theer yet.

SARAH. Never mind that. [*Slowly rises.*] A'm going to give it thee, lass, for a weddin'-gift. Tha'll tak' care of it, A knaw, and when thy eye catches it, 'appen tha'll spare me a thowt.

EMMA. Oh no, Mrs Ormerod, A couldn't think o' takkin' it.

SARAH. Art too proud to tak' a gift from me?

EMMA. No. Tha knaws A'm not.

SARAH. Then hold thy hush. A'll be back in a minute. Happen A'd best tidy masel' up too against Parson cooms.

EMMA. Can A help thee, Mrs Ormerod?

SARAH. No, lass, no. A can do a bit for masel'. My 'ands isn't that bad. A canna weave wi' 'em, but A can do all as A need to.

EMMA. Well, A'll do box up.

[*Crosses to table R. and gets cord.*

SARAH. Aye.

EMMA. All reeght.

[*Exit* SARAH. *A man's face appears outside at the window. He surveys the room, and then the face vanishes as he knocks at the door.*

Who's theer?

SAM [*without*]. It's me, Sam Horrocks. [EMMA *crosses L. and opens door.*] May A coom in?

EMMA. What dost want?

SAM [*on the doorstep*]. A want a word wi' thee, Emma Brierley. A followed thee oop from factory and A've bin waitin' out theer till A'm tired o' waitin'.

EMMA. Well, tha'd better coom in. A 'aven't time to talk wi' thee at door.

> [EMMA *lets him in, closes door, and, leaving him standing in the middle of the room, resumes work on her knees at the box.* SAM HORROCKS *is a hulking young man of a rather vacant expression. He is dressed in mechanic's blue dungarees. His face is oily and his clothes stained. He wears boots, not clogs. He mechanically takes a ball of oily black cotton-waste from his right pocket when in conversational difficulties and wipes his hands upon it. He has a red muffler round his neck without collar, and his shock of fair hair is surmounted by a greasy black cap, which covers perhaps one tenth of it.*

SAM [*after watching* EMMA's *back for a moment*]. Wheer's Mrs Ormerod ?

EMMA [*without looking up*]. What's that to do wi' thee ?

SAM [*apologetically*]. A were only askin'. Tha needn't be short wi' a chap.

EMMA. She's in scullery washin' 'er if tha wants to knaw.

SAM. Oh !

EMMA [*looking at him over her shoulder after a slight pause*]. Doan't tha tak' thy cap off in 'ouse, Sam Horrocks ?

SAM. Naw.

EMMA. Well, tha can tak' it off in this 'ouse or get t' other side o' door.

SAM [*takes off his cap and stuffs it in his left pocket after trying his right and finding the ball of waste in it*]. Yes, Emma.

> [EMMA *resumes work with her back towards him and waits for him to speak. But he is not ready yet.*

EMMA. Well, what dost want ?

SAM. Nought. . . . Eh, but tha art a gradely wench.

EMMA. What's that to do wi' thee ?

SAM. Nought.

EMMA. Then just tha mind thy own business, an' doan't pass compliments behind folks' backs.

SAM. A didn't mean no 'arm.

EMMA. Well ?

SAM. It's a fine day, isn't it ? For th' time o' th' year ?

EMMA. Aye.

SAM. A very fine day.

EMMA. Aye.

SAM [*desperately*]. It's a damned fine day.

EMMA. Aye.

SAM [*after a moment*]. Dost know my 'ouse, Emma ?

EMMA. Aye.

SAM. Wert ever in it ?

EMMA. Not sin' tha moother died.

SAM. Naw. A suppose not. Not sin' ma moother died. She were a fine woman, ma moother, for all she were bed-ridden.

EMMA. She were better than 'er son, though that's not saying much neither.

SAM. Naw, but tha does mind ma 'ouse, Emma, as it were when she were alive ?

EMMA. Aye.

SAM. A've done a bit at it sin' them days. Got a new quilt on bed from Co-op. Red un it is wi' blue stripes down 'er.

EMMA. Aye.

SAM. Well, Emma ?

EMMA [*over her shoulder*]. Well, what ? What's thy 'ouse an' thy quilt to do wi' me ?

SAM. Oh nought. . . . Tha doesn't 'elp a feller much, neither.

EMMA [*rising and facing him. SAM is behind corner table and backs a little before her*]. What's tha gettin' at, Sam Horrocks ? Tha's got a tongue in thy faice, hasn't tha ?

sam. A suppose so.   A doan't use it much though.

emma. No.   Tha's not much better than a tongue-tied idiot, Sam Horrocks, allays mooning about in th' engine-house in day-time an' sulkin' at 'ome neeght-time.

sam. Aye, A'm lonely sin' ma moother died.   She did 'ave a way wi' 'er, ma moother.   Th' 'ould plaice 'as not bin t' same to me sin' she went.   Day-time, tha knaws, A'm all reeght.   Tha sees, them engines, them an' me's pals. They talks to me an' A understands their ways.   A doan't some'ow seem to understand the ways o' folks like as A does th' ways o' them engines.

emma. Tha doesn't try.   T'other lads goes rattin' or dog-feeghtin' on a Sunday or to a football match of a Saturday afternoon.   Tha stays moonin' about th' 'ouse.   Tha's not likely to understand folks.   Tha's not sociable.

sam. Naw.   That's reeght enough.   A nobbut get laughed at when A tries to be sociable an' stand my corner down at th' pub wi' th' rest o' th' lads.   It's no use ma tryin' to soop ale, A can't carry th' drink like t'others. A knaws A've ways o' ma own.

emma. Tha has that.

sam. A'm terrible lonesome, Emma.   That theer 'ouse o' mine, it do want a wench about th' plaice.   Th' engines is all reeght for days, but th' neeghts is that lonesome-like tha wouldn't believe.

emma. Tha's only thasel' to blame.   It's nought to do wi' me, choosehow.

sam. Naw ?   A'd . . . A'd 'oped as 'ow it might 'ave, Emma.

emma [*approaching threateningly*]. Sam Horrocks, if tha doan't tell me proper what tha means A'll give tha such a slap in th' mouth.

sam [*backing before her*   Tha does fluster a feller, Emma. Just like ma moother.

EMMA. A wish A 'ad bin. A'd 'ave knocked some sense into thy silly yead.

SAM [*suddenly and clumsily kneels above chair L. of table*]. Wilt tha 'ave me, Emma ? A mak' good money in th' engine-house.

EMMA. Get oop, tha great fool. If tha didn't keep thasel' so close wi' tha moonin' about in th' engine-'ouse an' never speakin' a word to nobody tha'd knaw A were keepin' coompany wi' Joe Hindle.

SAM [*scrambling up*]. Is that a fact, Emma ?

EMMA. Of course it's a fact. Bann's 'ull be oop come Sunday fortneeght. We've not 'idden it neither. It's just like the great blind idiot that tha art not to 'a' seen it long enough sin'.

SAM. A wern't aware. By gum, A 'ad so 'oped as tha'd 'ave me, Emma.

EMMA [*a little more softly*]. A'm sorry if A've 'urt thee, Sam.

SAM. Aye. It were my fault. Eh, well, A think mebbe A'd best be goin'.

EMMA [*lifts box to L.*]. Aye. Parson's coomin' to see Mrs Ormerod in a minute.

SAM [*with pride*]. A knaw all about that, anyhow.

EMMA. She'm in a bad way. A dunno masel' as Parson can do much for 'er.

SAM. It's 'ard lines on an ould un. Well, yo'll not want me 'ere. A'll be movin' on. [*Getting his cap out*] No offence, Emma, A 'ope. A'd a've asked thee first if A'd knawn as 'e were after thee. A've bin trying' for long enough.

EMMA. No. Theer's no offence, Sam. Tha's a good lad if tha art a fool, an' mebbe tha's not to blame for that. Good-bye.

SAM. Good-bye, Emma. An' . . . an' A 'ope 'e'll mak'

thee 'appy.   A'd dearly like to coom to th' weddin' an' shake
'is 'and.   [MRS ORMEROD *heard off R.*

EMMA.   A'll see tha's asked.   Theer's Mrs Ormerod stirrin'.
Tha'd best be gettin'.

SAM.   All reeght.   Good-bye, Emma.

EMMA.   Good-bye, Sam.

> [*Exit* SAM *L. C.*   MRS ORMEROD *comes from the
> inside door.   She has a small blue teapot in her
> hand.*

SARAH.   Was anybody 'ere, Emma ?   A thowt A yeard
someun talkin', only my yearin' isn't what it used to be, an'
A warn't sure.

EMMA.   It were Sam Horrocks, Mrs Ormerod.

SARAH.   Yon lad of ould Sal Horrocks as died last year ?
'Im as isn't reeght in 'is yead ?

EMMA.   Aye.   'E's bin askin' me to wed 'im.

SARAH [*incensed*].   In my 'ouse ?   Theer's imperence for
thee, an' tha promised to another lad, an' all.   A'd 'ave set
about 'im wi' a stick, Emma.

EMMA.   'E didn't knaw about Joe.   It made me feel cruel-
like to 'ave to tell 'im.

SARAH.   'E'll get ower it.   Soom lass'll tak' 'im.

EMMA.   A suppose so.

SARAH [*coming down, putting the tea-pot in* EMMA's *hands*].
Well, theer's tea-pot.

EMMA [*meets* SARAH *R. C., examining tea-pot*].   It's beautiful.   Beautiful, it is, Mrs Ormerod.

SARAH.   Aye, it's a bit o' real china is that.   Tha'll tak'
care on't, lass, won't thee ?

EMMA.   A will an' all.

SARAH.   Aye.   A knaw it's safe wi' thee.   Mebbe safer
than it would be in workus.   A can't think well on yon
plaice.   A goa cold all ower at thowt of it.

> [*A knock at the door.*

EMMA. That'll be Parson.

SARAH [*crosses L. Smoothing her hair*]. Goa an' look through window first, an' see who 'tis.

EMMA [*puts tea-pot on table. Looking through window*]. It's not th' ould Parson. It's one o' them young curate chaps.

SARAH. Well, coom away from window an' sit thee down. It won't do to seem too eager. Let un knock again if it's not th' ould Parson.

[EMMA *leaves the window and goes to R. of table. The knock is repeated.*

[*Raising her voice*] Coom in so who tha art. Door's on latch.

[*Enter the* REV. FRANK ALLEYNE. *He is a young curate, a Londoner and an Oxford man, by association, training, and taste, totally unfitted for a Lancashire curacy, in which he is unfortunately no exception.*

ALLEYNE. Good afternoon, Mrs Ormerod.

SARAH. Good day to thee.

ALLEYNE. I'm sorry to say Mr Blundell has had to go to a missionary meeting, but he asked me to come and see you in his stead.

SARAH. Tha's welcoom, lad. Sit thee down.

[EMMA *comes below table L. Dusts a chair L. of table, which doesn't need it, with her apron.* ALLEYNE *raises a deprecatory hand.* SARAH's *familiarity, as it seems to him, offends him. He looks sourly at* EMMA *and markedly ignores her.*

ALLEYNE. Thank you ; no, I won't sit, I cannot stay long.

SARAH. Just as tha likes. It's all same to me.

[EMMA *stays by R. of table.*

ALLEYNE. How is it with you, Mrs Ormerod ?

SARAH. It might be worse. A've lost th' use o' my 'ands,

98

and they're takkin' me to workus, but A'm not dead yet, and that's summat to be thankful for.

ALLEYNE. Oh yes, yes, Mrs Ormerod. The—er—message I am to deliver is, I fear, not quite what Mr Blundell led you to hope for. His efforts on your behalf have—er—unfortunately failed. He finds himself obliged to give up all hope of aiding you to a livelihood. In fact—er—I understand that the arrangements made for your removal to the workhouse this afternoon must be carried out. It seems there is no alternative. I am grieved to be the bearer of bad tidings, but I am sure you will find a comfortable home awaiting you, Mrs—er—Ormerod.

SARAH. 'Appen A shall an' 'appen A shan't. Theer's no tellin' 'ow you'll favour a thing till you've tried it.

ALLEYNE. You must resign yourself to the will of Providence. The consolations of religion are always with us. Shall I pray with you?

SARAH. A never were much at prayin' when A were well off, an' A doubt the Lord ud tak' it kind o' selfish o' me if A coom crying' to 'Im now A'm 'urt.

ALLEYNE. He will understand. Can I do nothing for you?

SARAH. A dunno as tha can, thankin' thee all same.

ALLEYNE. I am privileged with Mr Blundell's permission to bring a little gift to you, Mrs Ormerod. [*Feeling in his coat-tails and bringing out a Testament.*] Allow me to present you with this Testament, and may it help you to bear your cross with resignation. [*He hands her the Testament.* SARAH *does not raise her hands, and it drops on her lap.* ALLEYNE *takes it again and puts it on the table.*] Ah, yes, of course . . . your poor hands . . . I understand.

SARAH. Thankee kindly. Readin' don't coom easy to me, an' my eyes aren't what they were, but A'll mak' most of it.

ALLEYNE. You will never read that in vain. And now,

dear sister, I must go. I will pray for strength for you. All will be well. Good day.

SARAH. Good day to thee. [*Exit* ALLEYNE.

EMMA. Tha doesn't look so pleased wi' tha gift, Mrs Ormerod.

SARAH. It's not square thing of th' ould Parson, Emma. 'E should a coom an' tould me 'isself. Looks like 'e were feart to do it. A never could abide them curate lads. We doan't want no grand Lunnon gentlemen down 'ere. 'E doan't understand us no more than we understand 'im. 'E means all reeght, poor lad. Sithee, Emma, A've bin a church-goin' woman all my days. A was browt oop to church, an' many's th' bit o' brass they've 'ad out o' me in my time. An' in th' end they send me a fine curate with a tuppenny Testament. That's all th' good yo get out o' they folks.

EMMA. We'm chapel to our 'ouse, an' 'e didn't forget to let me see 'e knaw'd it, but A doan't say as it's ony different wi' chapels, neither. They get what they can outer yo, but yo mustn't look for nothin' back, when th' pinch cooms. [*Clock outside strikes three.*] Sakes alive, theer's clock goin' three. My dinner 'ull be nice an' cold.

SARAH. Eh, what's that, lass? Dost mean to tell me tha's bin clemmin' all this time?

EMMA. A coom 'ere straight from factory.

SARAH. Then tha doesn't move till tha's 'ad summat to eat.

EMMA. My dinner's ready for me at whoam, Mrs Ormerod.

SARAH. Then just look sharp an' get it, tha silly lass. Tha's no reeght to go wi'out thy baggin'.

EMMA [*putting her shawl on*]. All reeght. A'm off.

[*Picking up teapot.*

SARAH. Tha's bin a world o' coomfort to me, Emma. It'll be 'arder to bear when tha's gone. Th' thowt's too much for me. Eh, lass, A'm feart o' yon great gaunt building wi' th' drear windows.

EMMA. 'Appen ma moother 'ull coom in. Tha'll do wi' a bit o' coompany. A'll ask her to coom an' fetch thee a coop o' tea by an' bye. [*A knock at the door.*

SARAH. Who's theer ?

SAM [*without*]. It's only me, Mrs Ormerod.

EMMA. A do declare it's that Sam Horrocks again.

SARAH. Sam Horrocks ! What can th' lad be after now ? [*Calling*] Hast tha wiped thy boots on scraper ?

SAM. Yes, Mrs Ormerod.

SARAH. Coom in then. [EMMA *in L. corner. Enter* SAM.] Tak' thy cap off.

SAM. Yes, Mrs Ormerod.

SARAH. What dost want ?

SAM. A've soom business 'ere. A thowt A'd find thee by thysel'. A'll coom again. [*Bolting nervously for the door.*

SARAH. Let that door be. Dost say tha's got business 'ere ?

SAM. Aye, wi' thee. A'd like a word wi' thee private.

[EMMA *moves to open door.*

SARAH. All reeght. Emma's just goin' to 'er dinner.

EMMA [*speaking through door*]. A'll ask my moother to step in later on, Mrs Ormerod, and thank thee very much for th' tea-pot.

SARAH. A'll be thankful if she'll coom. [*Exit* EMMA *with tea-pot.*] Now, Sam Horrocks, what's the matter wi' thee ?

SAM [*dropping the cotton waste he is fumbling with and picking it up*]. It's a fine day for th' time o' th' year.

SARAH. Didst want to see me private to tell me that, lad ?

SAM. Naw, not exactly.

SARAH. Well, what is it then ? Coom, lad, A'm waitin' on thee. Art tongue-tied ? Can't tha quit mawlin' yon bit o' waste an' tell me what 'tis tha wants ?

SAM [*desperately*]. Mebbe it'll not be so fine in th' mornin'.

SARAH. A'll tell thee what A'd do to thee if A 'ad the use o' my 'ands, my lad. A'd coom aside thee and A'd box thy ears. If tha's got business wi' me, tha'd best state it sharp or A'll be showin' thee the shape o' my door.

SAM. Tha do fluster a feller so as A doan't knaw wheer A am. A've not been nagged like that theer sin' my ould moother died.

SARAH. A've 'eerd folk say Sal Horrocks were a slick un wi' 'er tongue.

SAM [*admiringly*]. She were that. Rare talker she were. She'd lie theer in 'er bed all day as it might be in yon corner, an' call me all th' names she could put her tongue to, till A couldn't tell ma reeght 'and from ma left. [*Still reminiscent*] Wonnerful sperrit, she 'ad, considerin' she were bed-ridden so long. She were only a little un an' cripple an' all, but by gum she could sling it at a feller if 'er tea weren't brewed to 'er taste. Talk! She'd talk a donkey's yead off, she would.

SARAH [*on her mettle*]. An' A'll talk thy silly yead off an' all if tha doan't get sharp to tellin' me what tha wants after in my 'ouse, tha great mazed idiot.

SAM. Eh, but she were a rare un.

SARAH. The lad's daft aboot his moother.

SAM [*detachedly, looking at window. Pause*]. Wunnerful breeght the sky is, to-day.

SARAH. Tha great 'ulkin' fool. A'd tak' a broomstick to thee if—if A'd the use o' my 'ands.

SAM. Now, if that isn't just what ma moother used to say.

SARAH. Dang thy moother. An' A doan't mean no disrespect to 'er neither. She's bin in 'er grave this year an' more, poor woman.

SAM. A canna 'elp thinkin' 'to 'er all same. Eh, but she were wunnerful.

SARAH. An' A'd be wunnerful too. A'd talk to thee. A'd call thee if A were thy moother an' A'd to live aside 'o thee neeght an' day.

SAM [*eagerly*]. Eh, by gum, but A wish tha would.

SARAH. Would what ?

SAM. Would coom an' live along wi' me.

SARAH. Tha great fool, what dost mean ? Art askin' me to wed thee ?

SAM. A didn't mean to offend thee, Mrs Ormerod. A'm sorry A spoke. A allays do wrong thing. But A did so 'ope as tha might coom. Tha sees A got used to Moother. A got used to 'earin' 'er cuss me. A got used to doin' for 'er an' A've nought to do in th' evenings now. It's terrible lonesome in th' neeght-time. An' when notion coom to me, A thowt as A'd mention un to thee casual.

SARAH. Dost mean it, Sam Horrocks ? Dost tha know what tha's sayin', or is tha foolin' me ?

SAM. O' course A mean it. Tha sees A'm not a marryin' sort. Th' lasses won't look at me. A'm silly Sam to them, A knaws it. A've a slate loose, A shan't never get wed. A thowt A'd mebbe a chance wi' yon lass as were 'ere wi' thee, but hoo towld me A were too late. A allays were slow. A left askin' too long an' A've missed 'er. A gets good money, Mrs Ormerod, but A canna talk to a young wench. They maks me go 'ot and cowld all over. An' when curate towld me as tha was to go to workus, A thowt A'd a chance wi' thee. A knaw'd it weren't a big chance, because my plaice ain't much cop after what tha's bin used to 'ere. A've got no fine fixin's nor big chairs an' things like as tha used to 'ave. Eh, but A would 'ave loved to do for thee as A used to do for ma moother, an' when A yeerd thee talkin' now an' callin' me a fool an' th' rest, by gum, A just yearned to 'ave thee for allays. Tha'd fill 'er plaice wunnerful well. A'd just a' loved to adopt thee.

SARAH. To adopt me?

SAM. Ay, for a moother. A'm sorry tha can't see thy way to let me. A didn't mean no offence.

[Turning to the door.

SARAH. 'Ere, lad, tha tell me this. If A'd said tha might tak' me for thy moother, what wouldst ha' done?

SAM. Why, kissed thee, an' takken thee oop in ma arms whoam to thy bed. It's standin' ready in yonder wi' clean sheets an' all, an' a new quilt from Co-op. A 'opes you'll pardon th' liberty o' mentioning it.

SARAH. A new quilt, Sam? What's colour?

SAM. Red, wi' blue stripes down 'er.

SARAH. A'm not a light weight, tha knows.

SAM. A'd carry thee easy—" Strong in th' arm and weak in th' yead." It's an ould sayin', but it's a good un, an' it fits.

SARAH. Wilt tha try, Sam Horrocks? God bless thee, wilt tha try, lad?

SAM. Dost mean it, Mrs Ormerod? Dost mean tha'll coom? Tha's not coddin' a feller, art tha?

SARAH. No, A'm not coddin'. Kiss me, Sam, my son.

[He kisses her and lifts her in his arms.

SAM. By gum, but that were good. A'll coom back fur thy box.

SARAH. Carry me careful, tha great luny. A'm not a sack o' flour.

SAM. Eh, but A likes to year thee talk. Yon was real mootherly, it were. *[Exit through door, carrying her.*

CURTAIN AT CLINK OF LATCH

THE RISING OF THE MOON

By Lady Gregory

CHARACTERS

Sergeant
Policeman X
Policeman B
A Ragged Man

LADY GREGORY, one of the originators of the Irish National Theatre in Dublin, is a playwright of astonishing fertility and great technical resource. She has perfected and uses a Kiltartan dialect which, while less beautiful than the dialect of Synge, is equally well adapted to her purpose. But although her name is strongly associated with rollicking peasant farces such as " Spreading the News," " The Jackdaw," " The Workhouse Ward," and " Hyacinth Halvey," there is both charm and the passion of Irish nationalism in " The Rising of the Moon "—a play which in purpose and accomplishment goes beyond the exhibition of closely observed Irish character in farcical circumstance. The circumstance can, indeed, be anything but farcical, as, for example, in " The Gaol Gate." In " The Story brought by Brigit " she wrote, by a plausible extension of an Irish legend, a Kiltartan Passion play.

THE RISING OF THE MOON [1]

SCENE: *Side of a quay in a seaport town. Some posts and chains. A large barrel. Enter three* POLICEMEN. *Moonlight.*

> [SERGEANT, *who is older than the others, crosses the stage to R. and looks down steps. The others put down a pastepot and unroll a bundle of placards.*

POLICEMAN B. I think this would be a good place to put up a notice. [*He points to barrel.*

POLICEMAN X. Better ask him. [*Calls to* SERGEANT.] Will this be a good place for a placard? [*No answer.*

POLICEMAN B. Will we put up a notice here on the barrel? [*No answer.*

SERGEANT. There's a flight of steps here that leads to the water. This is a place that should be minded well. If he got down here, his friends might have a boat to meet him; they might send it in here from outside.

POLICEMAN B. Would the barrel be a good place to put a notice up?

SERGEANT. It might; you can put it there. [*They paste the notice up.*

SERGEANT [*reading it*]. Dark hair—dark eyes, smooth face, height five feet five—there's not much to take hold of in that—it's a pity I had no chance of seeing him before he broke out of gaol. They say he's a wonder, that it's he

[1] Published by Messrs G. P. Putnam's Sons (paper covers, 1s. net). Applications regarding amateur performances of this play should be addressed to Messrs Samuel French, Ltd., 26 Southampton Street, Strand, London, W.C.2, or 25 West 45th Street, New York.

makes all the plans for the whole organization. There isn't another man in Ireland would have broken gaol the way he did. He must have some friends among the gaolers.

POLICEMAN B. A hundred pounds is little enough for the Government to offer for him. You may be sure any man in the force that takes him will get promotion.

SERGEANT. I'll mind this place myself. I wouldn't wonder at all if he came this way. He might come slipping along there [*points to side of quay*], and his friends might be waiting for him there [*points down steps*], and once he got away it's little chance we'd have of finding him ; it's maybe under a load of kelp he'd be in a fishing boat, and not one to help a married man that wants it to the reward.

POLICEMAN X. And if we get him itself, nothing but abuse on our heads for it from the people, and maybe from our own relations.

SERGEANT. Well, we have to do our duty in the force. Haven't we the whole country depending on us to keep law and order ? It's those that are down would be up and those that are up would be down, if it wasn't for us. Well, hurry on, you have plenty of other places to placard yet, and come back here then to me. You can take the lantern. Don't be too long now. It's very lonesome here with nothing but the moon.

POLICEMAN B. It's a pity we can't stop with you. The Government should have brought more police into the town, with *him* in gaol, and at assize time too. Well, good luck to your watch. [*They go out.*

SERGEANT [*walks up and down once or twice and looks at placard*]. A hundred pounds and promotion sure. There must be a great deal of spending in a hundred pounds. It's a pity some honest man not to be the better of that.

[A RAGGED MAN *appears at left and tries to slip past.*
SERGEANT *suddenly turns.*

THE RISING OF THE MOON

SERGEANT. Where are you going ?

MAN. I'm a poor ballad-singer, your honour. I thought to sell some of these [*holds out bundle of ballads*] to the sailors.

[*He goes on.*

SERGEANT. Stop ! Didn't I tell you to stop ? You can't go on there.

MAN. Oh, very well. It's a hard thing to be poor. All the world's against the poor !

SERGEANT. Who are you ?

MAN. You'd be as wise as myself if I told you, but I don't mind. I'm one Jimmy Walsh, a ballad-singer.

SERGEANT. Jimmy Walsh ? I don't know that name.

MAN. Ah, sure, they know it well enough in Ennis. Were you ever in Ennis, Sergeant ?

SERGEANT. What brought you here ?

MAN. Sure, it's to the assizes I came, thinking I might make a few shillings here or there. It's in the one train with the judges I came.

SERGEANT. Well, if you came so far, you may as well go farther, for you'll walk out of this.

MAN. I will, I will ; I'll just go on where I was going.

[*Goes towards steps.*

SERGEANT. Come back from those steps; no one has leave to pass down them to-night.

MAN. I'll just sit on the top of the steps till I see will some sailor buy a ballad off me that would give me my supper. They do be late going back to the ship. It's often I saw them in Cork carried down the quay in a hand-cart.

SERGEANT. Move on, I tell you. I won't have anyone lingering about the quay to-night.

MAN. Well, I'll go. It's the poor have the hard life ! Maybe yourself might like one, Sergeant. Here's a good sheet now. [*Turns one over.*] *Content and a Pipe*—that's

not much. *The Peeler and the Goat*—you wouldn't like that.
Johnny Hart—that's a lovely song.

SERGEANT. Move on.

MAN. Ah, wait till you hear it. [*Sings*]:

" There was a rich farmer's daughter lived near the town
of Ross ;
She courted a Highland soldier, his name was Johnny
Hart ;
Says the mother to her daughter, ' I'll go distracted
mad
If you marry that Highland soldier dressed up in
Highland plaid.' "

SERGEANT. Stop that noise.

[MAN *wraps up his ballads and shuffles towards the
steps.*

SERGEANT. Where are you going ?

MAN. Sure, you told me to be going, and I am going.

SERGEANT. Don't be a fool. I didn't tell you to go that
way ; I told you to go back to the town.

MAN. Back to the town, is it ?

SERGEANT [*taking him by the shoulder and shoving him
before him*]. Here, I'll show you the way. Be off with you.
What are you stopping for ?

MAN [*who has been keeping his eye on the notice, points to
it*]. I think I know what you're waiting for, Sergeant.

SERGEANT. What's that to you ?

MAN. And I know well the man you're waiting for—I
know him well—I'll be going. [*He shuffles on.*

SERGEANT. You know him ? Come back here. What sort
is he ?

MAN. Come back is it, Sergeant ? Do you want to have
me killed ?

SERGEANT. Why do you say that ?

MAN. Never mind. I'm going. I wouldn't be in your shoes if the reward was ten times as much. [*Goes on off stage to L.*] Not if it was ten times as much.

SERGEANT [*rushing after him*]. Come back here, come back. [*Drags him back.*] What sort is he? Where did you see him?

MAN. I saw him in my own place, in the County Clare. I tell you you wouldn't like to be looking at him. You'd be afraid to be in the one place with him. There isn't a weapon he doesn't know the use of, and as to strength, his muscles are as hard as that board [*slaps barrel*].

SERGEANT. Is he as bad as that?

MAN. He is then.

SERGEANT. Do you tell me so?

MAN. There was a poor man in our place, a sergeant from Ballyvaughan.—It was with a lump of stone he did it.

SERGEANT. I never heard of that.

MAN. And you wouldn't, Sergeant. It's not everything that happens gets into the papers. And there was a police-man in plain clothes, too. . . . It is in Limerick he was. . . . It was after the time of the attack on the police barrack at Kilmallock. . . . Moonlight . . . just like this . . . water-side. . . . Nothing was known for certain.

SERGEANT. Do you say so? It's a terrible country to belong to.

MAN. That's so, indeed! You might be standing there, looking out that way, thinking you saw him coming up this side of the quay [*points*], and he might be coming up this other side [*points*], and he'd be on you before you knew where you were.

SERGEANT. It's a whole troop of police they ought to put here to stop a man like that.

MAN. But if you'd like me to stop with you, I could be look-ing down this side. I could be sitting up here on this barrel.

SERGEANT. And you know him well, too?

MAN. I'd know him a mile off, Sergeant.

SERGEANT. But you wouldn't want to share the reward?

MAN. Is it a poor man like me, that has to be going the roads and singing in fairs, to have the name on him that he took a reward? But you don't want me. I'll be safer in the town.

SERGEANT. Well, you can stop.

MAN [*getting up on barrel*]. All right, sergeant. I wonder, now, you're not tired out, Sergeant, walking up and down the way you are.

SERGEANT. If I'm tired I'm used to it.

MAN. You might have hard work before you to-night yet. Take it easy while you can. There's plenty of room up here on the barrel, and you see farther when you're higher up.

SERGEANT. Maybe so. [*Gets up beside him on barrel, facing right. They sit back to back, looking different ways.*] You made me feel a bit queer with the way you talked.

MAN. Give me a match, Sergeant [*he gives it and* MAN *lights pipe*]; take a draw yourself? It'll quiet you. Wait now till I give you a light, but you needn't turn round. Don't take your eye off the quay for the life of you.

SERGEANT. Never fear, I won't. [*Lights pipe. They both smoke.*] Indeed it's a hard thing to be in the force, out at night and no thanks for it, for all the danger we're in. And it's little we get but abuse from the people, and no choice but to obey our orders, and never asked when a man is sent into danger, if you are a married man with a family.

MAN [*sings*]:

" As through the hills I walked to view the hills and
        shamrock plain,
    I stood awhile where nature smiles to view the rocks and
        streams,

On a matron fair I fixed my eyes beneath a fertile vale,
As she sang her song it was on the wrong of poor old
    Granuaile."

SERGEANT. Stop that; that's no song to be singing in
these times.

MAN. Ah, Sergeant, I was only singing to keep my heart
up. It sinks when I think of him. To think of us two
sitting here, and he creeping up the quay, maybe, to get
to us.

SERGEANT. Are you keeping a good look-out?

MAN. I am; and for no reward too. Amn't I the foolish
man? But when I saw a man in trouble, I never could help
trying to get him out of it. What's that? Did something
hit me?   [*Rubs his heart.*

SERGEANT [*patting him on the shoulder*]. You will get your
reward in heaven.

MAN. I know that, I know that, Sergeant, but life is
precious.

SERGEANT. Well, you can sing if it gives you more courage.

MAN [*sings*]:

" Her head was bare, her hands and feet with iron bands
    were bound,
  Her pensive strain and plaintive wail mingles with the
    evening gale,
  And the song she sang with mournful air, I am old
    Granuaile.
  Her lips so sweet that monarchs kissed . . ."

SERGEANT. That's not it. . . . " Her gown she wore was
stained with gore." . . . That's it—you missed that.

MAN. You're right, Sergeant, so it is; I missed it. [*Repeats line.*] But to think of a man like you knowing a song
like that.

SERGEANT. There's many a thing a man might know and might not have any wish for.

MAN. Now, I dare say, Sergeant, in your youth, you used to be sitting up on a wall, the way you are sitting up on this barrel now, and the other lads beside you, and you singing *Granuaile* ? . . .

SERGEANT. I did then.

MAN. And the *Shan Bhean Bhocht* ? . . .

SERGEANT. I did then.

MAN. And the *Green on the Cape* ?

SERGEANT. That was one of them.

MAN. And maybe the man you are watching for to-night used to be sitting on the wall, when he was young, and singing those same songs. . . . It's a queer world. . . .

SERGEANT. Whisht ! . . . I think I see something coming. . . . It's only a dog.

MAN. And isn't it a queer world ? . . . Maybe it's one of the boys you used to be singing with that time you will be arresting to-day or to-morrow, and sending into the dock. . . .

SERGEANT. That's true indeed.

MAN. And maybe one night, after you had been singing, if the other boys had told you some plan they had, some plan to free the country, you might have joined with them . . . and maybe it is you might be in trouble now.

SERGEANT. Well, who knows but I might ?   I had a great spirit in those days.

MAN. It's a queer world, Sergeant, and it's little any mother knows when she sees her child creeping on the floor what might happen to it before it has gone through its life, or who will be who in the end.

SERGEANT. That's a queer thought now, and a true thought.   Wait now till I think it out. . . . If it wasn't for the sense I have, and for my wife and family, and for me joining the force the time I did, it might be myself now would be after breaking gaol and hiding in the dark, and it might be him that's hiding in the dark and that got out of gaol would be sitting up where I am on this barrel. . . . And it might be myself would be creeping up trying to make my escape from himself, and it might be himself would be keeping the law, and myself would be breaking it, and myself would be trying maybe to put a bullet in his head, or to take up a lump of a stone the way you said he did . . . no, that myself did. . . . Oh! [*Gasps. After a pause.*] What's that ? [*Grasps* MAN's *arm.*]

MAN [*jumps off barrel and listens, looking out over water*]. It's nothing, Sergeant.

SERGEANT. I thought it might be a boat. I had a notion there might be friends of his coming about the quays with a boat.

MAN. Sergeant, I am thinking it was with the people you were, and not with the law you were, when you were a young man.

SERGEANT. Well, if I was foolish then, that time's gone.

MAN. Maybe, Sergeant, it comes into your head sometimes, in spite of your belt and your tunic, that it might have been as well for you to have followed Granuaile.

SERGEANT. It's no business of yours what I think.

MAN. Maybe, Sergeant, you'll be on the side of the country yet.

SERGEANT [*gets off barrel*]. Don't talk to me like that. I have my duties and I know them. [*Looks round.*] That was a boat ; I hear the oars.

[*Goes to the steps and looks down.*

MAN [*sings*] :

> " O, then, tell me, Shawn O'Farrell,
>   Where the gathering is to be.
>   In the old spot by the river
>   Right well known to you and me ! "

SERGEANT. Stop that ! Stop that, I tell you !

MAN [*sings louder*] :

" One word more, for signal token,
 Whistle up the marching tune,
 With your pike upon your shoulder,
 At the Rising of the Moon."

SERGEANT. If you don't stop that, I'll arrest you.

[*A whistle from below answers, repeating the air.*

SERGEANT. That's a signal. [*Stands between him and steps.*] You must not pass this way. . . . Step farther back. . . . Who are you ? You are no ballad-singer.

MAN. You needn't ask who I am ; that placard will tell you. [*Points to placard.*]

SERGEANT. You are the man I am looking for.

MAN [*takes off hat and wig.* SERGEANT *seizes them*]. I am. There's a hundred pounds on my head. There is a friend of mine below in a boat. He knows a safe place to bring me to.

SERGEANT [*looking still at hat and wig*]. It's a pity ! It's a pity. You deceived me. You deceived me well.

MAN. I am a friend of Granuaile. There is a hundred pounds on my head.

SERGEANT. It's a pity, it's a pity !

MAN. Will you let me pass, or must I make you let me ?

SERGEANT. I am in the force. I will not let you pass.

MAN. I thought to do it with my tongue. [*Puts hand in breast.*] What is that ?

Voice of POLICEMAN X *outside*. Here, this is where we left him.

SERGEANT. It's my comrades coming.

MAN. You won't betray me . . . the friend of Granuaile. *Slips behind barrel.*]

Voice of POLICEMAN B. That was the last of the placards.

POLICEMAN X [*as they come in*]. If he makes his escape, it won't be unknown he'll make it.

[SERGEANT *puts hat and wig behind his back.*

POLICEMAN B. Did anyone come this way ?

SERGEANT [*after a pause*]. No one.

POLICEMAN B. No one at all ?

SERGEANT. No one at all.

POLICEMAN B. We had no orders to go back to the station ; we can stop along with you.

SERGEANT. I don't want you. There is nothing for you to do here.

POLICEMAN B. You bade us to come back here and keep watch with you.

SERGEANT. I'd sooner be alone. Would any man come this way and you making all that talk ? It is better the place to be quiet.

POLICEMAN B. Well, we'll leave you the lantern anyhow.

[*Hands it to him.*

SERGEANT. I don't want it. Bring it with you.

POLICEMAN B. You might want it. There are clouds coming up and you have the darkness of the night before you yet. I'll leave it over here on the barrel. [*Goes to barrel.*

SERGEANT. Bring it with you, I tell you. No more talk.

POLICEMAN B. Well, I thought it might be a comfort to you. I often think when I have it in my hand and can be flashing it about into every dark corner [*doing so*] that it's the same as being beside the fire at home, and the bits of bogwood blazing up now and again.

[*Flashes it about, now on the barrel, now on* SERGEANT.

SERGEANT [*furious*]. Be off, the two of you, yourselves and your lantern !

[*They go out.* MAN *comes from behind barrel. He and* SERGEANT *stand looking at one another.*

SERGEANT. What are you waiting for ?

MAN. For my hat, of course, and my wig. You wouldn't wish me to get my death of cold ? [SERGEANT *gives them.*

MAN [*going towards steps*]. Well, good night, comrade, and thank you. You did me a good turn to-night, and I'm obliged to you. Maybe I'll be able to do as much for you when the small rise up and the big fall down . . . when we all change places at the Rising [*waves his hand and disappears*] of the Moon.

SERGEANT [*turning his back to audience and reading placard*]. A hundred pounds reward ! A hundred pounds ! [*Turns towards audience.*] I wonder, now, am I as great a fool as I think I am ?

CURTAIN

THE KING'S WAISTCOAT

A PLAY IN ONE ACT

By Olive Conway

CHARACTERS

Lord Francis Webling
Felicity Hammond
Bob Repington
Lady Susan Harcourt
Isaac Hammond
Zachariah Hammond
Servant

Miss Olive Conway's " Becky Sharp," an adaptation of the Waterloo chapters of *Vanity Fair* included in the First Series of *One-Act Plays of To-day*, proved to be one of the outstanding successes of that volume, and the demand for it from amateur producing societies has been exceptional. The following is an example of Miss Conway's work when she is not indebted for material to a Thackeray. " The King's Waistcoat " is a picture of manners during the reign of Charles II. It is a ' costume ' play, and good one-act ' costume ' plays are rare. Historically and dramatically it is a presentation of Puritan manners *versus* Cavalier manners (coarse, if witty, some of their manners were), and it is also a satire upon the king-worship of an earlier day than ours.

THE KING'S WAISTCOAT[1]

1670

*The scene is the chief room of a manor-house owned by
Isaac Hammond, an old Puritan. Its appointments are
as severe as the dress of its users. The door is C.;
window looking on garden L.; while R. is a sideboard
with pewter.*

FELICITY HAMMOND *sits by a table;* ZACHARIAH HAMMOND
*stands by her, her cousin, a good-looking boy in a heavy,
earnest way. If he is a bit of a fanatic, he is too sincere
to be priggish.*

ZACHARIAH [*appealingly*]. These are my last three days before I sail, Felicity. You make them heavy with afflictions.

FELICITY [*delicately sly*]. The Lord chasteneth whom He
loveth, Cousin Zachariah.

ZACHARIAH. You speak that cunningly. A man who did
not know you well, might think you mocked. [*Moves away,
then turns appealingly.*] Felicity, you see the strait you bring
me to. I am goaded to madness. I suspect a raillery in
every word you utter—you, whom I love.

FELICITY. It is a sad case, Cousin.

ZACHARIAH. Do you ease it? Even now, when I remind
you that in three days I sail for the Colonies, what assurance
do you give me?

Applications regarding amateur performances of this play should
be addressed to Messrs Samuel French, Ltd., 26 Southampton Street,
Strand, London, W.C.2, or 25 West 45th Street, New York.

FELICITY. You have so much assurance of your own, Cousin, that I do not see the need for liberality.

ZACHARIAH. You twit me. Yes, and in the very accent of the scented courtier who corrupts this house by——

FELICITY. Oh, but Lord Francis has ceased to be a courtier. He has foresworn the Court.

ZACHARIAH. He has not foresworn the Court's abominations. He stinks of the Court as a devil stinks of brimstone. He scents ; he is bewigged, bejewelled, and begemmed, wears satins and brocades and——

FELICITY. He must wear them or go naked. Having foresworn the town, he will no doubt get apparel undeserving of your censorship, when he is well enough to see a tailor.

ZACHARIAH. Is a man who broke his wrist six weeks ago too ill to send for a tailor ? He imposes on my uncle, feigning an illness that is past, and you defend him. Felicity, I should go happy to Bristol for my voyage were it not for Lord Francis Webling. Before he came, all that God purposed for us two was in a fair way of dutiful accomplishment. I see Satan's work in the coming of this lord.

FELICITY. Truly a carriage accident and a broken wrist are not amongst the blessings of Providence.

ZACHARIAH. Felicity, you make it plain with every word you speak how much you have consorted with the ungodly. You practise their levities. You talk their blasphemies.

FELICITY. Nay, Cousin, but I agreed with you, an accident which injures a lord is surely not a work of God.

ZACHARIAH. If the accident injured past mending, it might be.

FELICITY. Oh, you are uncharitable.

ZACHARIAH. Well, then the accident was Satan's work. Satan sent him here. But you keep him, Cousin. You abet the devil and——

THE KING'S WAISTCOAT

[*Enter* ISAAC HAMMOND, *C., an old man, walking with a stick, with a pious but slightly cunning expression of face. Still he is mellow and benign.*

ISAAC [*conversationally, not in surprise*]. You here, Zachariah?

ZACHARIAH [*turning hotly*]. Yes, Uncle. Here where there used to be a welcome for the godly.

ISAAC. And surely there is. [*Sitting.*

ZACHARIAH. I judge things as I find them. I find the carnal-minded have the warmer welcome, and six weeks are not long enough for them to outstay it.

ISAAC. Lord Francis must stay till he be fit to travel from us, Zachariah.

ZACHARIAH. Is he to travel? Felicity tells me he means to live in the country.

ISAAC. It has been God's will that under my roof he should see the error of his ways. He is to abjure the town.

ZACHARIAH. And to live near here? [ISAAC *agrees.*] And you approve? You value as a neighbour one who has wallowed in all the pollutions of the Court, one whose speech proclaims him of the sons of Anti-Christ?

ISAAC. He is the sinner who repented.

ZACHARIAH. No. A wolf whom you welcome as a lamb though he have not even troubled to change his skin.

ISAAC. Zachariah! This is disrespectful to my understanding.

ZACHARIAH. I do not doubt your understanding, Uncle. I doubt your honesty.

ISAAC [*rising*]. Nephew!

ZACHARIAH. I will speak my mind. I say you are lukewarm in the faith. I thought it when you shirked to go with me to America, where there is freedom of religion. I thought you weak in faith when you refused to let Felicity and me be wed before I went, but pleaded I must first make a home for her in the wilderness, then either send for her or come, so that God only knows when I may marry her. And I say you are worse than weak, you are a time-server, now that you are gentle with this interloper, who for aught you know is a Papist, because he is a lord and therefore has some interest at Court. Uncle, take heed. To bid for the protection of this profligate is to compromise with hell.

ISAAC. This is not to be borne.

ZACHARIAH. Then lift suspicion from you. Spare me the duty of bearing witness against you in the congregation.

ISAAC. You would do that?

ZACHARIAH. Send him away.

ISAAC. All in good time, Nephew, all in good time.

ZACHARIAH. To-day!

ISAAC. He shall go when humanity and Christian courtesy allow. I am not a barbarian to turn a sick man from my roof.

ZACHARIAH. So! He stays, and I go to sea knowing he is in the same house with Felicity, knowing that she, being woman and a weak vessel, is attracted by the outward showing of a man and will not look beneath the surface.

FELICITY. I am indeed a poor thing, Cousin.

ZACHARIAH. Felicity, will you drive all my doubts away? Will you marry me before I go?

FELICITY. Weak, silly as I am?

ISAAC. I have answered that already, Zachariah!

ZACHARIAH. And the answer is still the same? I am to go, leaving Felicity to the devices of this spangled piece of pranked-out suppleness?

ISAAC. Am I to be dictated to by you?

ZACHARIAH. No. By your conscience. Ask your conscience if it is fitting for one of God's chosen to harbour the

124

Amalekite. He grows upon you like a canker. Cut him off! Here! This hour!

ISAAC. Nephew, you strut like a cock in a chicken run. You pert blusterer, will you call my conscience to account? Listen to me; I am master here, and Lord Francis has my cordial leave to stay as long as he desire.

ZACHARIAH. Then I must cut his staying short, myself.

ISAAC. You will forbear from meddling.

ZACHARIAH. I have God's precedent for meddling with Satan's handiwork.

ISAAC. You insolent——

ZACHARIAH. Still, I will snatch this brand from the burning——

> [*Enter* LORD FRANCIS WEBLING, *in the extreme of elaborate fashion. His right wrist is carried in a sling. Lace handkerchief in his left hand. He is pale, but rather with the paleness of habitual dissipation than of illness.*

ISAAC [*going to him*]. How does your lordship feel to-day?

> [ZACHARIAH *goes up to window, staying there, turning his back.*

WEBLING. Pale, Mr Hammond, pale. I had great hopes of myself till I looked in the mirror. But mirrors have no obligingness; they always speak the truth, and I am constrained to feel extremely pale to-day. [*He bows.*] Your servant, Miss Felicity. There is small need to ask what answer *your* mirror made when it looked back into that rose-garden, your face.

FELICITY. At least it did not flatter me, Lord Francis.

WEBLING. It knew better than to attempt the impossible. [*Looks at* ZACHARIAH.] Do I identify the back as Cousin Zachariah's? I am your humble servant, sir.

> [ZACHARIAH *makes no motion.* WEBLING *raises voice.*

Mr Zachariah, your servant.

[ZACHARIAH *shuffles but does not turn.* WEBLING *sighs and sits.*

Indeed, the one great hardship I foresee in a country life is to grow accustomed to the manners of the bucolics.

ISAAC. We are not all to be judged by a peevish boy.

WEBLING. I am happy to acknowledge it, Mr Hammond. There are sharp contrasts in the country where, naturally, there are swine and, amazingly, there are such pearls as never gleamed in any Court.

ZACHARIAH [*turning and coming to him*]. Lord Francis Webling, you have insulted me.

WEBLING [*rising*]. In London, sir, I should have said the prior insult was that which your back offered me, but I am a stranger to the country and backs may be as much the mode as faces are in town.

ZACHARIAH. Will you come to plain words, sir? I hate you.

WEBLING. You appear to find hatred a most absorbing emotion, Mr Zachariah. Must I remind you there is a lady present?

ZACHARIAH [*striking him*]. Now do you understand me, sir? Will you fight or must I brand you coward as well as villain?

ISAAC. This brawling——

WEBLING. Nay, Mr Hammond, I vow the boy is positively heroical. But I will not fight you, Mr Zachariah, and for the reason that when I fight, I fight right-handedly.

[*Pointing with left hand to his sling.*

ZACHARIAH. Oh, Satan protects his own.

FELICITY. You speak of Satan! You who strike an injured man.

ZACHARIAH. Felicity! Uncle left me no other way.

FELICITY. And this way fails. Oh, you disgrace us all.

ISAAC. Leave the house, Zachariah. Leave instantly and never return.

ZACHARIAH. Felicity!

FELICITY. Go. [*Exit* ZACHARIAH *quite brokenly*.

ISAAC. I will make certain he is gone.   That, Lord Francis, is the best apology I can make. [WEBLING *bows*.

[*Exit* ISAAC.

[WEBLING *sits and astounds* FELICITY *by taking his right hand out of the sling and fanning his face with handkerchief*.

WEBLING. I vow I never admired myself before.   But I am newly apprenticed to self-restraint.   I still find it over-heating.

FELICITY. Lord Francis!   Your wrist!

WEBLING. I test its suppleness.

FELICITY. Supple!   You have sheltered from my cousin behind a lie.

WEBLING. Sheltered?   But do you not observe my wrist is sound?   I have saved his life.

FELICITY. How?

WEBLING. How?   Why, is our Zachariah a duellist?

FELICITY. God forbid.

WEBLING. Then God forbid that I should fight with him. I . . . I used to kill my men in duels, Felicity.

FELICITY. Oh!

WEBLING. I had no self-restraint.   Now, I ask you to perceive I have.

FELICITY. I perceive you have deceived us wickedly about your wrist.

WEBLING. Deception?   Yes.   But was it wicked?   Was it not a venial sin that procured me another week under your roof, poppet?   Will you not call it the last and smallest of my hypocrisies, and forgive it?

FELICITY. Lord Francis, did you really kill a man in a duel?

WEBLING. More than once. [*She looks at him admiringly.*] You should look horrified at my iniquity.

FELICITY [*trying to, failing, and bending her head*]. Yes.

WEBLING. I'll kiss your hand for that. [*Kisses it.*] What a very woman. What an Eve it is ! Confess, child, you had rather the monster you have tamed was a miracle of infamy than only a little bad.

FELICITY [*shyly*]. It is more creditable to me. If . . . if I really have—tamed you.

WEBLING. Adorable creature ! Tame ! It's possible an oath will stray into my conversation now and then, and it's sure I shan't attain the simple beauty of manner of a rustic Zachariah. But on my soul, Felicity, I have but the one ambition now, to make myself worthy of your sweet purity.

FELICITY. I think that God is very kind to me.

WEBLING [*sincerely*]. May God help me to deserve you.

[MANSERVANT *enters.*

SERVANT. To see Lord Francis Webling. Mr Repington and Lady Susan Harcourt.

WEBLING. Good God ! The devil and his doxy.

FELICITY. Lord Francis !

WEBLING. I warned you I should lapse, and a lapse is not surprising when such people fall upon one from the skies.

SERVANT. From Winton Hall, your lordship.

WEBLING. Then they've not fallen from heaven. They've risen from hell if Winton Hall deserves its reputation. I'll see them. [*Exit* SERVANT.] But you must not. They're of the Court.

FELICITY. The Court !

WEBLING. Yes. In its way, this is a sort of test. The town pursues me to the country. Fear nothing, child. It shall not catch me.

[*He hands her to the door. Exit* FELICITY.
[WEBLING *becomes busy with a pocket mirror, arrang-*

ing his wig. Enter BOB REPINGTON *and* LADY
SUSAN HARCOURT, *both stout, florid, coarsely hand-
some people in riding costume, shown in by the*
SERVANT.

SERVANT. Mr Repington. Lady Susan Harcourt.

LADY SUSAN. Harcutt, you imbecile. Have they *no* culture in the country ? [*Strikes him with switch.*]
                    [*The* SERVANT *gapes helplessly and exit.*

BOB [*crossing to embrace* WEBLING, *who evades him*]. You
damned fox, Frankie Webling ! But we smoked you. We
ran you to earth.

WEBLING [*bowing*]. Your servant, Mr Repington. Yours,
Lady Susan.

BOB. Here's a glacial frigidity. Why, my old rip, my
lusty sot, we've ridden twenty miles to see thee.

WEBLING. I am honoured.

BOB. And I am dusty. Get me a pint of Burgundy,
Frank.

LADY SUSAN. Get me a quart.

WEBLING. They do not keep it in this house. There is
ale and I believe I may trespass enough on my host's indul-
gence to order for you. I should warn you it is mild.
                                    [*Going to ring.*

LADY SUSAN. Mild ale ! I'd rather choke.

BOB. Have you lived here six weeks on ale ?

LADY SUSAN. Ale and kisses, Bob. He mortifies the flesh
in one direction that he may indulge it the more in another.

BOB. Aye, that's the secret. Bring her out, Frank. Let's
see the angel of this stoical ale-drinking paradise.

LADY SUSAN. She should be worth the seeing if you've
eschewed Burgundy for her.

WEBLING. You misapprehend.

BOB. Curse it, Frank, a man of your kidney doesn't rot in
the country for nothing.

WEBLING. You may remember I was dismissed the Court.

LADY SUSAN. You'll recover from that. Charles asked for you the other day.

WEBLING. No doubt to dot the *i*'s of my dismissal.

BOB. Or to recall you, lad. You've grown melancholic in the country. Why shouldn't he have asked for you to recall you ?

WEBLING. I do not wish to be recalled.

BOB. Oh, you've the pride of Lucifer. But you'll know soon what the King wanted.

WEBLING. How ?

BOB. Because he's an accomplished monarch, Frank. His Majesty can read.

WEBLING. You wrote to him ?

BOB. The very hour I heard that you were here. [WEBLING *looks sourly at him.*] Curse me, if that ain't the frostiest face of gratitude I ever saw in my life. You've grown faint-hearted on a diet of small-ale. What if you did leave Court under the cloud of his Majesty's displeasure ? The sun never shines brighter than when it shows forth after an eclipse.

WEBLING. You thought to do me a service, Bob, and I suppose that I must thank you——

BOB. Oddslife, Susan, he supposes he must thank us ! Why, you whey-faced ingrate, we're the very impersonation of the milk of human kindness.

WEBLING. The truth is, I hoped never to hear of the Court again.

LADY SUSAN. Lud, Repington, we're visiting a lunatic.

WEBLING. I think you're visiting a man that has been cured of lunacy.

BOB. By becoming a country bumpkin ? You're dreaming.

WEBLING. May I never wake.

BOB. Didst ever dice all night, Frank ?

WEBLING. You know I did.

BOB. And afterwards strolled into St James's Park in the cool of the dawn and bought new milk of the milkmaid that has a cow there ? It's monstrous pleasant to be simple when the playhouse and the gaming rooms are round the corner, but simplicity when the reasonable requirements of a man of quality are not within call is a nauseating insipid idea. A man that's had success at Court can't sit down in the country and breed cabbages. Positively you don't know how waistcoats are cut this last month.

WEBLING [*interested*]. There's been a change of fashion since this ? [*Indicates his waistcoat.*]

BOB. Split me, a revolution. The King appeared one day with——

LADY SUSAN. Don't tell him, Bob, let him come to town to find out.

WEBLING. Nay, but if I am out of date, I implore you——

LADY SUSAN. Out of date ? You are obsolete ! In six weeks, Frank. Think what you'll be in six months.

BOB. He'll frighten rooks.

WEBLING. I—— [*With an effort*] I shall do very well. New fashions do not interest me.

BOB. 'Twas to celebrate a conquest that Charles donned the waistcoat.

WEBLING. A conquest ! The King has a new mistress ?

LADY SUSAN. Oh, lud, Lord Francis, your bumpkinly plain-speaking makes me blush.

WEBLING [*bowing*]. From this moment, I am famous. But tell me, who is it that the King——? No, his Majesty's amours bore me.

BOB. You exhibit unspeakable mental degradation, Webling. Six weeks in the house of a crop-eared Puritan——

WEBLING [*interrupting angrily*]. My host, Repington.

BOB. Six weeks with such a host have sunk you to the level of not caring to know who loves who at Court. The beasts in the field have more intellectual interests than you. Rot it, Frank, if you had to have a carriage accident, had you no more taste than to be thrown out at the gates of a notorious Puritan?

WEBLING. I did not have to have my accident, Repington. Seeing a lady in Mr Hammond's garden as I drove past, I contrived my accident by putting my cane between the spokes of the wheels.

LADY SUSAN. I vowed there was a wench in it, Bob.

BOB. Bring her to town, Frank. You dog! You selfish, licentious dog! You discover a jewel in a pig-sty and want her to glitter for yourself alone.

WEBLING. My wife, Repington, who at the moment is still Mistress Felicity Hammond——

BOB. Your wife! Lud, Webling, what an unspeakably wanton thought.

WEBLING. My wife——

BOB. No, man. It's stark lunacy. Charles may forgive you the past, but he'll never forgive you a marriage with a psalm-singer.

WEBLING. I shall hope to survive his displeasure.

BOB. It ain't natural. It's a perverted alliance. I shall have to wear a domino when I come to call on you in town.

WEBLING. I secure you from that inconvenience by not living in town.

LADY SUSAN. You can't live in the country for ever.

BOB. It's heathenish to find a treasure and to bury it. If Mistress Hammond has half the beauty you imply—you must give the town the chance to quizz her.

WEBLING. Thank you. I'll spare her that.

BOB. Gad, he's afraid to trust his Puritan.

WEBLING [*half draws sword, then replaces it. In cold anger*]. Mr Repington, two months ago I would have run you through for that. See that you don't force me to resort to a weapon I have discarded.

LADY SUSAN. Lud, the man's serious.

WEBLING. For the future I live in the country, Lady Susan.

LADY SUSAN. Until Charles sends for you.

WEBLING. His Majesty dismissed me with too much firmness for me to have any expectation of such event. Nor do I desire to be restored to favour.

LADY SUSAN. Not desire recall ?

WEBLING. That is my sentiment.

LADY SUSAN. Bob, I can stomach most things, but disloyalty makes me heave. Is there any Burgundy nearer than Winton Hall to wash the taste of this odious fellow away ?

BOB. We passed an inn on the road.

[WEBLING *opens door.*

LADY SUSAN. It was a mistake we shan't repeat. [*At door to* WEBLING.] If you come out with me I shall scream. You have no principles. [*Exit* LADY SUSAN.

BOB [*snapping his fingers at* WEBLING]. Long live the King.

WEBLING. With all my heart.

BOB. And that's a damned dishonest sentiment from you. Your heart's in pawn to a Puritan, to a low, prudish, canting——

WEBLING [*hand on sword warningly*]. Mr Repington.

BOB. Your servant, sir. [*Goes to door, then turns.*] I honour you with my profound contempt. [*Exit* BOB.

[WEBLING *produces a scent bottle from pocket, scents handkerchief and smells it. Still not finding the aroma of the Court overcome, he goes to window and opens it. He sees* FELICITY *in the garden.*

WEBLING. Of us two it's me that God is kind to, Felicity. I open the window for fresh air, and I find you.

FELICITY [*at window*]. Has she—the Court gone?

WEBLING. That is why I wanted air—and you.

FELICITY. Shall I come in?

WEBLING. I should not like you to meet them in the hall.

FELICITY. I'll come this way. [*Climbing in.*]

WEBLING [*handing her*]. Child, you are wonderful.

FELICITY. Because I can climb a window-sill?

WEBLING. A window-sill? You climb high heaven and take me with you. You come, and at one bound from the very dregs, I am a brother to the stars.

FELICITY. And you are not to leave me?

WEBLING. Leave you?

FELICITY. I was afraid of the grand lady and gentleman.

WEBLING. Lady! Gentleman! Rats from the stews of St James! I kept my sword off him, and admired myself for becoming consummate master of the art of self-restraint.

FELICITY. You quarrelled!

WEBLING. I'm turned scrupulous about the company I keep since I met you, Felicity. 'Twas nothing but the last severing of my connection with the Court. I'm clear of the Court now, clear of it and all its vices. [*Takes snuff.*] Ready for my life with you that's going to be as simple as a daisy. [*Snuff has, perhaps, rested on his shoulder. He is not satisfied to flick at it with his handkerchief. The hand-mirror comes into use to spy it out as he goes on.*] Simplicity. Gad, how I yearn for it! How I know that I was made for it! There is wonderful rightness for me here. I really must send for my tailor. My clothes grow antique.

FELICITY. There is a tailor in the village.

WEBLING. The decorator of Zachariah's person? No, child, there are no tailors in the country. Indeed, there is but one in the town—the one I owe.

FELICITY. Shall you be very simple, then?

WEBLING. I'm going to be married. Would you have me married in a smock? To be simple, child, is not to be crude.

FELICITY. I'm . . . I'm crude.

WEBLING. You! You are clean. You are pure. If you have a particle of rusticity, it becomes you. Egad, a thought! and mark how I grow countrified already. 'Tis a thrifty thought. We'll have the tailor bring a dressmaker for you.

FELICITY. No! No!

WEBLING. Nay, but you shall not thwart my thrift. Do you not see, child, how we avoid expense? They come together in the same carriage and one posting bill will pay for two. Pen, paper! I must see about it instantly.

[*He sits to write.* FELICITY *stands with doubt frightening her.* WEBLING *has hardly begun writing when* ISAAC *enters, followed by* SERVANT, *who stays by door.*

ISAAC [*excitedly*]. Lord Francis! Lord Francis! There is a fellow just alighted at the door, ridden to you from London, a Court messenger.

WEBLING [*bored*]. Really!

FELICITY [*fearfully*]. Oh! The Court!

WEBLING [*rising*]. I withstood Repington, Felicity, I can withstand a messenger.

SERVANT [*to* ISAAC]. Shall he come in, sir?

WEBLING. A messenger from the Court in here? I think not, sirrah!

SERVANT. He bears a letter to your lordship.

WEBLING. Truly? But from the Court. One needs a long spoon when one sups with the devil. [*Very elaborately he takes a pewter salver and sprinkles scent on it.*] You allow me, Mr Hammond? By this means, we may hope to escape infection, Felicity. [*Gives salver to* SERVANT.] Bid him place the letter on that. Then bring it to me.

SERVANT. Yes, my lord. [*Exit* SERVANT.

ISAAC. But is this respectful to a messenger of the Court?

WEBLING. You underrate my subtlety. Do you not perceive that if the King sends insults in the letters I have not rushed to swallow 'em?

ISAAC. But if he sent a reconciliation that would advance us all.

WEBLING. Why, neither have I run for it like a beggar after a coach. But I warrant you it is the insults. Charles jeers by nature as a lawyer lies.

[SERVANT *re-enters with letter on salver.* WEBLING *takes it up in his handkerchief, looks at it and immediately becomes reverential.*

Oddsfish, the superscription is writ in his Majesty's own hand. This is a sublimity of condescension! Charles, my king whom I disparaged, I don't deserve such honour—unless indeed it be writ in his own hand to make the insults more direct.

[*The* SERVANT *goes out as* WEBLING *speaks.*
[WEBLING *breaks the seal.*

Egad, it's the insult.

FELICITY [*relieved*]. Ah, thank God for that.

WEBLING [*reading*]. " Sirrah, what's this I hear of thee housed by a notorious malignant that was on the devil's side in the late rebellious wars? "

ISAAC [*interrupting*]. I have recanted. I have sworn loyalty.

WEBLING [*reading*]. " But they tell me of an accident at the malignant's gates, and if thou hast suffered both thy own pain and his prayers, thou art punished enough for thy late misconduct at Court. I would tell thee of a waistcoat I have devised. I like it and then dislike it. Mayhap all I need to set my mind at ease is thy commendation. I need thee, Francis. Come to me instantly. Charles." [WEB-LING *kisses the letter.*] Charles, my king!

[*During this reading* ZACHARIAH *has entered and stands unseen by any of them by the door.*

FELICITY [*going to him*]. Francis!

WEBLING. Yes, child, I must go at once.

FELICITY. It is to the Court.

WEBLING. The King commands and I obey. [*Turns from her.*]

[*She holds her hands out towards him in vain. At the door he sees* ZACHARIAH.

ZACHARIAH. Now will you fight with me, Lord Francis Webling?

WEBLING. I can't spare time for killing clodhoppers.

[*Exit* WEBLING.

FELICITY. Zachariah! You here!

ZACHARIAH. I spoke to the messenger, Felicity, and—I guessed.

FELICITY. Can you forgive me? [*Fiercely*] Zachariah. You must. Marry me. Marry me at once and take me with you to America.

[ZACHARIAH *takes her hand. He might intend to kiss her, but restrains the impulse and instead draws her to her knees as he goes down on his.*

ZACHARIAH. Let us thank God together for all His mercies.

[ISAAC *hesitates, then kneels apart from them.*

CURTAIN

THE DEAR DEPARTED

A COMEDY IN ONE ACT

BY STANLEY HOUGHTON

CHARACTERS

MRS SLATER ⎱ *sisters*
MRS JORDAN ⎰

HENRY SLATER ⎱ *their husbands*
BEN JORDAN ⎰

VICTORIA SLATER, *a girl of ten*

ABEL MERRYWEATHER

The action takes place in a provincial town on a Saturday afternoon.

This play was first produced at the Gaiety Theatre, Manchester, by Miss Horniman's company on November 2, 1908, with the following cast:

Mrs Slater	ADA KING
Victoria Slater	ENID MEEK
Henry Slater	HENRY AUSTIN
Mrs Jordan	LOUISE HOLBROOK
Ben Jordan	JOSEPH A. KEOGH
Abel Merryweather	EDWARD LANDOR

STANLEY HOUGHTON died in 1913, and one of the most promising dramatists was cut off at the age of thirty-two. He was a Manchester business man, a dramatic critic for the *Manchester Guardian*, and in his leisure hours wrote plays, the most noteworthy being "Independent Means," "The Younger Generation," and "Hindle Wakes." The last brought him fame, for although it is essentially a Lancashire play it achieved (like Mr Brighouse's "Hobson's Choice") great popularity in London and in America.

Stanley Houghton's one-act plays are excellent. The theme of "The Dear Departed" was suggested by a French story by Guy de Maupassant, but the play is so completely 'soaked in Lancashire' that it is difficult to associate with any other setting. "Master of the House" and "Fancy Free" reveal the dramatist in other entirely different moods.

THE DEAR DEPARTED[1]

*The scene is the sitting-room of a small house in a lower middle-
class district of a provincial town. On the spectator's left
is the window, with the blinds down. A sofa is in front of
it. On his right is a fireplace with an armchair by it. In
the middle of the wall facing the spectator is the door into
the passage. To the left of the door a cheap, shabby chest
of drawers, to the right a sideboard. In the middle of the
room is the table, with chairs round it. Ornaments and a
cheap American clock are on the mantelpiece, in the hearth
a kettle. By the sideboard a pair of gaudy new carpet
slippers. The table is partly laid for tea, and the neces-
saries for the meal are on the sideboard, as also are copies
of an evening paper and of " Tit-Bits " and " Pearson's
Weekly." Turning to the left through the door takes you
to the front door ; to the right, upstairs. In the passage
a hat-stand is visible.*

When the curtain rises MRS SLATER *is seen laying the table.
She is a vigorous, plump, red-faced vulgar woman, prepared
to do any amount of straight talking to get her own way.
She is in black, but not in complete mourning. She listens
a moment and then goes to the window, opens it and calls
into the street.*

MRS SLATER [*sharply*]. Victoria, Victoria ! D'ye hear ?
Come in, will you ?

[1] Applications regarding amateur performances of this play should
be addressed to Messrs Samuel French, Ltd., 26 Southampton Street,
Strand, London, W.C.2, or 25 West 45th Street, New York.

141

[MRS SLATER *closes window and puts the blind straight and then returns to her work at the table.* VICTORIA, *a precocious girl of ten, dressed in colours, enters.*

MRS SLATER. I'm amazed at you, Victoria; I really am. How you can be gallivanting about in the street with your grandfather lying dead and cold upstairs I don't know. Be off now, and change your dress before your Aunt Elizabeth and your Uncle Ben come. It would never do for them to find you in colours.

VICTORIA. What are they coming for? They haven't been here for ages.

MRS SLATER. They're coming to talk over poor Grandpa's affairs. Your father sent them a telegram as soon as we found he was dead. [*A noise is heard.*] Good gracious, that's never them. [MRS SLATER *hurries to the door and opens it.*] No, thank goodness! it's only your father.

[HENRY SLATER, *a stooping, heavy man with a drooping moustache, enters. He is wearing a black tail coat, grey trousers, a black tie, and a bowler hat. He carries a little paper parcel.*

HENRY. Not come yet, eh?

MRS SLATER. You can see they haven't, can't you? Now, Victoria, be off upstairs and that quick. Put your white frock on with a black sash. [VICTORIA *goes out.*

MRS SLATER [*to* HENRY]. I'm not satisfied, but it's the best we can do till our new black's ready, and Ben and Elizabeth will never have thought about mourning yet, so we'll outshine them there. [HENRY *sits in the armchair by the fire.*] Get your boots off, Henry; Elizabeth's that prying she notices the least speck of dirt.

HENRY. I'm wondering if they'll come at all. When you and Elizabeth quarrelled she said she'd never set foot in your house again.

MRS SLATER. She'll come fast enough after her share of what Grandfather's left. You know how hard she can be when she likes. Where she gets it from I can't tell.

[MRS SLATER *unwraps the parcel* HENRY *has brought. It contains sliced tongue, which she puts on a dish on the table.*]

HENRY. I suppose it's in the family.

MRS SLATER. What do you mean by that, Henry Slater?

HENRY. I was referring to your father, not to you. Where are my slippers?

MRS SLATER. In the kitchen; but you want a new pair, those old ones are nearly worn out. [*Nearly breaking down*] You don't seem to realize what it's costing me to bear up like I am doing. My heart's fit to break when I see the little trifles that belonged to Grandfather lying around, and think he'll never use them again. [*Briskly*] Here! you'd better wear these slippers of Grandfather's now. It's lucky he'd just got a new pair.

HENRY. They'll be very small for me, my dear.

MRS SLATER. They'll stretch, won't they? I'm not going to have them wasted. [*She has finished laying the table.*] Henry, I've been thinking about that bureau of Grandfather's that's in his bedroom. You know I always wanted to have it after he died.

HENRY. You must arrange with Elizabeth when you're dividing things up.

MRS SLATER. Elizabeth's that sharp she'll see I'm after it, and she'll drive a hard bargain over it. Eh, what it is to have a low money-grubbing spirit!

HENRY. Perhaps she's got her eye on the bureau as well.

MRS SLATER. She's never been here since Grandfather bought it. If it was only down here instead of in his room, she'd never guess it wasn't our own.

HENRY [*startled*]. Amelia! [*He rises.*]

MRS SLATER. Henry, why shouldn't we bring that bureau down here now ? We could do it before they come.

HENRY [*stupefied*]. I wouldn't care to.

MRS SLATER. Don't look so daft. Why not ?

HENRY. It doesn't seem delicate, somehow.

MRS SLATER. We could put that shabby old chest of drawers upstairs where the bureau is now. Elizabeth could have that and welcome. I've always wanted to get rid of it. [*She points to the drawers.*]

HENRY. Suppose they come when we're doing it.

MRS SLATER. I'll fasten the front door. Get your coat off, Henry ; we'll change it.

[MRS SLATER *goes out to fasten the front door.* HENRY *takes his coat off.* MRS SLATER *reappears.*

MRS SLATER. I'll run up and move the chairs out of the way.

[VICTORIA *appears, dressed according to her mother's instructions.*

VICTORIA. Will you fasten my frock up the back, Mother ?

MRS SLATER. I'm busy ; get your father to do it.

[MRS SLATER *hurries upstairs, and* HENRY *fastens the frock.*

VICTORIA. What have you got your coat off for, Father ?

HENRY. Mother and me is going to bring Grandfather's bureau down here.

VICTORIA [*after a moment's thought*]. Are we pinching it before Aunt Elizabeth comes ?

HENRY [*shocked*]. No, my child. Grandpa gave it your mother before he died.

VICTORIA. This morning ?

HENRY. Yes.

VICTORIA. Ah ! He was drunk this morning.

HENRY. Hush ; you mustn't ever say he was drunk, now

THE DEAR DEPARTED

[HENRY *has fastened the frock, and* MRS SLATER
appears carrying a handsome clock under her arm.

MRS SLATER. I thought I'd fetch this down as well. [*She
puts it on the mantelpiece.*] Our clock's worth nothing and
this always appealed to me.

VICTORIA. That's grandpa's clock.

MRS SLATER. Chut! Be quiet! It's ours now. Come,
Henry, lift your end. Victoria, don't breathe a word to
your aunt about the clock and the bureau.

[*They carry the chest of drawers through the doorway.*

VICTORIA [*to herself*]. I thought we'd pinched them.

[*After a short pause there is a sharp knock at the front
door.*

MRS SLATER [*from upstairs*]. Victoria, if that's your aunt
and uncle you're not to open the door.

[VICTORIA *peeps through the window.*

VICTORIA. Mother, it's them!

MRS SLATER. You're not to open the door till I come down.
[*Knocking repeated.*] Let them knock away. [*There is a
heavy bumping noise.*] Mind the wall, Henry.

[HENRY *and* MRS SLATER, *very hot and flushed, stagger
in with a pretty old-fashioned bureau containing a
locked desk. They put it where the chest of
drawers was, and straighten the ornaments, etc.
The knocking is repeated.*

MRS SLATER. That was a near thing. Open the door,
Victoria. Now, Henry, get your coat on. [*She helps
him.*]

HENRY. Did we knock much plaster off the wall?

MRS SLATER. Never mind the plaster. Do I look all right?
[*Straightening her hair at the glass*] Just watch Elizabeth's
face when she sees we're all in half mourning. [*Throwing
him "Tit-Bits"*] Take this and sit down. Try and look as
if we'd been waiting for them.

145

[HENRY *sits in the armchair and* MRS SLATER *left of
    table. They read ostentatiously.* VICTORIA
    ushers in BEN *and* MRS JORDAN. *The latter is a
    stout, complacent woman with an impassive face
    and an irritating air of being always right. She
    is wearing a complete and deadly outfit of new
    mourning crowned by a great black hat with
    plumes.* BEN *is also in complete new mourning,
    with black gloves and a band round his hat. He
    is rather a jolly little man, accustomed to be
    humorous, but at present trying to adapt himself to
    the regrettable occasion. He has a bright, chirpy
    little voice.* MRS JORDAN *sails into the room and
    solemnly goes straight to* MRS SLATER *and kisses her.
    The men shake hands.* MRS JORDAN *kisses* HENRY.
    BEN *kisses* MRS SLATER. *Not a word is spoken.*
    MRS SLATER *furtively inspects the new mourning.*

MRS JORDAN. Well, Amelia, and so he's gone at last.

MRS SLATER. Yes, he's gone. He was seventy-two a fort-
night last Sunday.

[*She sniffs back a tear.* MRS JORDAN *sits on the left of
    the table.* MRS SLATER *on the right.* HENRY *in
    the armchair.* BEN *on the sofa with* VICTORIA
    near him.

BEN [*chirpily*]. Now, Amelia, you mustn't give way.
We've all got to die some time or other. It might have
been worse.

MRS SLATER. I don't see how.

BEN. It might have been one of us.

HENRY. It's taken you a long time to get here, Elizabeth.

MRS JORDAN. Oh, I couldn't do it. I really couldn't do it.

MRS SLATER [*suspiciously*]. Couldn't do what?

MRS JORDAN. I couldn't start without getting the mourning. [*Glancing at her sister.*]

146

MRS SLATER. We've ordered ours, you may be sure. [*Acidly*] I never could fancy buying ready-made things.

MRS JORDAN. No? For myself it's such a relief to get into the black. And now perhaps you'll tell us all about it. What did the doctor say?

MRS SLATER. Oh, he's not been near yet.

MRS JORDAN. Not been near?

BEN [*in the same breath*]. Didn't you send for him at once?

MRS SLATER. Of course I did. Do you take me for a fool? I sent Henry at once for Dr Pringle, but he was out.

BEN. You should have gone for another. Eh, Eliza?

MRS JORDAN. Oh, yes. It's a fatal mistake.

MRS SLATER. Pringle attended him when he was alive and Pringle shall attend him when he's dead. That's professional etiquette.

BEN. Well, you know your own business best, but——

MRS JORDAN. Yes—it's a fatal mistake.

MRS SLATER. Don't talk so silly, Elizabeth. What good could a doctor have done?

MRS JORDAN. Look at the many cases of persons being restored to life hours after they were thought to be 'gone.'

HENRY. That's when they've been drowned. Your father wasn't drowned, Elizabeth.

BEN [*humorously*]. There wasn't much fear of that. If there was one thing he couldn't bear it was water.

[*He laughs, but no one else does.*

MRS JORDAN [*pained*]. Ben! [BEN *is crushed at once.*]

MRS SLATER [*piqued*]. I'm sure he washed regular enough.

MRS JORDAN. If he did take a drop too much at times, we'll not dwell on that, now.

MRS SLATER. Father had been 'merry' this morning. He went out soon after breakfast to pay his insurance.

BEN. My word, it's a good thing he did.

MRS JORDAN. He always was thoughtful in that way. He was too honourable to have 'gone' without paying his premium.

MRS SLATER. Well, he must have gone round to the Ring-o'-Bells afterwards, for he came in as merry as a sandboy. I says, "We're only waiting Henry to start dinner." "Dinner," he says, "I don't want no dinner, I'm going to bed!"

BEN [*shaking his head*]. Ah! Dear, dear.

HENRY. And when I came in I found him undressed sure enough and snug in bed. [*He rises and stands on the hearth-rug.*]

MRS JORDAN [*definitely*]. Yes, he'd had a 'warning.' I'm sure of that. Did he know you?

HENRY. Yes. He spoke to me.

MRS JORDAN. Did he say he'd had a 'warning'?

HENRY. No. He said, "Henry, would you mind taking my boots off; I forgot before I got into bed."

MRS JORDAN. He must have been wandering.

HENRY. No, he'd got 'em on all right.

MRS SLATER. And when we'd finished dinner I thought I'd take up a bit of something on a tray. He was lying there for all the world as if he was asleep, so I put the tray down on the bureau—[*correcting herself*] on the chest of drawers—and went to waken him. [*A pause.*] He was quite cold.

HENRY. Then I heard Amelia calling for me, and I ran upstairs.

MRS SLATER. Of course we could do nothing.

MRS JORDAN. He was 'gone'?

HENRY. There wasn't any doubt.

MRS JORDAN. I always knew he'd go sudden in the end.

[*A pause. They wipe their eyes and sniff back tears.*

MRS SLATER [*rising briskly at length; in a businesslike*

tone]. Well, will you go up and look at him now, or shall we have tea ?

MRS JORDAN. What do you say, Ben ?

BEN. I'm not particular.

MRS JORDAN [*surveying the table*]. Well then, if the kettle's ready we may as well have tea first.

> [MRS SLATER *puts the kettle on the fire and gets tea ready.*

HENRY. One thing we may as well decide now ; the announcement in the papers.

MRS JORDAN. I was thinking of that. What would you put ?

MRS SLATER. At the residence of his daughter, 235 Upper Cornbank Street, etc.

HENRY. You wouldn't care for a bit of poetry ?

MRS JORDAN. I like " Never Forgotten." It's refined.

HENRY. Yes, but it's rather soon for that.

BEN. You couldn't very well have forgot him the day after.

MRS SLATER. I always fancy " A loving husband, a kind father, and a faithful friend."

BEN [*doubtfully*]. Do you think that's right ?

HENRY. I don't think it matters whether it's right or not.

MRS JORDAN. No, it's more for the look of the thing.

HENRY. I saw a verse in the *Evening News* yesterday. Proper poetry it was. It rhymed.

> [*He gets the paper and reads.*

" Despised and forgotten by some you may be
But the spot that contains you is sacred to we."

MRS JORDAN. That'll never do. You don't say " Sacred to we."

HENRY. It's in the paper.

MRS SLATER. You wouldn't say it if you were speaking properly, but it's different in poetry.

HENRY. Poetic licence, you know.

MRS JORDAN. No, that'll never do. We want a verse that says how much we loved him and refers to all his good qualities and says what a heavy loss we've had.

MRS SLATER. You want a whole poem. That'll cost a good lot.

MRS JORDAN. Well, we'll think about it after tea, and then we'll look through his bits of things and make a list of them. There's all the furniture in his room.

HENRY. There's no jewellery or valuables of that sort.

MRS JORDAN. Except his gold watch. He promised that to our Jimmy.

MRS SLATER. Promised your Jimmy! I never heard of that.

MRS JORDAN. Oh, but he did, Amelia, when he was living with us. He was very fond of Jimmy.

MRS SLATER. Well. [*Amazed.*] I don't know!

BEN. Anyhow, there's his insurance money. Have you got the receipt for the premium he paid this morning?

MRS SLATER. I've not seen it.

[VICTORIA *jumps up from the sofa and comes behind the table.*

VICTORIA. Mother, I don't think Grandpa went to pay his insurance this morning.

MRS SLATER. He went out.

VICTORIA. Yes, but he didn't go into the town. He met old Mr Tattersall down the street, and they went off past St Philips's Church.

MRS SLATER. To the Ring-o'-Bells, I'll be bound.

BEN. The Ring-o'-Bells?

MRS SLATER. That public-house that John Shorrock's widow keeps. He is always hanging about there. Oh, if he hasn't paid it——

BEN. Do you think he hasn't paid it? Was it overdue?

MRS SLATER. I should think it was overdue.

MRS JORDAN. Something tells me he's not paid it. I've a 'warning,' I know it ; he's not paid it.

BEN. The drunken old beggar.

MRS JORDAN. He's done it on purpose, just to annoy us.

MRS SLATER. After all I've done for him, having to put up with him in the house these three years. It's nothing short of swindling.

MRS JORDAN. I had to put up with him for five years.

MRS SLATER. And you were trying to turn him over to us all the time.

HENRY. But we don't know for certain that he's not paid the premium.

MRS JORDAN. I do. It's come over me all at once that he hasn't.

MRS SLATER. Victoria, run upstairs and fetch that bunch of keys that's on your grandpa's dressing table.

VICTORIA [*timidly*]. In Grandpa's room ?

MRS SLATER. Yes.

VICTORIA. I—I don't like to.

MRS SLATER. Don't talk so silly. There's no one can hurt you. [VICTORIA *goes out reluctantly*.] We'll see if he's locked the receipt up in the bureau.

BEN. In where ? In this thing ? [*He rises and examines it.*]

MRS JORDAN [*also rising*]. Where did you pick that up, Amelia ? It's new since last I was here.

[*They examine it closely.*

MRS SLATER. Oh—Henry picked it up one day.

MRS JORDAN. I like it. It's artistic. Did you buy it at an auction ?

HENRY. Eh ! Where did I buy it, Amelia ?

MRS JORDAN. Yes, at an auction.

BEN [*disparagingly*]. Oh, second-hand.

MRS JORDAN. Don't show your ignorance, Ben. All artistic things are second-hand. Look at those old masters.

[*VICTORIA returns, very scared. She closes the door after her.*

VICTORIA. Mother! Mother!

MRS SLATER. What is it, child?

VICTORIA. Grandpa's getting up.

BEN. What?

MRS SLATER. What do you say?

VICTORIA. Grandpa's getting up.

MRS JORDAN. The child's crazy.

MRS SLATER. Don't talk so silly. Don't you know your grandpa's dead?

VICTORIA. No, no; he's getting up. I saw him.

[*They are transfixed with amazement; BEN and MRS JORDAN left of table; VICTORIA clings to MRS SLATER, right of table; HENRY near fireplace.*

MRS JORDAN. You'd better go up and see for yourself, Amelia.

MRS SLATER. Here—come with me, Henry.

[*HENRY draws back terrified.*

BEN [*suddenly*]. Hist! Listen.

[*They look at the door. A slight chuckling is heard outside. The door opens, revealing an old man clad in a faded but gay dressing-gown. He is in his stockinged feet. Although over seventy he is vigorous and well coloured; his bright, malicious eyes twinkle under his heavy, reddish-grey eyebrows. He is obviously either GRANDFATHER ABEL MERRYWEATHER or else his ghost.*

ABEL. What's the matter with little Vicky? [*He sees BEN and MRS JORDAN.*] Hello! What brings you here? How's yourself, Ben?

THE DEAR DEPARTED

[ABEL *thrusts his hand at* BEN, *who skips back smartly and retreats with* MRS JORDAN *to a safe distance below the sofa.*

MRS SLATER [*approaching* ABEL *gingerly*]. Grandfather, is that you ? [*She pokes him with her hand to see if he is solid.*]

ABEL. Of course it's me. Don't do that, 'Melia. What the devil do you mean by this tomfoolery ?

MRS SLATER [*to the others*]. He's not dead.

BEN. Doesn't seem like it.

ABEL [*irritated by the whispering*]. You've kept away long enough, Lizzie ; and now you've come you don't seem over-pleased to see me.

MRS JORDAN. You took us by surprise, Father. Are you keeping quite well ?

ABEL [*trying to catch the words*]. Eh ? What ?

MRS JORDAN. Are you quite well ?

ABEL. Ay, I'm right enough but for a bit of a headache. I wouldn't mind betting that I'm not the first in this house to be carried to the cemetery. I always think Henry there looks none too healthy.

MRS JORDAN. Well, I never !

[ABEL *crosses to the armchair and* HENRY *gets out of his way to the front of the table.*

ABEL. 'Melia, what the dickens did I do with my new slippers ?

MRS SLATER [*confused*]. Aren't they by the hearth, Grandfather ?

ABEL. I don't see them. [*Observing* HENRY *trying to remove the slippers.*] Why, you've got 'em on, Henry.

MRS SLATER [*promptly*]. I told him to put them on to stretch them, they were that new and hard. Now, Henry.

[MRS SLATER *snatches the slippers from* HENRY *and gives them to* ABEL, *who puts them on and sits in armchair.*

MRS JORDAN [*to* BEN]. Well, I don't call that delicate, stepping into a dead man's shoes in such haste.

> [HENRY *goes up to the window and pulls up the blind.*
> VICTORIA *runs across to* ABEL *and sits on the floor at his feet.*

VICTORIA. Oh, Grandpa, I'm so glad you're not dead.

MRS SLATER [*in a vindictive whisper*]. Hold your tongue, Victoria.

ABEL. Eh ? What's that ? Who's gone dead ?

MRS SLATER [*loudly*]. Victoria says she's sorry about your head.

ABEL. Ah, thank you, Vicky, but I'm feeling better.

MRS SLATER [*to* MRS JORDAN]. He's so fond of Victoria.

MRS JORDAN [*to* MRS SLATER]. Yes ; he's fond of our Jimmy, too.

MRS SLATER. You'd better ask him if he promised your Jimmy his gold watch.

MRS JORDAN [*disconcerted*]. I couldn't just now. I don't feel equal to it.

ABEL. Why, Ben, you're in mourning ! And Lizzie too. And 'Melia, and Henry and little Vicky ! Who's gone dead ? It's some one in the family. [*He chuckles.*]

MRS SLATER. No one you know, Father. A relation of Ben's.

ABEL. And what relation of Ben's ?

MRS SLATER. His brother.

BEN [*to* MRS SLATER]. Dang it, I never had one.

ABEL. Dear, dear. And what was his name, Ben ?

BEN [*at a loss*]. Er—er. [*He crosses to front of table.*

MRS SLATER [*R. of table, prompting*]. Frederick.

MRS JORDAN [*L. of table, prompting*]. Albert.

BEN. Er—Fred—Alb—Isaac.

ABEL. Isaac ? And where did your brother Isaac die ?

BEN. In—er—in Australia.

ABEL. Dear, dear. He'd be older than you, eh ?

BEN. Yes, five years.

ABEL. Ay, ay. Are you going to the funeral ?

BEN. Oh, yes.

MRS SLATER *and* MRS JORDAN. No, no.

BEN. No, of course not.   [*He retires to* L.

ABEL [*rising*]. Well, I suppose you've only been waiting for me to begin tea. I'm feeling hungry.

MRS SLATER [*taking up the kettle*]. I'll make tea.

ABEL. Come along, now ; sit you down and let's be jolly.

> [ABEL *sits at the head of the table, facing spectators.* BEN *and* MRS JORDAN *on the left.* VICTORIA *brings a chair and sits by* ABEL. MRS SLATER *and* HENRY *sit on the right. Both the women are next to* ABEL.

MRS SLATER. Henry, give Grandpa some tongue.

ABEL. Thank you. I'll make a start.

> [*He helps himself to bread and butter.*
> [HENRY *serves the tongue and* MRS SLATER *pours out tea. Only* ABEL *eats with any heartiness.*

BEN. Glad to see you've got an appetite, Mr Merryweather, although you've not been so well.

ABEL. Nothing serious. I've been lying down for a bit.

MRS SLATER. Been to sleep, Grandfather ?

ABEL. No, I've not been to sleep.

MRS SLATER *and* HENRY. Oh !

ABEL [*eating and drinking*]. I can't exactly call everything to mind, but I remember I was a bit dazed, like. I couldn't move an inch, hand or foot.

BEN. And could you see and hear, Mr Merryweather ?

ABEL. Yes, but I don't remember seeing anything particular. Mustard, Ben. [BEN *passes the mustard.*]

MRS SLATER. Of course not, Grandfather. It was all your fancy. You must have been asleep.

ABEL [*snappishly*]. I tell you I wasn't asleep, 'Melia. Damn it, I ought to know.

MRS JORDAN. Didn't you see Henry or Amelia come into the room ?

ABEL [*scratching his head*]. Now let me think——

MRS SLATER. I wouldn't press him, Elizabeth. Don't press him.

HENRY. No. I wouldn't worry him.

ABEL [*suddenly recollecting*]. Ay, begad ! 'Melia and Henry, what the devil did you mean by shifting my bureau out of my bedroom ?

[HENRY *and* MRS SLATER *are speechless.*

D'you hear me ? Henry ! 'Melia !

MRS JORDAN. What bureau was that, Father ?

ABEL. Why, my bureau, the one I bought——

MRS JORDAN [*pointing to the bureau*]. Was it that one, Father ?

ABEL. Ah, that's it. What's it doing here ? Eh ?

[*A pause. The clock on the mantelpiece strikes six. Every one looks at it.*

Drat me if that isn't my clock, too. What the devil's been going on in this house ? [*A slight pause.*

BEN. Well, I'll be hanged.

MRS JORDAN [*rising*]. I'll tell you what's been going on in this house, Father. Nothing short of robbery.

MRS SLATER. Be quiet, Elizabeth.

MRS JORDAN. I'll not be quiet. Oh, I call it double-faced.

HENRY. Now, now, Elizabeth.

MRS JORDAN. And you, too. Are you such a poor creature that you must do every dirty thing she tells you ?

MRS SLATER [*rising*]. Remember where you are, Elizabeth.

HENRY [*rising*]. Come, come. No quarrelling.

BEN [*rising*]. My wife's every right to speak own mind.

MRS SLATER. Then she can speak it outside, not here.

ABEL [*rising; thumping the table*]. Damn it all, will some one tell me what's been going on.

MRS JORDAN. Yes, I will. I'll not see you robbed.

ABEL. Who's been robbing me ?

MRS JORDAN. Amelia and Henry. They've stolen your clock and bureau. [*Working herself up*] They sneaked into your room like a thief in the night and stole them after you were dead.

HENRY *and* MRS SLATER. Hush ! Quiet, Elizabeth !

MRS JORDAN. I'll not be stopped. After you were dead, I say.

ABEL. After who was dead ?

MRS JORDAN. You.

ABEL. But I'm not dead.

MRS JORDAN. No, but they thought you were.

[*A pause.* ABEL *gazes round at them.*

ABEL. Oho ! So that's why you're all in black to-day. You thought I was dead. [*He chuckles.*] That was a big mistake. [*He sits and resumes his tea.*]

MRS SLATER [*sobbing*]. Grandfather.

ABEL. It didn't take you long to start dividing my things between you.

MRS JORDAN. No, Father ; you mustn't think that. Amelia was simply getting hold of them on her own account.

ABEL. You always were a keen one, Amelia. I suppose you thought the will wasn't fair.

HENRY. Did you make a will ?

ABEL. Yes, it was locked up in the bureau.

MRS JORDAN. And what was in it, Father ?

ABEL. That doesn't matter now. I'm thinking of destroying it and making another.

MRS SLATER [*sobbing*]. Grandfather, you'll not be hard on me.

ABEL. I'll trouble you for another cup of tea, 'Melia ; two lumps and plenty of milk.

MRS SLATER. With pleasure, Grandfather. [*She pours out the tea.*]

ABEL. I don't want to be hard on anyone. I'll tell you what I'm going to do. Since your mother died, I've lived part of the time with you, 'Melia, and part with you, Lizzie. Well, I shall make a new will, leaving all my bits of things to whoever I'm living with when I die. How does that strike you?

HENRY. It's a bit of a lottery, like.

MRS JORDAN. And who do you intend to live with from now?

ABEL [*drinking his tea*]. I'm just coming to that.

MRS JORDAN. You know, Father, it's quite time you came to live with us again. We'd make you very comfortable.

MRS SLATER. No, he's not been with us as long as he was with you.

MRS JORDAN. I may be wrong, but I don't think Father will fancy living on with you after what's happened to-day.

ABEL. So you'd like to have me again, Lizzie?

MRS JORDAN. You know we're ready for you to make your home with us for as long as you please.

ABEL. What do you say to that, 'Melia?

MRS SLATER. All I can say is that Elizabeth's changed her mind in the last two years. [*Rising*] Grandfather, do you know what the quarrel between us was about?

MRS JORDAN. Amelia, don't be a fool; sit down.

MRS SLATER. No, if I'm not to have him, you shan't either. We quarrelled because Elizabeth said she wouldn't take you off our hands at any price. She said she'd had enough of you to last a lifetime, and we'd got to keep you.

ABEL. It seems to me that neither of you has any cause to feel proud about the way you've treated me.

MRS SLATER. If I've done anything wrong, I'm sure I'm sorry for it.

MRS JORDAN. And I can't say more than that, too.

ABEL. It's a bit late to say it, now. You neither of you cared to put up with me.

MRS SLATER *and* MRS JORDAN. No, no, Grandfather.

ABEL. Ay, you both say that because of what I've told you about leaving my money. Well, since you don't want me I'll go to some one that does.

BEN. Come, Mr Merryweather, you've got to live with one of your daughters.

ABEL. I'll tell you what I've got to do. On Monday next I've got to do three things. I've got to go to the lawyer's and alter my will; and I've got to go to the insurance office and pay my premium ; and I've got to go to St Philips's Church and get married.

BEN *and* HENRY. What !

MRS JORDAN. Get married !

MRS SLATER. He's out of his senses.

[*General consternation.*

ABEL. I say I'm going to get married.

MRS SLATER. Who to ?

ABEL. To Mrs John Shorrocks who keeps the Ring-o'-Bells. We've had it fixed up a good while now, but I was keeping it for a pleasant surprise. [*He rises.*] I felt I was a bit of a burden to you, so I found some one who'd think it a pleasure to look after me. We shall be very glad to see you at the ceremony. [*He gets to the door.*] Till Monday, then. Twelve o'clock at St Philips's Church. [*Opening the door*] It's a good thing you brought that bureau downstairs, 'Melia. It'll be handier to carry across to the Ring-o'-Bells on Monday. [*He goes out.*

THE CURTAIN FALLS

'OP-O'-ME-THUMB

A PLAY IN ONE ACT

By Frederick Fenn and Richard Pryce

CHARACTERS

Madame Jeanne Marie Napoleon
de Gallifet Didier
Clem (Mrs) Galloway
Rose Jordan
Celeste
Amanda Afflick
Horace Greensmith

This play was first produced by the Stage Society at the Court Theatre, London, on March 14, 1904, with the following cast:

Madame Jeanne Marie Napoleon de Gallifet Didier	Marianne Caldwell
Clem (Mrs) Galloway . .	Annie Goward
Rose Jordan	Margaret Busse
Celeste	Florence Lloyd
Amanda Afflick. . .	Hilda Trevelyan
Horace Greensmith. . .	H. Nye Chart

THE following play was written by Messrs Frederick Fenn and Richard Pryce in collaboration. The former has written a number of popular plays, the best known being " The Convict on the Hearth," " Judged by Appearances," and " The Nelson Touch " ; and he composed a good comic opera, " Amasis," in 1906. His father was Manville Fenn, the novelist whose books make such a stirring appeal to boys.

Mr Richard Pryce is a novelist with a lengthy list of books and plays to his name, among them being an excellent stage adaptation of Mr Arnold Bennett's novel *Helen with the High Hand.*

'OP-O'-ME-THUMB [1]

SCENE: *Working room at* MADAME DIDIER's *laundry in Soho.*
In front of the large shop window that gives on to the street
there hangs a lace curtain. Upon the glass of the upper
half of a door " Madame Didier, Blanchisserie Française "
may be read backwards.

It is Saturday evening before an August Bank Holiday.
MADAME *with goffering irons is finishing a cap at stage*
back L. ROSE JORDAN *stands on a chair putting paper*
packets of collars and cuffs into pigeon holes. CLEM
(MRS) GALLOWAY *is mending socks, etc., at small table*
R. CELESTE *is sitting on a centre table marking off*
collars, etc., in account book, or slipping pink tissue paper
into a stack of shirts, and singing as she swings her
feet.

CELESTE. Eve in her garden she was a lady,
    She never grew old n' fady.
    She might 'a' bin there to-day-dy,
    But *she* was inquisitive.
    I'd never 'a bin s' crazy,
    You wait till I'm 'alf a daisy,
    See me with a chance to be lazy.
    I'd keep you all alive !

MADAME. You have make out zose bills, Celeste ?

[1] Applications regarding amateur performances of this play should
be addressed to Messrs Samuel French, Ltd., 26 Southampton Street,
Strand, London, W.C.2, or 25 West 45th Street, New York.

CELESTE [*nodding*].

> Oh wait till I'm 'alf a daisy,
> Snakes! I'd send 'em all back to blazy.
> *You* give me the chance to be lazy,
> I'd——

CLEM. Couldn't be much lazier than what you are now, I should think—daisy or no daisy.

CELESTE. Couldn't I? I'd have a bit of a try!

[*Resumes.*]

> Oh when I'm a real lady,
> *In* a barouche I shall parady——

[*She breaks off suddenly.*] Where's Amanda?

CLEM [*sarcastically*]. Want a little 'elp with y' singin'?

CELESTE. Where *is* Amanda?

ROSE. Gone to Strahan's.

CELESTE. What for?

ROSE. They never sent them things they wrote about.

CELESTE [*stopping in her work*]. Do they expect us to do 'em this time o' day!

MADAME [*coming down*]. No. No. Like always you excite yourself for nothing. Go on. Go on. What is Monday? 'Oliday, is it not? Very well. They close. I close. I 'ave the things 'ere for Tuesday, *hein?* You mind your business. Always wanting to know.

CELESTE [*appeased*]. Well, you never do know with shops. It wouldn't be the first time. It was Strahan wanted the collars dressed in two hours last week, wasn't it, for some customer or other. I wouldn't 'a' done 'em, I know. Oh ho. [*She hums to herself for a moment or two.*] Well, well. When I'm married and 'ave a 'usband to keep me——

MADAME. Keep you! Bah, you know nothing, you. A man wants a wife who will work. *Mon Dieu*, if one is to be lazy it will not be the wife. Look at me.

164

CLEM (MRS) GALLOWAY [*who has gone up to table at back to fetch more things and who now comes down*]. You're right, madam. 'Usbands is all very well in their way, as I should be the first to deny, me of course bein' different and independent so to speak, but when it comes to which is to do the work——

CELESTE. Listen to Clem.

CLEM. Not so much of y'r Clem. Mrs Galloway, if you please. You seem to forget who I am. I've got me ring, I 'ave, *and* me lines if I do come 'ere to oblige—Mr Galloway 'avin' poor 'ealth—besides private means, bein' a pensioneer.

CELESTE. Pensioneer! Fourpence a day, isn't it, dear?— and gone before twelve, they tell me, at the Pig and Whistle. A fine pensioneer! You wait until I bring mine along.

CLEM. Yes, I dare say there'll be some waitin' to do. What's your 'usband goin' to be if I may make so bold to inquire?

CELESTE. 'Aven't quite made up me mind. But I'm just about tired of this. I'm not sure as I shan't go and be a actress for a change, and stand in the limelight and 'ave bokays thrown at me—'ere chuck us some of those things, Rose—[*begins to work frantically*]—and—and 'ave lords waitin' at the stage door to take the 'orses out of me carriage——

CLEM [*laughs*]. You'll be wantin' to be a child of myst'ry next, like Amanda.

CELESTE [*pausing, seriously*]. Do you think she is?

CLEM. Is what?

CELESTE. A child of myst'ry—what she says, I mean. You know—all that about 'er father and about them jewels as somebody gives 'er. Do you know she washed that there shirt again last week. She says it'll be fetched one of these days and then there'll be a surprise for us.

ROSE. Surprise! Garn! A little image like 'er? Ain't room for much up 'er sleeve. Little 'aporth o' mis'ry!

CELESTE [*thoughtfully*]. Well, I don't know. Things *do* 'appen, y' know. I wonder 'oo 'er father reelly is. [*Mystified*] She's so close about 'im, ain't she? And then there *is* that shirt—there's no goin' against that.

CLEM [*shortly*]. Lots of customers forgets things.

CELESTE. Yes, but the care she takes of it. It's bin 'ere best part of a year, and I don't know 'ow many times she 'asn't dressed it. There may be something in it, y' know.

ROSE [*pulling a long paper parcel out of one of the large pigeon holes—reading*]. "Mr 'Orris Greensmith, to be called for." [*Opening the paper a little and looking inside*] Blest if I don't believe she's done it up again. It 'ad pink paper in last week and now it's blue. 'Ve we got any blue paper, madam? No. I thought not.

CLEM [*interested*]. She must 'a' bought it.

CELESTE. There.

ROSE. Well! *It'll* never be fetched. If 'e's 'er mash why doesn't 'e come 'ere and fetch it?

CELESTE. She says it's a sort of a token, see? while 'e's away. Something to 'old by, she says. And then, 'e does send 'er things.

CLEM [*weightily*]. 'As any body seen 'em?

CELESTE. N-no, but there was a brooch, I b'lieve, and a necktie.

CLEM [*coming to the table C. to fetch scissors L. and pausing in her work to gossip*]. Well, why doesn't she wear 'em? That's it, y' see. Why doesn't she wear 'em?

CELESTE [*as if struck by this for the first time*]. Yes. Why doesn't she?

CLEM [*sits at table R. and talks confidentially*]. That's where the test comes in. Why doesn't she wear 'em— 'stead of that bit of crape, say? Not that I've anything

to say against that. She 'as plenty of deaths in 'er family
—that I will say for 'er.

ROSE [*contemptuously*]. Lots of people 'as relations die.
Anyone can.

CLEM [*generously*]. No, give everybody their due, I say,
and she does 'ave her afflictions. I've been bereaved meself
and I know what it is.

ROSE. Crape's cheap enough. And she don't ask us to
none of 'er funerals.

CLEM [*forgetting* AMANDA *and showing an inclination to lose
herself in pleasant retrospect*]. Fun'rals—the fun'rals I've
been to in my time! There was me sister's 'usband [*she
goes back to her place* R. *as she speaks*]—all my family's
married well, that I am thankful to say—and when she lost
'im she done the thing 'andsome I tell y'. [*To* CELESTE]
Gimme them vests—no—there by the socks. Under y'
nose, stupid! There was as many as three mournin'
coaches an' a 'earse with plumes—and the 'atbands!—
well!—and afterwards we——

CELESTE. That'll do, Clem. We know all about that—
and y' cousins too as died at 'Ighb'ry. It's Amanda I'm
talking about, not you. I wonder whether she could show
us one of them presents. Good mind to ask 'er. Why
don't she come in?

ROSE. Gone a errand, I tell y'.

CELESTE. Well, she might be back be now, I should think.
Talk about 'ares and tortoise shells! I'd 'a' done it on me
'ead. She's a fair crawler, Amanda is.

ROSE [*laconically*]. Legs is short.

CELESTE. So's time, and I don't want to be 'ere all night.

MADAME [*coming down*]. She is little, but she is good.
She work. She does not talk, talk, talk. She is not singing
when she should be working. Where should I be, me, with
another like you? And this Saturday and I forced to go

167

out at five! Five, *mon Dieu*, and it wants but ten minutes. [*She goes up L. C.*]

CELESTE [*absently*]. I wonder whether she's got anybody to take 'er out a Monday. Think she 'as?

ROSE. It'd be a funny sort o' feller as 'd want to. [*She looks over her shoulder towards the glass door.*] 'Ere she is. 'Ere's Mandy.

[*The door R. is pushed open and AMANDA AFFLICK comes in backwards pulling after her a washing basket nearly as large as herself. She is an odd, forlorn-looking little figure with big eyes and a pathetic expression. She has yet an air of being quite capable of taking care of herself.*

ROSE. Well, Craipe.

MADAME. Ah, you have come back. You have brought the money. [*AMANDA hands her a paper and some loose change.*] That is right. Now I may go and you will help these good for nothings to finish. [*She takes the cap on its stand and puts it on end of table back, then goes into inner room L. whence she returns a moment or two later with her cloak.*]

CELESTE [*to AMANDA*]. Didn't 'appen to meet ch' father, did y'?

CLEM. We thought perhaps as you was gone s' long that you'd ran away with that mash o' yours—'im as goes without 'is shirt. 'Orris Whatsaname.

AMANDA. Oh. Did y'? [*She sidles past CLEM who is leaning over a basket and giving her an intentional 'shove,' sends her sprawling across it.*] Now then, Mrs, can't y' make room for a lady?

CLEM [*getting up, and angry*]. They don't teach y' manners in the work'us, do they, Clumsy?

AMANDA. You'll find out when you get there, dear.

ROSE [*linking arms with CELESTE L., coming towards*

AMANDA *in front of table C.*]. We've got a new bow to-day.
[*She points to a band of black crape round* AMANDA's *arm.*]

CELESTE. So she 'as! Where did y' git that, S'rimp?
[AMANDA *arranges the bow on her arm, pulling out the ends.*]

AMANDA. I've been doin' a little shoppin' this afternoon,
and I bought this Rembrandt in case you was took off
sudden, S'leste. S'leste! [*She gives a little chuckle.*] It is
a name, ain't it? Where did y' git it? Off the front of
a shop, eh?

> Pretty Celeste
> 'Ad a very weak chest.
> If 'er chest 'd been stronger
> Me tale 'd been longer.

> > [*She hoists herself on the table.*
> [CLEM *and* ROSE *laugh shrilly.* CELESTE *flushes.*

CELESTE. Weak chest y'self. What's wrong with my
chest?

AMANDA [*sitting on table*]. Bit narrer, dear, isn't it?
But p'raps it's the cut o' y' bodice. Some of those bodice-
'ands can spoil things a treat, can't they?

CELESTE. What do y' know about it. You shut y' face.
You! you ain't got no figger, you never dresses, you ain't
got enough 'air to go in a locket, and every feller I know
says as you're a bloomin' little monkey without a stick. So,
now, there!

MADAME [*bustling into outdoor things and interposing to
prevent the quarrel developing*]. Now, now, now! One
would think that in life there was nothing to do. You
quarrel, you talk, you sing. Do I sing? *Mon Dieu*, no.
Celeste she sing till she make my 'ead ache, and then it is
you. [*To* AMANDA, *who gets off table*] And you all talk,
talk, talk like I don't know what. For shame. Now I go,
and you, Celeste, will go to Madame Jones with 'er things—
they are listed, eh?—and Mrs Galloway will take M.

Gigot 'is waistcoat, and Rose, you will not forget Miss Smeet's dress. She must 'ave it to-night. Now quick all of you. Amanda will wait for me. I shall not be long. Now attention! No more singing, do you 'ear? You can sing if you want, in the street, and then you will be run in for drink to punish you. [*She goes out L.*]

[ROSE *jumps off her chair.*

ROSE. Is she gone? Lord, I wish it was Monday! I shan't git up all to-morrow so's to rest meself. Do 'ope it'll be fine.

CLEM. I expect it will. Makes such a difference, bank 'oliday, don't it? P'tickler when it's 'Am'stead.

ROSE. Course it's 'Am'stead. What d' *you* think.

CLEM [*crossing to* ROSE *and* CELESTE *R.*]. We should 'a' gone there too, only for Mr Galloway 'avin' a aunt at Greenwich—though of course bein' married I'm different, so to speak. We shall go be tram, I expect, and then there's th' 'ill in the Park, an' the 'eath close by an' all. But I don't know as I shouldn't like to be goin' with y'.

ROSE [*half ignoring her*]. Wish you was, dear. [*Turning to* CELESTE] S'leste, you an' Albert will be ready, won't you? You must be 'ere first thing, cause of me and my friend pickin' y' up.

[CLEM *goes up L., presently returns to her work R.*

CELESTE. We'll be ready. Rather. What ho! [*Seeing* AMANDA, *who has been looking from one to another and who stands a little bit wistfully outside the group*] Well, Mandy, got some one to take y' out Monday, eh?

AMANDA [*starts and pulls herself together*]. I—I don't know as I can go out at all a Monday. Y' see, prop'ly speakin' I'm in mournin'.

CELESTE. You're always in mournin' 'oliday time—you was at Easter, too. I believe meself——

AMANDA [*quickly*]. Well, so I was. I lost me aunt on

the mother's side just before Good Friday. This [*she touches crape bow*] is for me cousin's niece as passed away quietly last week in—in Kensington. We—we 'ad been estranged for some time, but now she is gone I bear 'er no malice, and she shall never 'ave it to say as I didn't pay 'er proper respect. And besides I don't know as I care to go out in my circumstances.

CELESTE. Your circumstances! What are they?

AMANDA. Oh, well—till—till 'e comes for me, y' know.

ROSE. Till 'e comes for 'is shirt, eh?—the tall 'andsome stranger as none of us 'as never seen—n' never won't. [*She jumps on a chair again and takes out parcel.*] Garn. You've made it all up about 'im, I believe. "Mr 'Orris Green-smith, to be called for"! "Miss Amanda Afflick, to be called for"! That's more like it. 'Ere, Clem! Ketch. [*She pitches parcel to* MRS GALLOWAY.]

AMANDA [*starting forward*]. Give it 'ere.

CLEM [*holding it high*]. Y' been washin' it again, Crapie, 'aven't y'?

AMANDA. Give it 'ere. 'Tain't yours.

CLEM. Ketch, S'leste. [*She throws it to* CELESTE.]

CELESTE. Better not wash it any more. It's gettin' so thin it'll blow away one of these days.

AMANDA [*fiercely*]. Give it me.

CELESTE. Not so fast.

AMANDA. Give it to me!

CELESTE. Tell us the truth, then. You been coddin' us about it all this time, 'aven't you? 'Orris or whatever 'e's called 'as left it 'ere didn't take no notice of y' at all, now did 'e?

AMANDA [*at back of centre table as* CELESTE *dances round with shirt*]. Didn't 'e? P'raps 'e's never wrote to me neither, letters and letters on scented paper with crests and coats o' arms—and sealing wax too. You're jealous, all the lot o' y'! Give it 'ere. You'll mess it. Oh, [*half cry-ing*] you'll mess it and 'e might come for it to-day. Give it 'ere.

CLEM. Let 'er 'ave it, S'leste.

CELESTE [*holds it high*]. If I do will y' show me that brooch?

AMANDA. What brooch?

CELESTE. You know. The one you told us about. The minnycher set in diamonds.

AMANDA [*affecting unconcern*]. Oh, 'aven't I shown it to y'?

CELESTE. No, n' none of 'is presents. If I give it y', will y'?

AMANDA [*hesitates*]. I—I don't know where I put it.

CELESTE. Well then, the bracelet with the turquoise.

AMANDA. I—I lent that to me cousin for 'er niece's funeral. She 'asn't sent it back yet.

CELESTE. Well then, one of the other things then—some present as 'e's give y', will y'?

AMANDA. Give me my shirt.

CELESTE. Will y', then?

AMANDA. All right.

CELESTE. There y' are, Kipper! Ketch!

[AMANDA *catches the shirt and with her back to the others gently fondles it for a moment as a mother might fondle a child. Then pulling a chair for-ward and climbing it she puts the parcel safely away on a shelf.*

CELESTE. Seein's believin', y' know, and when we've seen —no 'anky-panky mindje!—some jewel or something.

AMANDA. All right.

CLEM [*indulgently*]. Let 'er alone, S'leste. That'll do.

AMANDA [*standing on chair to put away the shirt, turns fiercely*]. 'Ere, what's it got to do with you? You keep

172

your oar out of my wheel. I can take care of meself, Mrs Clementina William Galloway. You think just because I'm not twelve feet 'igh and six foot round like some people as I can't 'old me own with a pack of chatterin' girls like S'leste 'ere and Rose Allelujah Jordan. One more river to cross! What ho! I spurn the lot of you. You're no more to me than a herd of buzzin' flies. [*Quieting down*] I go 'ome from 'ere and I set on the sofa and read 'is letters, and all what 'appens in this 'ouse o' bondage is no more to me than a dream of the night!

CLEM. Does 'e know what your temper is?

ROSE. Little spitfire!

AMANDA. There, dear, I don't mean it. Only y' see when y'r 'ead's full of more important things and there's wonderful changes loomin' before y' it's apt to make y' a bit 'asty. There, Clem, [*goes to her*] I didn't mean to be cross. One of these days you shall know all.

CELESTE [*impressed in spite of herself*]. When did y' 'ear from 'im last?

AMANDA. Wednesday week—no, Tuesday it would be.

ROSE. Did 'e send y' anything then?

AMANDA. 'E's goin' to.

CELESTE. Something nice!   [AMANDA *nods*.

CELESTE. Is it a ring?

AMANDA. No.

CLEM. 'E's too sharp for that, eh, Mandy?

AMANDA. Better than that. [*Gets on the table again.*] It's—it's a hairloom—one of those things you wear in it at the op'ra.

CELESTE. I know—a tarara.

AMANDA. Yes. [*The girls stop working and loll on the table listening open-mouthed.*] It sticks in y'r 'ead with spikes and it's got diamonds and em'rals and stars all round—it sticks up like a crown and it glitters—fit to blind y'.

173

CELESTE. 'E must 'ave a lot o' money.

ROSE. Seems to chuck it about, don't 'e ?

CELESTE. But you ain't *seen* 'im again ?

AMANDA. No. But 'e's comin'.

CELESTE. 'Ere ?

AMANDA. Yes. There's a understandin', y' see. There's clouds on the horizon—that why there's all this mystery. But when 'e fetches 'is shirt—it's a sort of a sign, see—I shall know that bright days are in store.

CLEM [*joining the table group after affecting indifference*]. But what I want to know is—me of course 'avin' a 'ome of me own and bein' in a responsible p'sition so to speak—what I want to know—is 'e going to marry y' ?

AMANDA. When 'e's asked me father.

ROSE. Asked y' father ?

AMANDA. Everybody respectable does that. A young fella comes along and 'e says, isn't she beautiful, 'e says, I'd die for 'er, I wish she'd walk on me, through my 'eart first. But 'e don't say nothing to 'er, not till 'e's been to 'er father—if 'e's any class, y' know.

ROSE. But you're not beautiful. I'm a lot better-lookin' than what you are and I shouldn't like any chap to go to my father.

AMANDA [*sweetly*]. Of course if y' father 'appens to be doin' a bit in 'Olloway it makes a difference.

ROSE. 'Olloway ! Jail bird y'self ! I don't believe a word of it. I don't believe——

CELESTE. Easy, Rose. [*Pulling her away*] Let's 'ear. [*To* AMANDA] 'As 'e seen y' father ?

AMANDA. Not yet—because—because of law suits, and then there's a missin' will, y' see.

CELESTE. Missin' will ?

AMANDA [*setting herself again on table C.*]. Well, there should be be rights, but I think we've got over that. Y' see, it’s like this : My father wanted me to grow up without any rank or pearls or carriages so as I shall be loved just for myself alone——

CLEM. She’s coddin’. She’s only a workus girl and never ’ad no father.

AMANDA. I’m not. It’s true. I’ve thought about it and dreamt about it till I know it’s true. Besides you’ll see. I’m goin’ to ’im in oh such a little while.

CELESTE. And what about ’Orris ?

AMANDA. I shall ask ’im if ’e loves me passionately, and if ’e says yes, I shall lay one white jew’ld ’and in ’is, and look into ’is pleadin’ eyes and say, ’Orris, because you loved me truly when I was pore and in disguise, you shall ’ave your reward.

CELESTE [*to the others*]. It sounds all right, don’t it ?

CLEM [*rises*]. ’Ere, come along, girls. What’s the good o’ ’angin’ about listenin’ to all this rubbish when we got these things to take ’fore we can go. ’Ere, bustle up, S’leste. The old woman ’ll be back again mongdewing like Lord-save-us-all if she finds they ain’t gone. [CELESTE *and* ROSE *go into inner room to put on their hats and coats.*] You show us that present, Corpsie, or find some one to take y’ out a Monday, and then p’raps we’ll see about believin’ y’. Come, Rose. [*She goes into inner room L.*]

AMANDA [*absently and waving her hand*]. I have always loved you, ’Orris. Now your patience is rewarded. Rise and take me to my carriage.

ROSE [*putting on her hat and helping* CELESTE *with her coat as she and* CLEM *reappear with their things*]. Carriage ! You find somebody with a moke and a barrer to take y’ to ’Amstead.

AMANDA [*loftily*]. I’m not goin’ on Monday. Bank ’olidy ! It’s just for ordinary people as ’ave no prospex and nothing better to think of.

175

ROSE. Oh, indeed. [*She picks up basket back centre.*] Well, I 'ope, Miss Amander Afflick, as you'll enjoy yours all alone by y'r own self with nobody asked y' to go with 'em !

CLEM. Don't git run away with by a earl or anything like that while we're out.

CELESTE. So long, Corpsie. Y' got to show us one of them presents, y' know. 'Ere, wait for me, Rose.

[*They troop out L. with their packages.*

AMANDA [*when the door has closed behind them sits still for a moment or two. When she lifts her face it is seen to be working. To herself*]. Monday ! I should like to be goin' to 'Amstead—or anywheres. They might 'a' asked me to go with 'em. Somebody might. Nobody never won't. Never, never, never. 'Oo wants me ? 'Oo could ? I couldn't. Oh, well.

[*She sniffs drily and getting up and moving to rack climbs the chair again and takes down the rescued shirt. Very carefully and lovingly she refolds it in its covering, holds it to her for a moment and puts it back on the shelf. She is turning once more to the room when the door is flung open and* HORACE GREENSMITH *enters R. He is a young workman of sufficiently ordinary appearance, the type of navvy who may always be seen in London breaking up main thoroughfares with sledge-hammer and wedge.*

HORACE. 'Ere, two-foot-nothing. Where's Mother Didier ?

AMANDA [*getting off chair quickly*]. Oh, Mr Greensmith ! I thought you was dead. Oh ! [*Sits.*] Oh !

HORACE. Mr Greensmith ! You know my name. And who might you be to think I was dead ?

AMANDA. Oh—you must excuse me—but I did indeed. [*She puts her hand over her heart.*]

HORACE. Did y' ? Well, I'm jolly well not.

AMANDA [*faintly*]. Oh, it's like one from the grave. I shall be all right in a minute.

HORACE. Well, be quick about it. Now are y' better? Very well then, touchin' a shirt I left 'ere. Has the old woman sold it or lost it? Is she goin' to fork it out or does she want me to summons her for it? Go an' arsk 'er. Look slippy.

AMANDA. It's all right, Mr Greensmith. It's been took pertikler care of. [*Fetches it, and undoing the paper in which it is wrapped, displays the shirt to him proudly.*]

HORACE. Jeroosalem! Did y' wash it yesterday?

AMANDA. Yes, Mr Greensmith.

HORACE. Not so much o' y' Mr Greensmith. 'Oo told y' to wash it yesterday! Did the old woman twig I was comin'?

AMANDA. No, Mr—'Orris. I've washed it every week, *ever* since you left it so as to 'ave it ready for you.

HORACE. S'help me Jimmy, you must be 'ard up for something to do! Y' don't think I'm going to pay for all that, do y'?

AMANDA. Oh, no, Mr Greensmith. If you was to stuff the money down me throat wild horses wouldn't make me swallow it.

HORACE. H'm! Well, I ain't going to. What's the damage, anyhow?

AMANDA. We don't want you to pay anything, reelly.

HORACE. Oh, we don't, don't we! That suits me A1. You may stick over the door then, Washers by appointment to 'Orris Greensmith, Esquire. Do you do all y'r work like that? Is this a charitable institution or what is it?

AMANDA. Oh, no, Mr 'Orris, we aren't charitable, oh, not at all. You see we—that is, *I* thought we should never see you no more. You'd been away so long—there seemed nothing else to think——

HORACE. Well, I'm jiggered. Deaders on the free list, eh? 'Oly Moses!

AMANDA. You don't think it was a liberty, do you?

HORACE [*looks at her a moment and then bursts out laughing*]. Strike me silly if I ever came across anything quite as dotty before. I was dead, was I, and this was a blasted souvenir. 'Oo the blazes wanted a blasted souvenir of me? Not you!

AMANDA. I know it was a liberty, Mr Greensmith.

HORACE. 'Ere, 'andle me carefully. I shall faint.

AMANDA. I'm very sorry if you're angry.

HORACE. Was you 'ere when I come before?

AMANDA [*eagerly*]. Oh, yes, Mr 'Orris. It was at a quarter to five one Wednesday—don't you recklekt? It was in October, the 15th, and there was a crool fog all the morning. You was coughin' and saying things about the weather.

HORACE. Was I?

AMANDA. Don't you remember?

HORACE. I remember the fog—but then I remember a lot o' fogs.

AMANDA. I've thought of it every day since.

HORACE. 'Ere, what are you anyway?

AMANDA. I'm a orphin. I don't say so but I am—only to you I mean. I—what'll you think of me, Mr Green-smith?—I—I was born in the Union.

HORACE. I got no call to think one way or the other.

AMANDA. I wouldn't 'a' told no one else. But I couldn't tell you—well, what I tell the others.

HORACE. The others? Are there any more 'ere like you?

AMANDA. Oh, no, I don't think there's any others any-where like me.

HORACE. No, I dessay not.

AMANDA. Of course, I'm not very tall. We don't grow

much in the work'ouse—but some o' them large girls is very fickle, don't you think so, Mr Greensmith ?

HORACE. No girls is any good.

AMANDA. Oh, Mr 'Orris, you ain't married, are y' ?

HORACE. Not much.

AMANDA [*relieved*]. Oh—I thought jes' fer a moment— you mustn't mind me. Oh, I am glad.

HORACE. Married. Yah. Knows too much about it.

AMANDA. I'm glad ye're not married, anyway. Y' see, Mr Greensmith, if you won't think it a liberty what I am telling you, I always thought of you as a sort of fairy prince, y' see ; and they aren't never married, are they ?

HORACE [*stretches out one leg and looks at it dubiously*]. 'Ere, my 'ead 'll go if I stop much longer. A fairy— you've been ill, 'aven't you ?

AMANDA. Oh *no*, Mr 'Orris, I'm never ill. I'm very strong, and work ! Well, you should see me on a busy day ! It's only——

HORACE. Only what ?

AMANDA. Well, when you ain't got much of y'r own you do dream about beautiful things, don't you ? That's how I came to think of you.

HORACE. Thank you—very kind of you, don't mention it. [*Pause.*] Well, chuck us the shirt.

AMANDA [*brings it to him slowly*]. I suppose you'll send us some other things.

HORACE. Don't know ; can't say.

[AMANDA *furtively wipes one eye.*

HORACE. Hello. What's the matter with y' ?

AMANDA. Oh, nothing.

HORACE. What's that crape for ?

AMANDA. I *say* it's for relations.

HORACE. Oh, well, pull up your socks and grin, y' can't 'ave y' relations always, y' know.

AMANDA. I never 'ad no relations.

HORACE. Well, what d' y' wear the bow for then? Y' don't know what y're talking about. Y' wears it for your relations and you never 'ad none. Rottin' sort of goin' into mourning that. Where's y' father?

[AMANDA *shakes her head.*

HORACE. Oh, well—where's y' mother, anyway?

AMANDA. She's dead—she died when I was quite little— oh well, littler than I am now. But it ain't for 'er.

HORACE. 'Oo is it for?

AMANDA. You won't tell the other girls, will y'?

HORACE. No. What should I want t' go jawin' about you for?

AMANDA. You see, I tell *them* that I got a father who's rich—ever so rich—and who's coming to take me away, see, like in a story. I'm in disguise now, but one day 'e'll come and say " Apparel 'er in ermine," and then I shall go away and be a lady. I used to think he would really come, but now I guess 'e's dead, though I tell them 'e's comin'. I don't wear it for 'im though. I keep on changin' 'oo it's for. Y' see, I felt I must wear it. [*Looks up shyly.*] But I can take it off now, Mr 'Orris. [*A pause.*

HORACE. Well of all. . . . Give us the shirt.

AMANDA. Are y' goin' at once?

HORACE. Well, since you are so pressin' I got about 'alf a minute t' waste. *Now* then.

AMANDA. Nothin', I jes' wanted to see you. Y' can smoke if y' like.

HORACE. Make meself at 'ome, eh, and what for! [*Sits on table.*]

AMANDA [*coming near to him L., standing beside him*]. Y' said y' wasn't married. Are y' in love, Mr Greensmith?

HORACE. Oh, chuck it. What's that to do with you?

AMANDA. I want to know pertickler.

HORACE. Well, I ain't jes' now.

AMANDA. I expect lots o' girls is in love with you.

HORACE. Oh, yes. I can't 'ardly get down the street for em.

AMANDA. You wouldn't say I was pretty, would y', Mr Greensmith?

HORACE. I 'aven't thought about it.

AMANDA. You wouldn't think about it, would y'?

HORACE [*indulgently*]. W-ell——

AMANDA. Eh? but looks ain't everything, are they? Some o' them pretty girls they aren't content when one feller likes 'em, they wants a lot o' chaps to say as they're beautiful.

HORACE. Don't I know it? 'Orris Greensmith ain't goin' to be one of them.

AMANDA. You ain't very 'asty, are you?

HORACE. Middlin'. What's up?

AMANDA. I don't hardly like to tell y'.

HORACE. 'Ere, what y' been doin' of? [*Stops in act of lighting pipe and stares at her with match in his hand.*]

AMANDA [*wriggling in front of him*]. I want to tell y', Mr Greensmith, but I'm afraid you won't like it.

HORACE. Not knowing, can't say. Stand still, can't y'?

AMANDA. Y' might turn round, will y', and look out the winder? I don't like bein' looked at—then I'll tell y'.

HORACE [*stares at her hard a minute*]. Well, there ain't much to look at, is there? Now then. [*Turns round and lights up pipe.*]

AMANDA. Y' see—y' see—it's like this, Mr 'Orris. You comin' in and seein' me last year and never comin' 'ere again, all the girls what's 'ere says as 'ow you were in love with me.

HORACE [*turning round promptly*]. What! Me! Wodder they take me for? In love——! Lord save us.

AMANDA. Y' know girls will talk, Mr 'Orris.

HORACE. Yuss, they talks right enough if you give them 'alf a chance. Well, is that what y' wanted to tell me, 'cause if so y' could 'a' kep' it to y'self.

AMANDA. That ain't all.

HORACE. 'Ope y' jolly well told 'em I wasn't.

AMANDA. No. I didn't tell 'em that.

HORACE. D'y' mean to tell me a pack o' girls thinks as I—— [*Roars with laughter.* AMANDA *stands shamefaced and nervous.*]

AMANDA. I 'oped y' wouldn't laugh, Mr 'Orris.

HORACE. Wouldn't laugh. Ho no! but it is a bit thick, isn't it! So I'm in love with you, am I? Would y' like t' get on the table and then y'r lovin' 'usband could give y' a kiss. [AMANDA *begins to get on table.*

HORACE [*amazed*]. Did y' think I was really goin' to kiss y'?

AMANDA. I should like y' to kiss me, Mr 'Orris.

HORACE [*sinks into chair.*] Phew. 'Ere, I'm gettin' 'ot. Give us a chance. You go too quick fer me.

AMANDA [*squatting on the table and smoothing her dress and pulling it over her boots*]. I didn't know as gentlemen didn't like bein' kissed.

HORACE. 'Ere, let's look at y'. [*Pause.*

AMANDA [*looking at him diffidently.*] You are 'andsome, aren't you, Mr 'Orris, but I s'pose you know that.

HORACE. I've 'eard something about it.

AMANDA. That ain't all what I told y' jes' now.

HORACE. What!

AMANDA. All the other girls they've got fellers to give 'em things.

HORACE. You don't say so. Well, you ain't goin' to catch me——

AMANDA. Oh, no, but I didn't like their sayin' as nobody ever giv' me anything, so I bin tellin' them as you give me

lots an' 'eaps o' things—dimonds and joolery and watches—
'andsome, y' know. I didn't know as you'd come back. I'd
waited so long—and at last I went into mournin'—but I
kep' on sayin' about the presents and letters, and now I
'aven't even anything to be in mournin' for, and they'll say
as they always knew as I was kiddin', and [*sniffs*] they didn't
—they reelly thought it was true what I told them. I know
it was a liberty, Mr 'Orris, but I 'oped you wouldn't mind.

HORACE [*whistles. Slowly*]. They thinks as I've been
stuffing you up with presents.

AMANDA. Yes, Mr 'Orris.

HORACE. Well you've just about made a nice mess of
things, ain't y' ?

AMANDA. Couldn't you——

HORACE. Couldn't I do it really ? Not much.

AMANDA. I didn't mean that, but as you ain't dead
couldn't you go on sayin' nothin' and let me go on pretendin'—— ?

HORACE. No.

AMANDA. It wouldn't cost y' nothin'. Why won't y' ?

HORACE. Yes. Why won't I ?

AMANDA [*walking away very much downcast*]. I thought
you might like to oblige a lady.

HORACE. What next !

[AMANDA *goes up to window and dries her eyes with her
apron.*

HORACE. What 'r y' snuffling about, y' little beggar ?

AMANDA. Nothin', Mr 'Orris.

HORACE. They must be a precious lot o' mugs them girls
if they swaller a tale like that. I never heard o' such a
thing. [*He leans against table with his back to audience.*]

AMANDA. They didn't believe it for a long while, but now
they believes it, an' about me father, too.

HORACE. Father ! Didn't y' say he was a gonner——

AMANDA [*faintly and tearfully*]. I don't know, though I guess. But [*rather proudly*] they think I've got a father as rich as ever 'e could be, and 'andsome, more 'andsome even than you.

HORACE. Pretty sort o' father to leave you in this 'ole then.

AMANDA. They think 'e's comin' to fetch me.

HORACE. Best 'urry up, I should say.

AMANDA [*gives a little gesture*]. Oh, don't you see! I got nothing, Mr 'Orris—nothing. [*She subsides and burying her face in the hollow of her arm cries silently.*]

[*Pause.*

HORACE. 'Ere, funny, you needn't drown the place out. Tell 'em what you blasted well like. I don't care. [*Kicks a clothes basket.*] I don't care.

AMANDA. Oh, Mr 'Orris.

HORACE. Yes, oh, Mr 'Orris, but you don't catch me coming 'ere no more.

AMANDA. You won't come 'ere again!

HORACE. No fear. Is it likely? What d'ye take me for?

AMANDA. Then I don't know as I'll tell 'em anything then.

HORACE. Suit yourself.

AMANDA. I'd rather—oh, I don't care what they think.

HORACE. Look 'ere, nipper. [*He comes to her.*] I'm goin' to talk like a father to you. You're puttin' y'r money on the wrong 'orse—not as I'm a wrong'un mindje, but if you was to talk to some chaps like this——

AMANDA [*quickly*]. Oh, but I wouldn't.

HORACE. That's all right then. Now you give me my shirt and I'll be off and [*generously*] you tell those girls just what you damn well please.

AMANDA [*looking at the parcel lingeringly*]. You're goin' to take it?

HORACE. Time I did, isn't it?

AMANDA. I shan't 'ave nothin' to remember y' by.

HORACE. Would y' like a lock o' me 'air ? 'Ere—'ere's a present for y'. [*He takes a pin out of his tie.*] Gold pin, 42 carat, diamond mounted, pearl centre, em'rald border encrusted with rubies. [*Polishes it on his sleeve.*]. New cut 2-9. There, my dear.

AMANDA [*delighted*]. Oh, Mr 'Orris !

HORACE. Now we're quits.

AMANDA [*excitedly*]. I did want something to show to S'leste, and it is lovely, lovely, but—but——

HORACE. What now ?

AMANDA. It means as you're goin' for ever. Couldn't—couldn't you keep it and not——

HORACE. Not what ?

AMANDA. Not go. It—it's like you dyin' all over again.

HORACE. Well of all the treats——

AMANDA [*with a new thought*]. Where are y' goin' now ?

HORACE. 'Ome, I s'pose.

AMANDA. We—we do send things——

HORACE. What are y' drivin' at ?

AMANDA. Say I was to bring y' this. Or if you'd wait a little bit I might carry it out for you. It's nice strollin' in the summer evenin's, Mr 'Orris, and it'd be no trouble.

HORACE [*stooping, with his hands on his knees, and thus bringing his face on to a level with hers*]. Come with me, d' y' mean ?

AMANDA. Yes.

HORACE. Yes. We could go for strolls every evenin', eh ?

AMANDA [*with a long breath*]. Oh—ye-es.

HORACE [*mimicking her*]. Ye-es ! What d' y' think my friends 'd say ? Why, as we was walkin' out.

AMANDA. I wouldn't mind, Mr 'Orris.

HORACE. But what price me?

AMANDA. I shouldn't expect y' to marry me.

HORACE. Much obliged. Thank y'.

AMANDA. I didn't even dream as y'd marry me really.

HORACE. Well then, if you was to come messin' about with me what'd your girls 'ere say? You don't want to lose y' character, I s'pose.

AMANDA. *I* wouldn't mind, Mr 'Orris.

HORACE. So 'elp me Bob. You don't seem to mind anything. [*He walks half-way to the door and pauses.*] 'Ere. Are all o' you girls goin' out a Monday?

AMANDA. The others are, Rose and S'leste and Clem—that's Mrs Galloway.

HORACE. But what about you?

AMANDA. I—I'm supposed to be in mournin'.

HORACE. 'As nobody asked y'? [AMANDA *hangs her head.*

HORACE. 'As nobody asked y'?

AMANDA. I—[*she bites her lip*]—I can't pretend any more. [*Breaking down.*] No. Nobody's never asked me. [*She sobs.*] I s'pose now nobody never will. I see 'em all start times and times with their fellas. Oh, it don't matter. Only I didn't mean as *you* should know. [*Sits.*]

HORACE. Where are they goin'?

AMANDA [*sobbing gently*]. 'Amstead. Oh, it don't matter, Mr 'Orris.

HORACE. Yes, it do. [*He moves about restlessly for a minute, then stares at her intently.*] Look 'ere. Shall I take y'?

AMANDA. D' y' mean it?

HORACE. Did I say it? Very well then.

AMANDA. Oh, Mr 'Orris.

HORACE. I'll get a trap and we'll go to 'Amstead.

AMANDA [*in ecstasy*]. Oh, Mr 'Orris.

HORACE. All right. That's settled. I'll call for you 'ere at nine sharp Monday mornin'.

AMANDA. Y' won't change y' mind ?

HORACE. No. If I say I'll do a thing I'll do it.

AMANDA. And I may tell S'leste and the others.

HORACE. Tell the 'ole world if y' like. Tell all Soho.

AMANDA [*dancing and clapping her hands and singing*]. Oh, it'll be joyful, joyful, joyful, joyful ! I'll wear me blue dress that buttons up the back, and I've got a 'at as I hardly worn yet. Won't the other girls stare ! Not one of 'em's got a fella like you. Rose's Jim—why 'e's not much bigger than me. And S'leste's Albit—'e's only a dustman. And as for Mr Galloway—if 'e's sober be nine o'clock in the mornin' Clem'll 'ave something to be thankful for. Oh, Mr 'Orris. Sat'dy, Sundy, Mondy. A 'ole day to look forward in. There won't be a 'appier lady anywhere Monday than what I shall be. You'll be 'ere be nine. [*Coming back to him*] That's when the others go.

HORACE. D' they start from 'ere ?

AMANDA. Yes.

HORACE [*shifting his feet*]. Nine o'clock, that's all right, but I think it'd be better to meet by the Dispens'ry, see—in Paul Street.

AMANDA [*her face falling a little*]. Paul Street—right down there ?

HORACE. What's the matter with Paul Street ? Everyone knows the Dispens'ry. It's a good place to meet, ain't it ?

AMANDA. I should 'a' liked you to come 'ere.

HORACE. What's the difference ?

AMANDA [*reluctantly*]. I should 'a' liked 'em all to see me goin' off with y'. They won't more than 'alf believe else.

HORACE. Paul Street's much more convenient.

AMANDA. There won't be the crowd there is 'ere.

HORACE. No. That's it. We don't want no crowds, do we ? It'll be much better to go quietly from Paul Street, won't it ? You *be* there at nine and I'll come along and pick y' up. Then we shan't 'ave no waitin' about.

[AMANDA *looks at him slowly.*

HORACE. You could be at the corner, couldn't you, where thát little court is, and come out when I whistled ?

AMANDA [*still looking at him*]. Yes. I needn't show meself till you come.

HORACE. That's right. [*A little pause.*

HORACE. And er—I was thinking' there's such 'undreds of people goes to 'Amstead. We don't want to go there, do we ? What'd y' say to the forest ?

AMANDA. Eppin' ?

HORACE. Yes. I know a nice quiet little bit of it where we could go.

AMANDA [*meekly*]. I don't mind, Mr 'Orris. [*She walks away from him.*]

HORACE. All right then. Monday, nine o'clock. Paul Street. Blest if I wasn't goin' without me shirt after all. Ta-ta. [*Is about to go.*]

AMANDA [*calling him back just as he is at the door*]. Mr 'Orris.

HORACE. Yes.

AMANDA. I—I can't go after all.

HORACE [*coming back*]. Can't go !

AMANDA. No.

HORACE. What d' y' mean, can't go ?

AMANDA. What I say. I—[*recovering herself with an effort*]—I been pretendin'. Just to see what you'd do.

HORACE. Pretendin' !

AMANDA. Yes. [*Nervous and excited, but gaining confidence as she proceeds.*] You see I shouldn't be allowed to go out with strangers. My people wouldn't let me. I've been brought up different. I'm afraid you'll be very angry, but none of that about me bein' a orphin or born in the

Union is true. I'm the child of poor but respectable parents, and I've bin very strictly brought up, and so, though I'm very much obliged to you, Mr Greensmith, I mustn't accept your kind invitation.

HORACE. Strike me pink!

AMANDA. You don't mind me 'avin' a bit of a lark with y', do y'? It was so dull 'ere while the others was out. I couldn't 'elp it. Ha, ha, ha. If you was to see y'r own face! You got a soft 'eart, that I will say. Ha, ha, ha.

HORACE. Made a fool of me, 'ave y'? All right, my girl. Wait till I bring y' more washin' to do.

AMANDA. There, don't be angry.

HORACE. Angry! 'Oo's angry? It's enough to make anyone angry. Why——

AMANDA. Garn. You know very well as it's a relief.

HORACE. Relief?

AMANDA [*half hysterical*]. Not to 'ave to take me out—a little 'op-o'-me-thumb like me. Ain't it now? And 'ave everybody laughin' at y', and askin' y' what it was, and where y'd picked it up, and why they 'adn't drowned it when it was born. Ho, ho. It'd be a poor world, eh, if we didn't get a bit o' fun out of it some'ow, and some of us was meant to supply all the fun for the others, it's my opinion. Lord, when you thought I was cryin' I thought I should 'a died. Laugh! Whenever I think of it I shall most split meself. Y' don't mind, old man, do y'?

HORACE. I've a good mind to wring y' neck for y'.

AMANDA. No, don't do that. May I keep the pin?

HORACE. Keep what y' like.

AMANDA. I will then. Now say y' ain't angry before y' go.

HORACE. I'll be blowed if I do.

AMANDA. Jes' to show there's no ill-feelin'.

HORACE. Git out.

AMANDA. Say it. [*She stands looking up at him tremu-lously.*]

HORACE. 'Ere. [*Stares at her hard, then takes her hands and pulls her round to the light.*] Why! What'r ye playin' at ? Tell the truth and shame the devil. Twig ? I was a fool to say as I'd take y'. We wasn't made for each other—what d'ye call yerself 'op-o'-me-thumb ? but you're a game little 'un, and 'Orris Greensmith's goin' to sling 'is bloomin' 'ook. See! Now gi' us that kiss I asked y' for. [*Kisses her quickly and in shamefaced manner, but very kindly, then whips up hat and shirt and goes out quietly. She stands for a moment or two swaying. When she looks up he is gone.*]

AMANDA. 'E kissed me! [*Wonderingly*] 'E kissed me. O-oh. [*She looks round and begins mechanically to put the room tidy. Presently she bethinks her of the pin. She takes it out of the bosom of her dress where she has stuck it.*] 'E was ashamed of me, too. I s'pose I ought to spurn it. I ought really to 'a thrown it at 'is false feet and said : " Take back the jew'ls with which you 'ave loaded me, they are poisonin' me," but [*shaking her head and rubbing the stones on her sleeve to make them shine*] I can't. Oh, Mr 'Orris, you've broken my 'eart and stuck a pin in it. But you did kiss me. You can't take back y' kiss. I shan't wait to hear their talk. Me pretendin's over and done with. [*She pulls off her crape bow and holds it to her lips.*] There's nobody—nobody now for me to pretend. Oh, Mr 'Orris—Mr 'Orris. [*She crouches in a shabby little heap in the middle of the empty room as the*

CURTAIN FALLS

THE MONKEY'S PAW
A STORY IN THREE SCENES
By W. W. Jacobs
Dramatized by Louis N. Parker

CHARACTERS

Mr White
Mrs White
Herbert
Sergeant-major Morris
Mr Sampson

This play was first produced at the Haymarket Theatre, London, on October 6, 1903, with the following cast:

Mr White	Cyril Maude
Mrs White	Lena Ashwell
Herbert	Wilfred Forster
Sergeant-major Morris .	Sydney Valentine
Mr Sampson	Rudge Harding

Mr W. W. Jacobs has won a great reputation by his short stories, and it is as a writer of stories rather than of plays that we immediately think of him. Nevertheless, there is an obviously dramatic quality in his work which has attracted collaborators, and he has been fortunate in being associated with men who could skilfully transfer into good stage-plays the characteristic Jacobean quality of "The Ghost of Jerry Bundler," "The Monkey's Paw," and "The Boatswain's Mate."

The last, indeed, has enjoyed the ultimate dramatic honour of being made, by Dame Ethel Smythe, the subject of an opera. "Beauty and the Barge," by W. W. Jacobs and Louis N. Parker, is perhaps less successful as a piece of dramatic art than the one-act plays, but if we remember that Mr Jacobs' genius finds its natural expression in short stories this fact is not surprising. It is noteworthy, too, that, while Mr Jacobs uses the *macabre* only rarely and the humorous most frequently in his stories, the proportions seem to have become reversed in his plays.

THE MONKEY'S PAW [1]

SCENE: *The living-room of an old-fashioned cottage on the outskirts of Fulham. Set corner-wise in the left angle at the back a deep window; further front, L., three or four steps lead up to a door. Further forward a dresser, with plates, glasses, etc. R. C. at back an alcove with the street door fully visible. On the inside of the street door, a wire letter-box. On the right a cupboard, then a fire-place. In the centre a round table. Against the wall, L. back, an old-fashioned piano. A comfortable armchair each side of the fireplace. Other chairs. On the mantel-piece a clock, old china figures, etc. An air of comfort pervades the room.*

I

At the rise of the curtain, MRS WHITE, *a pleasant-looking old woman, is seated in the armchair below the fire, attending to a kettle which is steaming on the fire, and keeping a laughing eye on* MR WHITE *and* HERBERT. *These two are seated at the right angle of the table nearest the fire with a chessboard between them.* MR WHITE *is evidently losing. His hair is ruffled; his spectacles are high up on his forehead.* HERBERT, *a fine young fellow, is looking with satisfaction at the move he has just made.* MR WHITE *makes several attempts to move, but thinks*

---

[1] Applications regarding amateur performances of this play should be addressed to Messrs Samuel French, Ltd., 26 Southampton Street, Strand, London, W.C.2, or 25 West 45th Street, New York.

better of them. There is a shaded lamp on the table. The door is tightly shut. The curtains of the window are drawn ; but every now and then the wind is heard whistling outside.

MR WHITE [*moving at last, and triumphant*]. There, Herbert, my boy ! Got you, I think.

HERBERT. Oh, you're a deep 'un, Dad, aren't you ?

MRS WHITE. Mean to say he's beaten you at last ?

HERBERT. Lor, no ! Why, he's overlooked——

MR WHITE [*very excited*]. I see it ! Lemme have that back !

HERBERT. Not much. Rules of the game !

MR WHITE [*disgusted*]. I don't hold with them scientific rules. You turn what ought to be an innocent relaxation——

MRS WHITE. Don't talk so much, Father. You put him off——

HERBERT [*laughing*]. Not he !

MR WHITE [*trying to distract his attention*]. Hark at the wind.

HERBERT (*drily*). Ah ! I'm listening. Check.

MR WHITE [*still trying to distract him*]. I should hardly think Sergeant-major Morris'd come to-night.

HERBERT. Mate. [*Rises, goes up L.*]

MR WHITE [*with an outbreak of disgust and sweeping the chessmen off the board*]. That's the worst of living so far out. Your friends can't come for a quiet chat, and you addle your brains over a confounded——

HERBERT. Now, Father ! Morris'll turn up all right.

MR WHITE [*still in a temper*]. Lovers' Lane, Fulham ! Ho ! of all the beastly, slushy, out-o'-the-way places to live in——! Pathway's a bog, and the road's a torrent. [*To* MRS WHITE, *who has risen, and is at his side*] What's the County Council thinking of, that's what I want to know ?

Because this is the only house in the road it doesn't matter if nobody can get near it, I s'pose.

MRS WHITE. Never mind, dear. Perhaps you'll win to-morrow. [*She moves to back of table.*]

MR WHITE. Perhaps I'll—perhaps I'll—— What d'you mean? [*Bursts out laughing.*] There! You always know what's going on inside o' me, don't you, Mother?

MRS WHITE. Ought to, after thirty years, John.

> [*She goes to dresser, and busies herself wiping tumblers on tray there. He rises, goes to fireplace and lights pipe.*

HERBERT [*down C.*]. And it's not such a bad place, Dad, after all. One of the few old-fashioned houses left near London. None o' your stucco villas. Homelike, I call it. And so do you, or you wouldn't ha' bought it. [*Rolls a cigarette.*]

MR WHITE [*R., growling*]. Nice job I made o' that, too! With two hundred pounds owin' on it.

HERBERT [*on back of chair, C.*]. Why, I shall work that off in no time, Dad. Matter o' three years, with the rise promised me.

MR WHITE. If you don't get married.

HERBERT. Not me. Not that sort.

MRS WHITE. I wish you would, Herbert. A good, steady lad——

> [*She brings the tray with a bottle of whisky, glasses, a lemon, spoons, buns, and a knife to the table.*

HERBERT. Lot's o' time, Mother. Sufficient for the day —as the sayin' goes. Just now my dynamos don't leave me any time for love-making. Jealous they are, I tell you!

MR WHITE [*chuckling*]. I lay awake o' nights often, and think: If Herbert took a nap, and let his what-d'you-call-ums—dynamos, run down, all Fulham would be in darkness. Lord! what a joke! [*Gets R. C.*]

HERBERT. Joke! And me with the sack! Pretty idea of a joke you've got, I don't think.

[*Knock at outer door.*

MRS WHITE. Hark! [*Knock repeated, louder.*

MR WHITE [*going toward door*]. That's him. That's the Sergeant-major. [*He unlocks door, back.*]

HERBERT [*removes chessboard*]. Wonder what yarn he's got for us to-night. [*Places chessboard on piano.*]

MRS WHITE [*goes up right, busies herself putting the other armchair nearer fire, etc.*]. Don't let the door slam, John!

[MR WHITE *opens the door a little, struggling with it. Wind.* SERGEANT-MAJOR MORRIS, *a veteran with a distinct military appearance—left arm gone— dressed as a commissionaire, is seen to enter.* MR WHITE *helps him off with his coat, which he hangs up in the outer hall.*

MR WHITE [*at the door*]. Slip in quick! It's as much as I can do to hold it against the wind.

SERGEANT. Awful! Awful! [*Busy taking off his cloak, etc.*] And a mile up the road—by the cemetery—it's worse. Enough to blow the hair off your head.

MR WHITE. Give me your stick.

SERGEANT. If 'twasn't I knew what a welcome I'd get——

MR WHITE [*preceding him into the room*]. Sergeant-major Morris!

MRS WHITE. Tut! tut! So cold you must be! Come to the fire; do'ee, now.

SERGEANT. How are you, marm? [*To* HERBERT] How's yourself, laddie? Not on duty yet, eh? Day-week, eh?

HERBERT [*C.*]. No, sir. Night-week. But there's half an hour yet.

THE MONKEY'S PAW

SERGEANT [*sitting in the armchair above the fire, which* MRS WHITE *is motioning him toward.*]

[MR WHITE *mixes grog for* MORRIS.

Thank'ee kindly, marm. That's good—hah! That's a sight better than the trenches at Chitral. That's better than settin' in a puddle with the rain pourin' down in buckets, and the natives takin' pot-shots at you.

MRS WHITE. Didn't you have no umbrellas? [*Corner below fire, kneels before it, stirs it, etc.*]

SERGEANT. Umbrell——? Ho! ho! That's good! Eh, White? That's good. Did ye hear what she said? Umbrellas!—*And* goloshes! *and* hot-water bottles!—Ho, yes! No offence, marm, but it's easy to see you was never a soldier.

HERBERT [*rather hurt*]. Mother spoke out o' kindness, sir.

SERGEANT. And well I know it; and no offence intended. No, marm, 'ardship, 'ardship is the soldier's lot. Starvation, fever, and get yourself shot. That's a bit o' my own.

MRS WHITE. You don't look to've taken much harm—except—— [*Indicates his empty sleeve. She takes kettle to table, then returns to fire.*]

SERGEANT [*showing a medal hidden under his coat*]. And that I got this for. No, marm. Tough. Thomas Morris is tough.

[MR WHITE *is holding a glass of grog under the* SERGEANT'S *nose.*

And sober. What's this now?

MR WHITE. Put your nose in it; you'll see.

SERGEANT. Whisky? And hot? And sugar? And a slice o' lemon? No. I said I'd never—but seein' the sort o' night—— Well! [*Waving the glass at them*] Here's another thousand a year!

MR WHITE [*sits R. of table, also with a glass*]. Same to you and many of 'em.

SERGEANT [*to* HERBERT, *who has no glass*]. What? Not you?

HERBERT [*laughing and sitting across chair, C.*]. Oh! 'tisn't for want of being sociable. But my work don't go with it. Not if 'twas ever so little. I've got to keep a cool head, a steady eye, and a still hand. The fly-wheel might gobble me up.

MRS WHITE. Don't, Herbert. [*Sits in armchair below fire.*]

HERBERT [*laughing*]. No fear, Mother.

SERGEANT. Ah! you electricians!—Sort o' magicians, you are. Light! says you—and light it is. And, power! says you—and the trams go whizzin'. And, knowledge! says you —and words go 'ummin' to the ends o' the world. It fair beats me—and I've seen a bit in my time, too.

HERBERT [*nudges his father*]. Your Indian magic? All a fake, governor. The fakir's fake.

SERGEANT. Fake, you call it? I tell you, I've *seen* it.

HERBERT [*nudging his father with his foot*]. Oh, come, now! such as what? Come, now!

SERGEANT. I've seen a cove with no more clothes on than a babby, [*to* MRS WHITE] if you know what I mean—take an empty basket—empty, mind!—as empty as—as this nere glass——

MR WHITE. Hand it over, Morris. [*Hands it to* HERBERT, *who goes quickly behind table and fills it.*]

SERGEANT. Which was not my intentions, but used for illustration.

HERBERT [*while mixing*]. Oh, I've seen the basket trick; and I've read how it was done. Why, I could do it myself, with a bit o' practice. Ladle out something stronger.

[HERBERT *brings him the glass.*

SERGEANT. Stronger?—what do you say to an old fakir chuckin' a rope up in the air—in the *air*, mind you!—and swarming up it, same as if it was 'ooked on—vanishing clean out o' sight?—I've seen that.

THE MONKEY'S PAW

[HERBERT *goes to table, plunges a knife into a bun and offers it to the* SERGEANT *with exaggerated politeness.*

SERGEANT [*eyeing it with disgust*]. Bun——? What for?

HERBERT. That yarn takes it. [MR *and* MRS WHITE *delighted.*

SERGEANT. Mean to say you doubt my word?

MRS WHITE. No, no! He's only taking you off.—You shouldn't, Herbert.

MR WHITE. Herbert always was one for a bit o' fun!

[HERBERT *puts bun back on table, comes round in front, and moving the chair out of the way, sits cross-legged on the floor at his father's side.*

SERGEANT. But it's true. Why, if I chose, I could tell you things—— But there! you don't get no more yarns out o' me.

MR WHITE. Nonsense, old friend. [*Puts down his glass.*] You're not going to get shirty about a bit o' fun. [*Moves his chair nearer* MORRIS's.] What was that you started telling me the other day about a monkey's paw, or something? [*Nudges* HERBERT, *and winks at* MRS WHITE.]

SERGEANT [*gravely*]. Nothing. Leastways, nothing worth hearing.

MRS WHITE [*with astonished curiosity*]. Monkey's *paw*——?

MR WHITE. Ah—you was tellin' me——

SERGEANT. Nothing. Don't go on about it. [*Puts his empty glass to his lips—then stares at it.*] What? Empty again? There! When I begin thinkin' o' the paw, it makes me that absent-minded——

MR WHITE [*rises and fills glass*]. You said you always carried it on you.

SERGEANT. So I do, for fear o' what might happen. [*Sunk in thought*] Ay!—ay!

MR WHITE [*handing him his glass refilled*]. There. [*Sits again in same chair.*]

MRS WHITE. What's it for ?

SERGEANT. You wouldn't believe me, if I was to tell you.

HERBERT. *I* will, every word.

SERGEANT. Magic, then !—Don't you laugh !

HERBERT. I'm not.   Got it on you now ?

SERGEANT. Of course.

HERBERT. Let's see it.

> [*Seeing the* SERGEANT *embarrassed with his glass,* MRS
> WHITE *rises, takes it from him, places it on mantel-
> piece and remains standing.*

SERGEANT. Oh, it's nothing to look at. [*Hunting in his
pocket*] Just an ordinary—little paw—dried to a mummy.
[*Produces it and holds it towards* MRS WHITE.]   Here.

MRS WHITE [*who has leant forward eagerly to see it, starts
back with a little cry of disgust*].   Oh !

HERBERT. Give us a look. [MORRIS *passes the paw to* MR
WHITE, *from whom* HERBERT *takes it.*]   Why, it's all dried up !

SERGEANT. I said so.   [*Wind.*

MRS WHITE [*with a slight shudder*]. Hark at the wind !
[*Sits again in her old place.*]

MR WHITE [*taking the paw from* HERBERT].   And what might
there be special about it ?

SERGEANT [*impressively*]. That there paw has had a spell
put upon it !

MR WHITE. No ?   [*In great alarm he thrusts the paw back
into* MORRIS'S *hand.*]

SERGEANT [*pensively, holding the paw in the palm of his
hand*]. Ah !   By an old fakir. He was a very holy man.
He'd sat all doubled up in one spot, goin' on for fifteen year ;
thinkin' o' things.   And he wanted to show that fate ruled
people. That everything was cut and dried from the
beginning, as you might say.   That there warn't no gettin'
away from it.   And that, if you tried to, you caught it hot.
[*Pauses solemnly.*]   So he put a spell on this bit of a paw.

THE MONKEY'S PAW

It might ha' been anything else, but he took the first thing that came handy. Ah! He put a spell on it, and made it so that three people [*looking at them and with deep meaning*] could each have three wishes.

[*All but* MRS WHITE *laugh rather nervously.*

MRS WHITE. Ssh! Don't!

SERGEANT [*more gravely*]. But——! But, mark you, though the wishes was granted, those three people would have cause to wish they *hadn't* been.

MR WHITE. But how *could* the wishes be granted?

SERGEANT. He didn't say. It would all happen so natural, you might think it a coincidence if so disposed.

HERBERT. Why haven't you tried it, sir?

SERGEANT [*gravely, after a pause*]. I have.

HERBERT [*eagerly*]. You've had your three wishes?

SERGEANT [*gravely*]. Yes.

MRS WHITE. Were they granted?

SERGEANT [*staring at the fire*]. They were.   [*A pause.*

MR WHITE. Has anybody else wished?

SERGEANT. Yes. The first owner had his three wish—— [*Lost in recollection*] Yes, oh yes, he had his three wishes all right. I don't know what his first two were, [*very impressively*] but the third was for death. [*All shudder.*] That's how I got the paw.   [*A pause.*

HERBERT [*cheerfully*]. Well! Seems to me you've only got to wish for things that *can't* have any bad luck about 'em—— [*Rises.*]

SERGEANT [*shaking his head*]. Ah!

MR WHITE [*tentatively*]. Morris—if you've had your three wishes—it's no good to you, now—what do you keep it for?

SERGEANT [*still holding the paw; looking at it*]. Fancy, I s'pose. I did have some idea of selling it, but I don't think I will. It's done mischief enough already. Besides, people won't buy. Some of 'em think it's a fairy-tale. And some want to try it first, and pay after.

[Nervous laugh from the others.

MRS WHITE. If you could have another three wishes, would you ?

SERGEANT [*slowly—weighing the paw in his hand, and looking at it*]. I don't know—I don't know—— [*Suddenly, with violence, flinging it in the fire*] No ! I'm damned if I would ! *[Movement from all.*

MR WHITE [*rises and quickly snatches it out of the fire*]. What are you doing ? *[WHITE goes R. C.*

SERGEANT [*rising and following him and trying to prevent him*]. Let it burn ! Let the infernal thing burn !

MRS WHITE [*rises*]. Let it burn, Father !

MR WHITE [*wiping it on his coat-sleeve*]. No. If you don't want it, give it to me.

SERGEANT [*violently*]. I won't ! I won't ! My hands are clear of it. I threw it on the fire. If you keep it, don't blame me, whatever happens. Here ! Pitch it back again.

MR WHITE [*stubbornly*]. I'm going to keep it. What do you say, Herbert ?

HERBERT [*L. C., laughing*]. I say, keep it if you want to. Stuff and nonsense, anyhow.

MR WHITE [*looking at the paw thoughtfully*]. Stuff and nonsense. Yes. I wonder—[*casually*] I wish—— [*He was going to say some ordinary thing, like " I wish I were certain."*]

SERGEANT [*misunderstanding him ; violently*]. Stop ! Mind what you're doing. That's not the way.

MR WHITE. What *is* the way ?

MRS WHITE [*moving away, up R. C. to back of table, and beginning to put the tumblers straight, and the chairs in their places*]. Oh, don't have anything to do with it, John.

THE MONKEY'S PAW

[*Takes glasses on tray to dresser, L., busies herself there,
rinsing them in a bowl of water on the dresser, and
wiping them with a cloth.*

SERGEANT. That's what I say, marm. But if I warn't to
tell him, he might go wishing something he didn't mean to.
You hold it in your right hand, and wish aloud. But I warn
you! I warn you!

MRS WHITE. Sounds like *The Arabian Nights*. Don't you
think you might wish me four pair o' hands?

MR WHITE [*laughing*]. Right you are, Mother!—I
wish——

SERGEANT [*pulling his arm down*]. Stop it! If you must
wish, wish for something sensible. Look here! I can't
stand this. Gets on my nerves. Where's my coat? [*Goes
into alcove.*]

[MR WHITE *crosses to fireplace and carefully puts the
paw on mantelpiece. He is absorbed in it to the
end of the tableau.*

HERBERT. I'm coming your way, to the works, in a minute.
Won't you wait? [*Goes up C., helps* MORRIS *with his coat.*]

SERGEANT [*putting on his coat*]. No. I'm all shook up. I
want fresh air. I don't want to be here when you wish.
And wish you will as soon's my back's turned. I know. I
know. But I've warned you, mind.

MR WHITE [*helping him into his coat*]. All right, Morris.
Don't you fret about us. [*Gives him money.*] Here.

SERGEANT [*refusing it*]. No, I won't——

MR WHITE [*forcing it into his hand*]. Yes, you will. [*Opens
door.*]

SERGEANT [*turning to the room*]. Well, good night all. [*To*
WHITE] Put it in the fire.

ALL. Good night.

[*Exit* SERGEANT. MR WHITE *closes door, comes towards
fireplace, absorbed in the paw.*

HERBERT [*down L.*]. If there's no more in this than there is in his other stories, we shan't make much out of it.

MRS WHITE [*comes down R. C. to* WHITE]. Did you give him anything for it, Father?

MR WHITE. A trifle. He didn't want it, but I made him take it.

MRS WHITE. There, now! You shouldn't. Throwing your money about.

MR WHITE [*looking at the paw which he has picked up again*]. I wonder——

HERBERT. What?

MR WHITE. I wonder, whether we hadn't better chuck it on the fire?

HERBERT [*laughing*]. Likely! Why, we're all going to be rich and famous and happy.

MRS WHITE. Throw it on the fire, indeed, when you've given money for it! So like you, Father.

HERBERT. Wish to be an emperor, Father, to begin with. Then you can't be henpecked!

MRS WHITE [*going for him front of table with a duster*]. You young——! [*Follows him to back of table.*]

HERBERT [*running away from her round behind table*]. Steady with that duster, Mother!

MR WHITE. Be quiet, there! [HERBERT *catches* MRS WHITE *in his arms and kisses her.*] I wonder—— [*He has the paw in his hand.*] I don't know what to wish for, and that's a fact. [*He looks about him with a happy smile.*] I seem to've got all I want.

HERBERT [*with his hands on the old man's shoulders*]. Old Dad! If you'd only cleared the debt on the house, you'd be quite happy, wouldn't you! [*Laughing.*] Well—go ahead! —wish for the two hundred pounds: that'll just do it.

MR WHITE [*half laughing*]. Shall I? [*Crosses to R. C.*

HERBERT. Go on! Here!—I'll play slow music. [*Crosses to piano.*]

MRS WHITE. Don't 'ee, John. Don't have nothing to do with it !

HERBERT. Now, Dad ! [*Plays.*]

MR WHITE. I will ! [*Holds up the paw, as if half ashamed.*] I wish for two hundred pounds.

[*Crash on the piano. At the same instant* MR WHITE *utters a cry and lets the paw drop.*

MRS WHITE *and* HERBERT. What's the matter ?

MR WHITE [*gazing with horror at the paw*]. It moved ! As I wished, it twisted in my hand like a snake.

HERBERT [*goes down R., and picks the paw up*]. Nonsense, Dad. Why, it's as stiff as a bone. [*Lays it on the mantelpiece.*]

MRS WHITE. Must have been your fancy, Father.

HERBERT [*laughing*]. Well——? [*Looking round the room*] I don't see the money ; and I bet I never shall.

MR WHITE [*relieved*]. Thank God, there's no harm done ! But it gave me a shock.

HERBERT. Half-past eleven. I must get along. I'm on at midnight. [*Goes up C., fetches his coat, etc.*] We've had quite a merry evening.

MRS WHITE. I'm off to bed. Don't be late for breakfast, Herbert.

HERBERT. I shall walk home as usual. Does me good. I shall be with you about nine. Don't wait, though.

MRS WHITE. You know your father never waits.

HERBERT. Good night, Mother. [*Kisses her. She lights candle on dresser, L., goes upstairs and exit.*]

HERBERT [*coming to his father, R., who is sunk in thought*]. Good night, Dad. You'll find the cash tied up in the middle of the bed.

MR WHITE [*staring, seizes* HERBERT's *hand*]. It moved, Herbert.

HERBERT. Ah ! And a monkey hanging by his tail from the bed-post, watching you count the golden sovereigns.

MR WHITE [*accompanying him to the door*]. I wish you wouldn't joke, my boy.

HERBERT. All right, Dad. [*Opens door.*] Lord! What weather! Good night. [*Exit.*

[*The old man shakes his head, closes the door, locks it, puts the chain up, slips the lower bolt, has some difficulty with the upper bolt.*

MR WHITE. This bolt's stiff again! I must get Herbert to look to it in the morning.

[*Comes into the room, puts out the lamp, crosses towards steps; but is irresistibly attracted toward fireplace. Sits down and stares into the fire. His expression changes: he sees something horrible.*

MR WHITE [*with an involuntary cry*]. Mother! Mother!

MRS WHITE [*appearing at the door at the top of the steps with candle*]. What's the matter? [*Comes down R. C.*]

MR WHITE [*mastering himself. Rises*]. Nothing—I—haha!—I saw faces in the fire.

MRS WHITE. Come along.

[*She takes his arm and draws him toward the steps. He looks back frightened toward fireplace as they reach the first step.*

TABLEAU CURTAIN

II

Bright sunshine. The table, which has been moved nearer the window, is laid for breakfast. MRS WHITE *busy about the table.* MR WHITE *standing in the window looking off R. The inner door is open, showing the outer door.*

MR WHITE. What a morning Herbert's got for walking home!

MRS WHITE [*L. C.*]. What's o'clock ? [*Looks at clock on mantelpiece.*] Quarter to nine, I declare. He's off at eight. [*Crosses to fire.*]

MR WHITE. Takes him half an hour to change and wash. He's just by the cemetery now.

MRS WHITE. He'll be here in ten minutes.

MR WHITE [*coming to the table*]. What's for breakfast ?

MRS WHITE. Sausages. [*At the mantelpiece*] Why, if here isn't that dirty monkey's paw ! [*Picks it up, looks at it with disgust, puts it back. Takes sausages in dish from before the fire and places them on table.*] Silly thing ! The idea of us listening to such nonsense !

MR WHITE [*goes up to window again*]. Ay—the Sergeant-major and his yarns ! I suppose all old soldiers are alike——

MRS WHITE. Come, on, Father. Herbert hates us to wait. [*They both sit and begin breakfast.*

MRS WHITE. How could wishes be granted, nowadays ?

MR WHITE. Ah ! Been thinking about it all night, have you ?

MRS WHITE. You kept me awake, with your tossing and tumbling——

MR WHITE. Ay, I had a bad night.

MRS WHITE. It was the storm, I expect. How it blew !

MR WHITE. I didn't hear it. I was asleep and not asleep, if you know what I mean.

MRS WHITE. And all that rubbish about its making you unhappy if your wish *was* granted ! How could two hundred pounds hurt you, eh, Father ?

MR WHITE. Might drop on my head in a lump. Don't see any other way. And I'd try to bear that. Though, mind you, Morris said it would all happen so naturally that you might take it for a coincidence, if so disposed.

MRS WHITE. Well—it hasn't happened. That's all I know. And it isn't going to. [*A letter is seen to drop in the letter-box.*] And how you can sit there and talk about it—— [*Sharp postman's knock; she jumps to her feet.*] What's that?

MR WHITE. Postman, o' course.

MRS WHITE [*seeing the letter from a distance; in an awed whisper*]. He's brought a letter, John!

MR WHITE [*laughing*]. What did you think he'd bring? Ton o' coals?

MRS WHITE. John——! John——! Suppose——?

MR WHITE. Suppose what?

MRS WHITE. Suppose it was two hundred pounds!

MR WHITE [*suppressing his excitement*]. Eh!—Here! Don't talk nonsense. Why don't you fetch it?

MRS WHITE [*crosses and takes letter out of the box*]. It's thick, John—[*feels it*]—and—and it's got something crisp inside it. [*Takes letter to* WHITE, *R. C.*]

MR WHITE. Who—who's it for?

MRS WHITE. You.

MR WHITE. Hand it over, then. [*Feeling and examining it with ill-concealed excitement*] The idea! What a super-stitious old woman you are! Where are my specs?

MRS WHITE. Let me open it.

MR WHITE. Don't you touch it. Where are my specs?
[*Goes to R.*

MRS WHITE. Don't let sudden wealth sour your temper, John.

MR WHITE. *Will* you find my specs?

MRS WHITE [*taking them off mantelpiece*]. Here, John, here. [*As he opens the letter*] Take care! Don't tear it!

MR WHITE. Tear what?

MRS WHITE. If it was banknotes, John!

MR WHITE [*taking a thick, formal document out of the*

THE MONKEY'S PAW

envelope and a crisp-looking slip]. You've gone dotty.—
You've made me nervous. [*Reads.*] "Sir, Enclosed please
find receipt for interest on the mortgages of £200 on your
house, duly received."

> [*They look at each other.* MR WHITE *sits down to
> finish his breakfast silently.* MRS WHITE *goes to
> the window.*

MRS WHITE. That comes of listening to tipsy old soldiers.

MR WHITE [*pettish*]. What does?

MRS WHITE. You thought there was banknotes in it.

MR WHITE [*injured*]. I didn't! I said all along——

MRS WHITE. How Herbert will laugh, when I tell him!

MR WHITE [*with gruff good-humour*]. You're not going to tell
him. You're going to keep your mouth shut. That's what
you're going to do. Why, I should never hear the last
of it.

MRS WHITE. Serve you right. I shall tell him. You know
you like his fun. See how he joked you last night when
you said the paw moved.

> [*She is looking through the window towards R.*

MR WHITE. So it did. It did move. That I'll swear
to.

MRS WHITE [*abstractedly : she is watching something outside*]. You thought it did.

MR WHITE. I say it did. There was no thinking about it.
You saw how it upset me, didn't you?

> [*She doesn't answer.*

Didn't you?—Why don't you listen? [*Turns round.*] What
is it?

MRS WHITE. Nothing.

MR WHITE [*turns back to his breakfast*]. Do you see Herbert
coming?

MRS WHITE. No.

MR WHITE. He's about due. What *is* it?

209

MRS WHITE. Nothing. Only a man. Looks like a gentleman. Leastways, he's in black, and he's got a top-hat on.

MR WHITE. What about him ? [*He is not interested ; goes on eating.*]

MRS WHITE. He stood at the garden-gate as if he wanted to come in. But he couldn't seem to make up his mind.

MR WHITE. Oh, go on ! You're full o' fancies.

MRS WHITE. He's going—no ; he's coming back.

MR WHITE. Don't let him see you peeping.

MRS WHITE [*with increasing excitement*]. He's looking at the house. He's got his hand on the latch. No. He turns away again. [*Eagerly*] John ! He looks like a sort of a lawyer.

MR WHITE. What of it ?

MRS WHITE. Oh, you'll only laugh again. But suppose—suppose he's coming about the two hundred—— -

MR WHITE. You're not to mention it again !—You're a foolish old woman.—Come and eat your breakfast. [*Eagerly*] Where is he now ?

MRS WHITE. Gone down the road. He has turned back. He seems to've made up his mind. Here he comes !—Oh, John, and me all untidy ! [*Crosses to fire R.*]

[*Knock.*

MR WHITE [*to* MRS WHITE, *who is hastily smoothing her hair, etc.*]. What's it matter ? He's made a mistake. Come to the wrong house. [*Crosses to fireplace.*]

[MRS WHITE *opens the door.* MR SAMPSON, *dressed from head to foot in solemn black, with a top-hat, stands in the doorway.*

SAMPSON [*outside*]. Is this Mr White's ?

MRS WHITE. Come in, sir. Please step in.

[*She shows him into the room ; goes R. ; he is awkward and nervous.*

You must overlook our being so untidy ; and the room all

anyhow ; and John in his garden-coat. [*To* MR WHITE, *reproachfully*] Oh, John.

SAMPSON [*to* MR WHITE]. Morning. My name is Sampson.

MRS WHITE [*offering a chair*]. Won't you please be seated ?

[SAMPSON *stands quite still up C.*

SAMPSON. Ah—thank you—no, I think not—I think not. [*Pause.*]

MR WHITE [*awkwardly, trying to help him*]. Fine weather for the time o' year.

SAMPSON. Ah—yes—yes—— [*Pause ; he makes a renewed effort.*] My name is Sampson—I've come——

MRS WHITE. Perhaps you was wishful to see Herbert ; he'll be home in a minute. [*Pointing*] Here's his break-fast waiting——

SAMPSON [*interrupting her hastily*]. No, no ! [*Pause.*] I've come from the electrical works——

MRS WHITE. Why, you might have come *with* him.

[MR WHITE *sees something is wrong, tenderly puts his hand on her arm.*

SAMPSON. No—no—I've come—*alone*.

MRS WHITE [*with a little anxiety*]. Is anything the matter ?

SAMPSON. I was asked to call——

MRS WHITE [*abruptly*]. Herbert ! Has anything happened ? Is he hurt ? Is he hurt ?

MR WHITE [*soothing her*]. There, there, Mother. Don't you jump to conclusions. Let the gentleman speak. You've not brought bad news, I'm sure, sir.

SAMPSON. I'm—sorry——

MRS WHITE. Is he hurt ? [SAMPSON *bows.*

MRS WHITE. Badly ?

SAMPSON. Very badly. [*Turns away.*]

MRS WHITE [*with a cry*]. John——! [*She instinctively moves towards* MR WHITE.]

MR WHITE. Is he in pain?

SAMPSON. He is not in pain.

MRS WHITE. Oh, thank God! Thank God for that! Thank—— [*She looks in a startled fashion at* MR WHITE— *realizes what* SAMPSON *means, catches his arm and tries to turn him towards her.*] Do you mean——?

> [SAMPSON *avoids her look; she gropes for her husband: he takes her two hands in his, and gently lets her sink into the armchair above the fireplace, then he stands on her right, between her and* SAMPSON.

MR WHITE [*hoarsely*]. Go on, sir.

SAMPSON. He was telling his mates a story. Something that had happened here last night. He was laughing, and wasn't noticing and—and—(*hushed*) the machinery caught him——

> [*A little cry from* MRS WHITE, *her face shows her horror and agony.*

MR WHITE [*vague, holding* MRS WHITE's *hand*]. The machinery caught him—yes—and him the only child—it's hard, sir—very hard——

SAMPSON [*subdued*]. The Company wished me to convey their sincere sympathy with you in your great loss——

MR WHITE [*staring blankly*]. Our—great—loss——!

SAMPSON. I was to say further—[*as if apologizing*] I am only their servant—I am only obeying orders——

MR WHITE. Our—great—loss——

SAMPSON [*laying an envelope on the table and edging towards the door*]. I was to say, the Company disclaim all responsibility, but, in consideration of your son's services, they wish to present you with a certain sum as compensation. [*Gets to door.*]

MR WHITE. Our—great—loss—— [*Suddenly, with horror*] How—how much?

SAMPSON [*in the doorway*]. Two hundred pounds. [*Exit.*

[MRS WHITE *gives a cry. The old man takes no heed of her, smiles faintly, puts out his hands like a sightless man, and drops, a senseless heap, to the floor.* MRS WHITE *stares at him blankly and her hands go out helplessly towards him.*

TABLEAU CURTAIN

III

Night. On the table a candle is flickering at its last gasp. The room looks neglected. MR WHITE *is dozing fitfully in the armchair.* MRS WHITE *is in the window peering through the blinds towards L.*

[MR WHITE *starts, wakes, looks around him.*

MR WHITE [*fretfully*]. Jenny—Jenny.

MRS WHITE [*in the window*]. Yes.

MR WHITE. Where are you ?

MRS WHITE. At the window.

MR WHITE. What are you doing ?

MRS WHITE. Looking up the road.

MR WHITE [*falling back*]. What's the use, Jenny ? What's the use ?

MRS WHITE. That's where the cemetery is ; that's where we've laid him.

MR WHITE. Ay—ay—a week to-day—what o'clock is it ?

MRS WHITE. I don't know.

MR WHITE. We don't take much account of time now, Jenny, do we ?

MRS WHITE. Why should we ? He don't come home. He'll never come home again. There's nothing to think about——

MR WHITE. Or to talk about. [*Pause.*] Come away from the window ; you'll get cold.

MRS WHITE. It's colder where *he* is.

MR WHITE. Ay—gone for ever——

MRS WHITE. And taken all our hopes with him——

MR WHITE. And all our *wishes*——

MRS WHITE. Ay, and all our—— [*With a sudden cry*] John ! [*She comes quickly to him ; he rises.*

MR WHITE. Jenny ! For God's sake ! What's the matter ?

MRS WHITE [*with dreadful eagerness*]. The *paw* ! The monkey's paw !

MR WHITE [*bewildered*]. Where ? Where is it ? What's wrong with it ?

MRS WHITE. I want it ! You haven't done away with it ?

MR WHITE. I haven't seen it—since—why ?

MRS WHITE. I want it ! Find it ! Find it !

MR WHITE [*groping on the mantelpiece*]. Here ! Here it is ! What do you want of it ? [*He leaves it there.*]

MRS WHITE. Why didn't I think of it ? Why didn't *you* think of it ?

MR WHITE. Think of what ?

MRS WHITE. The *other two* wishes !

MR WHITE [*with horror*]. What ?

MRS WHITE. We've only had one.

MR WHITE [*tragically*]. Wasn't that enough ?

MRS WHITE. No ! We'll have one more. [WHITE *crosses to R. C.* MRS WHITE *takes the paw and follows him.*] Take it. Take it quickly. And wish——

MR WHITE [*avoiding the paw*]. Wish what ?

MRS WHITE. Oh, John ! John ! Wish our boy alive again !

MR WHITE. Good God ! Are you mad ?

MRS WHITE. Take it. Take it and wish. [*With a paroxysm of grief*] Oh, my boy ! My boy !

MR WHITE. Get to bed. Get to sleep. You don't know what you're saying.

MRS WHITE. We had the first wish granted—why not the second ?

MR WHITE [*hushed*]. He's been dead ten days, and—Jenny ! Jenny ! I only knew him by his clothing—if you wasn't allowed to see him then—how could you bear to see him *now* ?

MRS WHITE. I don't care. Bring him back.

MR WHITE [*shrinking from the paw*]. I daren't touch it !

MRS WHITE [*thrusting it in his hand*]. Here ! Here ! Wish !

MR WHITE [*trembling*]. Jenny !

MRS WHITE [*fiercely*]. WISH. [*She goes on frantically whispering " Wish."*]

MR WHITE [*shuddering, but overcome by her insistence*]. I—I—wish—my—son—alive again.

[*He drops it with a cry. The candle goes out. Utter darkness. He sinks into a chair.* MRS WHITE *hurries to the window and draws the blind back. She stands in the moonlight. Pause.*

MRS WHITE [*drearily*]. Nothing.

MR WHITE. Thank God ! Thank God !

MRS WHITE. Nothing at all. Along the whole length of the road not a living thing. [*Closes blind.*] And nothing, nothing, nothing left in our lives, John.

MR WHITE. Except each other, Jenny—and memories.

MRS WHITE [*coming back slowly to the fireplace*]. We're too old. We were only alive in him. We can't begin again. We can't feel anything now, John, but emptiness and darkness. [*She sinks into armchair.*]

MR WHITE. 'Tisn't for long, Jenny. There's that to look forward to.

MRS WHITE. Every minute's long, now.

MR WHITE [*rising*]. I can't bear the darkness !

MRS WHITE. It's dreary—dreary.

MR WHITE [*crosses to dresser*]. Where's the candle ? [*Finds it and brings it to table.*] And the matches ? Where are the matches ? We mustn't sit in the dark. 'Tisn't wholesome. [*Lights match ; the other candlestick is close to him.*] There. [*Turning with the lighted match toward* MRS WHITE, *who is rocking and moaning*] Don't take on so, Mother.

MRS WHITE. I'm a mother no longer.

MR WHITE [*lights candle*]. There now ; there now. Go on up to bed. Go on, now—I'm a-coming.

MRS WHITE. Whether I'm here or in bed, or wherever I am, I'm with my boy, I'm with——

[*A low single knock at the street door.*

MRS WHITE [*starting*]. What's that !

MR WHITE [*mastering his horror*]. A rat. The house is full of 'em.

[*A louder single knock ; she starts up. He catches her by the arm.*

Stop ! What are you going to do ?

MRS WHITE [*wildly*]. It's my boy ! It's Herbert ! I forgot it was a mile away ! What are you holding me for ? I must open the door !

[*The knocking continues in single knocks at irregular intervals, constantly growing louder and more insistent.*

MR WHITE [*still holding her*]. For God's sake !

MRS WHITE [*struggling*]. Let me go !

MR WHITE. Don't open the door !

[*He drags her towards left front.*

MRS WHITE. Let me go !

MR WHITE. Think what you might see !

MRS WHITE [*struggling fiercely*]. Do you think I fear the child I bore! Let me go! [*She wrenches herself loose and rushes to the door which she tears open.*] I'm coming, Herbert! I'm coming!

MR WHITE [*cowering in the extreme corner, left front*]. Don't 'ee do it! Don't 'ee do it!

[MRS WHITE *is at work on the outer door, where the knocking still continues. She slips the chain, slips the lower bolt, unlocks the door.*

MR WHITE [*suddenly*]. The paw! Where's the monkey's paw?

[*He gets on his knees and feels along the floor for it.*

MRS WHITE [*tugging at the top bolt*]. John! The top bolt's stuck. I can't move it. Come and help. Quick!

MR WHITE [*wildly groping*]. The paw! There's a wish left.

[*The knocking is now loud, and in groups of increasing length between the speeches.*

MRS WHITE. D'ye hear him? John! Your child's knocking!

MR WHITE. Where is it? Where did it fall?

MRS WHITE [*tugging desperately at the bolt*]. Help! Help! Will you keep your child from his home?

MR WHITE. Where did it fall? I can't find it—I can't find——

[*The knocking is now tempestuous, and there are blows upon the door as of a body beating against it.*

MRS WHITE. Herbert! Herbert! My boy! Wait! Your mother's opening to you! Ah! It's moving! It's moving!

MR WHITE. God forbid! [*Finds the paw.*] Ah!

MRS WHITE [*slipping the bolt*]. Herbert!

MR WHITE [*has raised himself to his knees; he holds the*

paw high]. I wish him dead. [*The knocking stops abruptly.*] I wish him dead and at peace !

MRS WHITE [*flinging the door open simultaneously*]. Herb——

[*A flood of moonlight. Emptiness. The old man sways in prayer on his knees. The old woman lies half swooning, wailing against the door-post.*

CURTAIN

NIGHT WATCHES

A COMEDY IN ONE ACT

By Allan Monkhouse

CHARACTERS

A Nurse
A Night Orderly
1st Soldier
2nd Soldier

Mr Allan Monkhouse's "Night Watches" (like "The Child in Flanders") was definitely inspired by the War, or at any rate by War conditions. It is a subject which the dramatist handled with great skill in a four-act play, "The Conquering Hero," which made a remarkable impression in 1924.

Mr Monkhouse has a penetrating insight in the human mind and heart. He has keen humour and writes excellent light comedy, but he frequently treats of tragic themes, and does so with a certain relentlessness that reminds us of Mr Galsworthy. The two playwrights have much in common technically, although their temperaments are widely different.

"The Education of Mr Surrage" and "Mary Broome" are other notable works of Mr Monkhouse, to which must be added "First Blood"— a tragedy based upon an industrial dispute—which has been published quite recently.

NIGHT WATCHES[1]

SCENE: *An anteroom to the wards in a small Red Cross Hospital. The door is at the back and it leads to a landing out of which the wards—a large and a small bedroom—open. In the room are a clock showing clearly the time—a few minutes after ten—a fire with an armchair before it, a coalscuttle, a low camp bed covered with a blanket, a small table on which is a tray covered with a table-cloth, a stand with a spirit lamp and kettle, etc. A* NURSE *enters with the* NIGHT ORDERLY. *He is an ordinary citizen of middle age; she is a comely woman of middle age.*

NURSE. This is your room. Plenty of coal, I think? It gets rather chilly in the middle of the night.

ORDERLY. Thank you very much. What about that bed? Am I supposed to go to sleep?

NURSE. Oh, I think so. Unless you're a heavy sleeper. Of course, you make your rounds every two or three hours. But you'll find all quiet, I think. We've no troublesome cases—unless—no, I don't think you'll be disturbed.

ORDERLY [*pointing to the tray*]. What's that?

NURSE. That's your tray. [*She half uncovers it, displaying teapot, loaf, etc.*] There are biscuits in this paper bag.

ORDERLY. I shan't want anything.

[1] Applications regarding amateur performances of this play should be addressed to Messrs Samuel French, Ltd., 26 Southampton Street, Strand, London, W.C.2, or 25 West 45th Street, New York.

NURSE. Yes, they all say that at first.

ORDERLY. No, but really——

NURSE. Here's the tea-caddy.

ORDERLY. I never take anything after dinner.

NURSE. And here's the toasting-fork.

ORDERLY. I don't think I shall want it.

NURSE [*looking into the kettle*]. You'd better light this spirit lamp in good time. It takes some time to boil. Or you could use the fire.

ORDERLY. You're very good. But——

NURSE. If you can spend a night with a good cup of tea staring at you, you're very different from most people.

ORDERLY [*relenting*]. Oh, I'm quite an ordinary person.

NURSE. Yes; most people are.

ORDERLY. I do rather like the idea of a round of hot buttered toast.

NURSE. I don't think you'll be satisfied with the idea.

ORDERLY. Perhaps not. Well, nurse, what are my instructions?

NURSE. You'd better read that paper on the wall.

ORDERLY. I see.

NURSE. The door just opposite is the big ward. Eight of them there. The little ward is the room at the end of the passage—to the right. [*She indicates it.*] Only two in that. They've been getting a little restless. I'm not sure that we shan't have to make a change there.

ORDERLY. What sort of a change?

NURSE. Well, we might put one of them in the big ward and somebody else in there. I think they're getting a bit on one another's nerves—those two. One of them's the deaf and dumb man, you know. You'd better have a look at him when you go round. But he's near the bell.

ORDERLY. A deaf and dumb man ?

NURSE. Dreadful, isn't it ? A shell burst near him ; he wasn't wounded, but he can't speak a word now and can't hear.

ORDERLY. Will he get right ?

NURSE. They hope so. There's a chance.

ORDERLY. Well, you're sure I needn't keep awake all the time ?

NURSE. I don't think you will.

ORDERLY. I'll spend the night pinching myself if you tell me to.

NURSE. Do it if you like.

ORDERLY. You're not going ?

NURSE. Yes.

ORDERLY. Won't you sit down and have half an hour's chat ? Have a cup of tea.

NURSE [*shakes her head smilingly*]. If there's anything wrong—anything you can't tackle—call me. There's a bell we've rigged up here to my room. See ? I think you've got everything. Good night.

ORDERLY. Good night, nurse. Thank you.

NURSE [*stands at the door, listening*]. They are all sleeping. Poor boys, poor boys. [*She goes. The* ORDERLY *looks after her wistfully. He takes a turn about the room, examines the toasting-fork, takes up a book, puts it down, sits in the armchair and begins to fill his pipe thoughtfully. The curtain falls for a moment to indicate the passage of time. When it rises the* ORDERLY *is dozing in the chair and the clock shows that it is half-past two. He rouses gradually and listens. A* SOLDIER *pushes the door open and looks in. His dress is a rough compromise between day and night. He is youngish, a typical private, now rather perturbed. His head is bandaged.*]

ORDERLY. What's up now ?

FIRST SOLDIER. 'Scuse me, sir. [*He salutes.*] May I have a word with you, sir ?

ORDERLY. Certainly. Come in.

FIRST SOLDIER [*advancing*]. I didn't ought to be put in there with 'im.

ORDERLY. In where ? With whom ?

FIRST SOLDIER. Little ward, they call it. There's only two of us ; me an' 'im.

ORDERLY. Little ward ? Well, but there's a deaf and dumb man there. He can't disturb you.

FIRST SOLDIER. Can't he ?

ORDERLY. How can he if he's—but perhaps you're the deaf and dumb man ?

FIRST SOLDIER [*laughs uneasily*]. About as much as 'e is.

ORDERLY. Do you mean to say that he's shamming ?

FIRST SOLDIER. I didn't say that. But he might be pretendin'.

ORDERLY. He might be—— What's the difference ?

FIRST SOLDIER. Well, one's worse than the other, isn't it ?

ORDERLY. D'you think so ? Shamming sounds worse, doesn't it ?

FIRST SOLDIER. Of course it does. I'd never say a man was shammin' unless I knew. It wouldn't be fair.

ORDERLY. But you'd say he was pretending ? Well, now, that's interesting. Sit down and explain the difference. Have a cigarette ?

FIRST SOLDIER. Thanky, sir. [*He takes one and sits down.*]

ORDERLY. Now, then.

FIRST SOLDIER. They wanted to get 'im out o' that big ward an' they did.

ORDERLY. Did they ? Why ?

FIRST SOLDIER. Deaf an' dumb, is 'e ?

ORDERLY. Well, isn't he ?

FIRST SOLDIER. Shall I tell y' somethin', sir ?

ORDERLY. Do.

FIRST SOLDIER. I'm not one to blab.

ORDERLY. No ; don't blab. Just tell me.

FIRST SOLDIER. What shall I tell y' ?

ORDERLY. Oh, heavens ! Tell me the difference between shamming and pretending.

FIRST SOLDIER. It's a rum thing. I never thought he was that sort of feller.

ORDERLY. What sort ?

FIRST SOLDIER. You think it's only pretendin' ?

ORDERLY. What's only pretending ?

FIRST SOLDIER. Shall I tell y' ?

ORDERLY. No ; not unless you like. Don't tell me anything. Go to bed.

FIRST SOLDIER. I'm bound to tell y'.

ORDERLY. Fire away, then.

FIRST SOLDIER. Calls himself deaf and dumb ?

ORDERLY. Does he ? Funny that he should call himself anything.

FIRST SOLDIER. He can talk right enough.

ORDERLY. How d'you know ?

FIRST SOLDIER. I've heard him. Others too. That's what they didn't like. Them in the big ward.

ORDERLY. When have you heard him ?

FIRST SOLDIER [*impressively*]. In his sleep.

ORDERLY. I see. I see.

FIRST SOLDIER. Thought y'd see.

ORDERLY. Has he done it often ?

FIRST SOLDIER. Pretty reg'lar.

ORDERLY. Can you make out what he says ?

FIRST SOLDIER. No, he's a bit too clever for that.

ORDERLY. Too clever ? Oh, come. How can that be ?

FIRST SOLDIER. Looks like pretendin' ? What ?

ORDERLY. And why not shamming? Why don't you call it shamming?

FIRST SOLDIER. I'll tell y'. Because he's deaf right enough.

ORDERLY. How d'you know?

FIRST SOLDIER. 'Cause y' may make a noise like hell behind 'im and he doesn't move. Y' may burst a paper bag agen 'is ear 'ole. He's deaf, 'e is, so I wouldn't go so far as to say 'e's shammin'.

ORDERLY. Yes, I begin to see the difference.

FIRST SOLDIER. Thought y' would.

ORDERLY. Now, look here. I don't think he's shamming or pretending or anything.

FIRST SOLDIER. I tell y' I've 'eard 'im many a time. It used to make me go creeps. It does still but I'm more vexed now. When y' curse 'im for it he can't 'ear a word.

ORDERLY. Look here. Have you—any of you—told him that he talks in his sleep?

FIRST SOLDIER. Tell 'im? 'E wouldn't 'ear.

ORDERLY. Yes, yes, yes; but you can write. He can read, I suppose?

FIRST SOLDIER. I don't set much store by that way of writin'.

ORDERLY. Now, that's no reason.

FIRST SOLDIER. I don't want 'im on to me.

ORDERLY. What d'you mean?

FIRST SOLDIER. You don't know what a feller like that'll do.

ORDERLY. What have you against him?

FIRST SOLDIER [testily]. 'Aven't I been tellin' y'?

ORDERLY. Not a word.

FIRST SOLDIER. Are you off your nut or am I?

ORDERLY. Both of us, perhaps.

FIRST SOLDIER. He gives out as 'e's dumb. Is 'e?

ORDERLY. Yes. When he's awake.

FIRST SOLDIER. Well, now——

ORDERLY. Let me explain—or try to. What is this dumbness? He has had a great shock and it has completely shattered—paralysed—of course, I don't understand it as a doctor would or a scientific man—it has put all his nerves wrong, it has cut off—or paralysed—the connections between his will—what he wants to do—and what he can do. D'you see? Well, he's all, as it were, dithering. And then he goes to sleep.

FIRST SOLDIER. Ah. That's it.

ORDERLY [*encouraged*]. He goes to sleep. And do you know—have you thought what a beautiful thing sleep is? We relax, we sink into nature, we—you don't read Shakespeare?

FIRST SOLDIER. I've 'eard tell of 'im.

ORDERLY. Well, he once wrote a play about a murderer.

FIRST SOLDIER [*starting*]. A murderer!

ORDERLY. Yes; and when this murderer knew that he would never sleep peacefully again he reeled off the most beautiful praises of sleep and what sleep could do—devil take you, I believe you're too stupid to understand.

FIRST SOLDIER. I'll understand if you'll talk sense.

ORDERLY. Yes. I beg your pardon. It's my fault. Well, sleep will do wonders. It will heal you, it will put things right for the time, it will help to put them right altogether. It accomplishes miracles. You awake—and there you are again.

FIRST SOLDIER. D'you believe all this yourself, sir?

ORDERLY. I think so. Yes.

FIRST SOLDIER.—You said a murderer.

ORDERLY. That was Macbeth. A chap called Macbeth.

FIRST SOLDIER. Talked in 'is sleep, did 'e?

ORDERLY. Well, his wife did. She was a murderer too.

FIRST SOLDIER. Yes, you may be sure there's summat wrong when they do that.

ORDERLY. No, no. The most innocent people may do it.

FIRST SOLDIER. Innercent, indeed! He's got a bad conscience, that chap.

ORDERLY. What is a bad conscience? It's only an uncomfortable mind. Most of you have that. Most of us, I should say.

FIRST SOLDIER. Are y' sayin' I've a bad conscience?

ORDERLY. No; but I can believe that if you've been out to the war and seen horrible things you have them on your mind. You may even talk in your sleep.

FIRST SOLDIER. That's a lie.

ORDERLY. You mustn't speak to me like that.

FIRST SOLDIER [saluting]. Beg y'r pard'n, sir.

ORDERLY. I'm not making myself out any better than you. I've a bad conscience.

FIRST SOLDIER. You, sir?

ORDERLY. Oh, this war finds us out. All the things that we might have done or left undone.

FIRST SOLDIER. D'you talk in y'r sleep?

ORDERLY [laughing]. Oh! I won't admit that.

FIRST SOLDIER. I sh'd think not.

ORDERLY. Now, look here. You're a fair-minded man. What have you against this poor chap in your room? Just look at it calmly as if you were judge or jury. What has he done?

FIRST SOLDIER. Y' talk of 'orrible things. I've seen some and I don't mention 'em—we tell y' a lot, but there are some things—we may 'av seen 'em or—we may 'av thought 'em. Better forget; better forget.

ORDERLY. Well, my dear fellow, that's just it. That should make you sympathize with him.

FIRST SOLDIER. Or we may 'av done 'em.

ORDERLY. Yes, I see.

FIRST SOLDIER. Y' can't be sure. Of anyone else I mean.

ORDERLY. Of course you can't. You can't be sure of anything. But you mustn't condemn others.

FIRST SOLDIER. What 'as that feller seen ? What 'as he done ? I'm alone with 'im in that little ward. I can't make out a word, but it's talkin' right enough. I've stood over 'im listenin'. It's 'orrible langwidge. I can't make out a word. 'Ardly.

ORDERLY. Oh! come, you know——

FIRST SOLDIER. He's done somethin'. I know 'e 'as.

ORDERLY. Oh, well, my friend, if it comes to that you've done a bit of killing or tried to.

FIRST SOLDIER. I 'ad to kill them bloody Germans.

ORDERLY. I know that. That's all right.

FIRST SOLDIER. It's all so 'orrible, sir, that you want things to be done right. You don't want any 'anky-panky.

ORDERLY. Yes, I see.

FIRST SOLDIER. Them Germans! I reckon they're all like 'im.

ORDERLY. How like him ?

FIRST SOLDIER. All talkin' in their sleep.

ORDERLY. That's a dreadful idea.

FIRST SOLDIER. An' there am I with 'im in the night. And in the big ward they're sleepin' peaceful. What did that Shakespeare say of sleep ?

ORDERLY. He said a lot of things.

FIRST SOLDIER. Tell me one.

ORDERLY. " The death of each day's life—— "

FIRST SOLDIER. An 'orrible idea. Damn 'im.

ORDERLY. You mustn't damn Shakespeare.

FIRST SOLDIER. I will if 'e talks like that. No disrespec' to you, sir. What else did 'e say ?

ORDERLY. "Sore labour's bath,
Balm of hurt minds, great nature's second course,
Chief nourisher in life's feast."

FIRST SOLDIER [*humbly*]. I don't understand. [*Resentfully*] Why, it might be 'im talkin' in 'is sleep. [*He jerks a thumb.*]

ORDERLY. Yes, he may be saying the most beautiful things.

FIRST SOLDIER. Nay, 'e's a devil, that feller is.

ORDERLY. Hullo! What's that?

FIRST SOLDIER. Begod, 'e's comin'.

[*They both look toward the door, and the* SECOND SOLDIER *appears there. He stands surveying them timidly and yet morosely. He wears an old dressing-gown over pyjamas.*]

ORDERLY. This is most irregular. I shall get into a row.

[*Seeing him speak, the* SECOND SOLDIER *straightens himself and salutes. Then he advances slowly into the room.*]

FIRST SOLDIER [*in a stentorian voice*]. Y're on fire.

[*The* SECOND SOLDIER *takes no notice.*]

ORDERLY. What the dickens d'you mean? You'll wake everybody.

FIRST SOLDIER. It's all right, sir. Best try 'im now and then. He might get back 'is 'earin' sudden. I think y' may talk free before 'im now.

ORDERLY. I don't know that I want to talk before him. I want you both to go back to bed.

FIRST SOLDIER. I'm not goin' back before 'e does.

ORDERLY. Why?

FIRST SOLDIER. Lyin' there in the dark and thinkin' 'e may come in.

[*The* SECOND SOLDIER *makes a gesture to indicate that he wants the other sent away. It is intended to be surreptitious, but the* FIRST SOLDIER *observes it.*]

230

Look at that! See 'im ? No, you don't.

> [*The* SECOND SOLDIER *fumbles in the pockets of his gown and produces a small slate and a pencil. He writes. The* FIRST SOLDIER *tries to see what he is writing, and there is a mild scuffle. The* SECOND SOLDIER *seeks the protection of the* ORDERLY, *who overlooks his writing and waves the* FIRST SOLDIER *away.*

Fair do's.

ORDERLY. Let him write.

FIRST SOLDIER. Yes, but let me see it.

ORDERLY. Why should you ?

FIRST SOLDIER. 'Tisn't polite to whisper in company.

ORDERLY. Whisper ?

FIRST SOLDIER. Same thing if you don't let me look.

ORDERLY [*looking at the slate*]. Well, the fact is he wants a little private conversation with me.

FIRST SOLDIER. Oh! Indeed! Wants me to go ? Well, I'm not 'avin' any. That's straight.

ORDERLY. If I tell you to go you'll have to.

FIRST SOLDIER. Cert'nly, sir, but he oughtn't to write about me be'ind my back.

ORDERLY. You've been talking about him behind his back.

FIRST SOLDIER. Yes, but he couldn't 'ear any'ow.

ORDERLY. What's that to do with it ?

FIRST SOLDIER. An' I can read writin'.

ORDERLY. Your distinctions are too fine for me.

> [*The* SECOND SOLDIER *has been writing on the slate and now hands it to the* ORDERLY, *who reads and laughs.*

FIRST SOLDIER. What's he say ?

ORDERLY. He says you're very restless and he thinks you have something on your mind.

FIRST SOLDIER. Well, I never.

ORDERLY. He says he doesn't know what you've been doing, but you must have a bad conscience.

FIRST SOLDIER. 'E's like them Germans. They always say as it's us does their dirty tricks. P'raps 'e is one.

ORDERLY. Now, you've no right to say that.

FIRST SOLDIER. No, sir; I 'aven't.

[*The* SECOND SOLDIER *grasps the slate again, rubs out his messages with fingers moistened at his mouth, and writes eagerly. The* FIRST SOLDIER *manages to overlook. He backs away.*

FIRST SOLDIER [*feebly*]. 'E says I'm a bad man.

ORDERLY [*looking at the slate as the* SECOND SOLDIER *writes*]. He says he caught you bending over him and going to stick something in him.

FIRST SOLDIER. 'E's a liar.

ORDERLY. And that you must be sent away.

FIRST SOLDIER. I'll bash 'is 'ed in.

ORDERLY. Silence.

[*The two* SOLDIERS *glare at one another, snarling and menacing. The* ORDERLY *steps between.*

FIRST SOLDIER. If 'e wants a scrap I'm 'is man.

ORDERLY. You two fools. [*To* FIRST SOLDIER] You should be sorry for the poor fellow. It's the old tale. Fear breeds cruelty.

FIRST SOLDIER. Fear!

ORDERLY. Yes, fear. You're brave enough when it comes to killing Germans, I dare say, but you're afraid of nothing at all. There's something here you can't understand, and, like a coward, you blame this poor fellow. You should help him. He's your comrade—your pal. It's the way with all of us. We fear and fear and then we'll do any beastly cruel thing.

[*He takes the slate and pencil and begins to write.*

FIRST SOLDIER [*sullenly*]. What 'r y' tellin' 'im ?

ORDERLY. Very much what I've been saying to you.

FIRST SOLDIER. I 'aven't touched 'im.

ORDERLY. Why! If you two fellows were back in the trenches together you'd die for one another.

> [*He gives the slate to the* SECOND SOLDIER, *who reads it, grabs the pencil, turns to the other side of the slate and writes furiously.*

FIRST SOLDIER. I dessay. What's 'e writin' now ?

ORDERLY. I don't know.

> [*The* SECOND SOLDIER *throws the slate on the table and moves towards the door. The* FIRST SOLDIER *tries to get it, but the* ORDERLY *is before him.*

FIRST SOLDIER. What's 'e say ?

ORDERLY [*angrily, in a loud voice, to* SECOND SOLDIER, *after reading*]. Don't be a fool. Deuce take it, I'm forgetting now.

FIRST SOLDIER. What *does* 'e say ?

ORDERLY. He says he'll blow his brains out.

FIRST SOLDIER [*daunted*]. I don't wish 'im no 'arm. Not a bit.

> [*The* ORDERLY *gets hold of the* SECOND SOLDIER *and leads him forward to a chair toward the front, where he sits down dejectedly. The* ORDERLY *picks up the slate.*

ORDERLY. Where's that pencil ?

> [*As he is looking for it the* FIRST SOLDIER, *who has been in a state of uncomfortable hesitancy, approaches the* SECOND SOLDIER *from behind and brings his mouth close to the other's ear.*

FIRST SOLDIER [*in a terrific voice*]. Bill!

> [*The* SECOND SOLDIER *starts slightly and then rises unsteadily. He turns slowly to look at the* FIRST SOLDIER.

FIRST SOLDIER [*in an awed voice*]. 'E 'eard me.

> [*Trembling, the* SECOND SOLDIER *stretches out his hand
> for the slate. The* ORDERLY *hands him the pencil,
> and he tries to write, but his agitation overcomes
> him and he sits down. In the meantime the* FIRST
> SOLDIER *empties the bag of biscuits and again
> approaches the* SECOND SOLDIER, *this time blow-
> ing out the bag into a balloon. He explodes
> it at the ear of the* SECOND SOLDIER, *who rises
> again and sees the torn bag. With an in-
> articulate cry he falls on the neck of the* FIRST
> SOLDIER.*

FIRST SOLDIER. I made 'im 'ear.

> [*They waltz round the room together, and passing the
> ORDERLY, drag him in. He joins in the dance,
> and they knock over a chair or two. The* NURSE,
> *in dressing-gown, etc., enters.*

NURSE. Well!

> [*They separate, looking rather sheepish, but the* FIRST
> SOLDIER *soon recovers, and cautiously gets hold of
> the poker and tongs.*

ORDERLY. You've caught us this time, nurse.

NURSE. Whatever are you doing? You'll wake everybody. Really, sir——

ORDERLY. Oh, you must forgive us, nurse. There's been
a great reconciliation. And more than that.

> [*The* SECOND SOLDIER *seizes the* NURSE's *arm. He
> simulates shouting, taps his ears and gesticulates
> explanations and delight.*

NURSE. Can he hear?

ORDERLY. Not much yet, but something.

> [*The* FIRST SOLDIER *makes a sudden and great clanging
> with the fireirons.*

NURSE. Whatever's that?

ORDERLY. Stop, confound you.

FIRST SOLDIER. Give 'im a bit o' pleasure.

[*The two* SOLDIERS *shake hands.*

NURSE. Well, I don't know what to say. It's most irregular.

ORDERLY. Report us, nurse ; report us. Blame me.

FIRST SOLDIER [*confidentially, to* ORDERLY]. 'E's not 'alf a bad chap. [*The two* SOLDIERS *shake hands.*

NURSE. Now, you two be off to bed. [*She gesticulates to the* SECOND SOLDIER.] Where's his slate ? The pencil ?

FIRST SOLDIER. Oh, never mind that ! 'E'll be talkin' d'rectly. 'E talks in 'is sleep now. My Gawd ! I used to be frightened of 'im. At nights you get thinkin'.

NURSE. Well, be off, be off, that's good boys.

[*They start off arm in arm.*

FIRST SOLDIER [*turning*]. What time may I start talkin' to 'im ?

NURSE. What time—— ?

FIRST SOLDIER. Yes, I'm goin' to make 'im 'ear proper in the mornin'.

NURSE. I'll box your ears if I hear a sound before eight o'clock.

FIRST SOLDIER. Well, look out then.

[*They go off laughing.*

ORDERLY. You'll have to report me.

NURSE. Shall I ?

ORDERLY. Won't you ? We must have awakened all of them.

NURSE. It wasn't quite so bad as shells bursting, after all.

ORDERLY. Well, do you want a full explanation ?

NURSE. It'll do in the morning. You can make a report. But I think I know. [*She goes to the door and listens.*] They're all sleeping quietly.

ORDERLY. Good lads !

NURSE. They've all sorts of fancies. They're so different in the daytime. Now—they're breathing like one. Even those two—very soon they'll be asleep.

ORDERLY. We're groping among strange things, nurse.

NURSE. I don't know that I understand you. They're like children to me. These two naughty ones—-well, you know what I mean.

ORDERLY. Do I ? Don't let us understand everything.

NURSE. Good night, again.

ORDERLY. Good night, nurse.

NURSE [going]. You have a cup of tea now and that toast.

ORDERLY. Am I one of your children too ?

NURSE. Are you wounded and ill ?

ORDERLY. No ; only rather melancholy.

NURSE [she shakes her head]. Try a cup of tea.

[She goes out. The ORDERLY gazes after her. Then he lifts up the teapot and looks at it. The curtain falls.

THE CHILD IN FLANDERS

A NATIVITY PLAY IN A PROLOGUE, FIVE TABLEAUX, AND AN EPILOGUE

By Cicely Hamilton

Music arranged by Theodore Flint

CHARACTERS

In the Prologue and Epilogue :

Private Whittaker, *an Englishman*
Private Murdoch, *an Australian*
Daoud Khan, *an Indian trooper*
Joseph Garnier, *a French peasant*
His New-born Son

The scene of the Prologue and Epilogue is laid in Garnier's cottage, a few miles behind the trenches.

The action of the Prologue and Tableaux is supposed to pass on a Christmas Eve during the War, of the Epilogue on Christmas Day.

Seen in the Vision are : The Virgin Mary ; St Joseph ; the Angel Gabriel ; another Angel ; the Three Shepherds ; the Three Kings ; a Little Boy, *attendant on the old King.*

Note.—All three soldiers wear overcoats, so that the only distinctive features of the Australian and Indian uniform are the hat and turban. Whittaker should wear a ' tin hat.' All have packs and rifles.

Miss CICELY HAMILTON came prominently into notice by the production of " Diana of Dobson's," a bitter-sweet comedy about a shop-assistant ; and running through most of her dramatic work is the note—sometimes a little embittered—of serious purpose.

"Just to Get Married" contributed to that movement which resulted in the enfranchisement of women in this country. During the War Miss Hamilton was actively associated with the Lena Ashwell organization under the Y.M.C.A. for providing drama at the base-camps overseas. "The Child in Flanders" is the work of one who saw the War at close quarters.

Miss Hamilton is a writer, a public speaker, and an actress as well as a dramatist. She has over twenty books to her credit, and her novel *William, an Englishman,* was accorded the Femina Prize in 1920.

THE CHILD IN FLANDERS[1]

PROLOGUE

Overture

O Little Town of Bethlehem (Choir).
Solemn Melody (Orchestra).
The Trail that leads to Home (Orchestra alone through verse and refrain, then repeat refrain, orchestra and men's voices, beginning loud and dying away in distance. Orchestra should leave it to the voices before end, the impression to be that of men singing as they march. Curtain rises on last notes).

As the curtain rises JOSEPH GARNIER *is kneeling beside the hearth pouring water from a pot into a cup. He stirs the mixture carefully, rises and goes out, carrying the cup, into room R. A lighted candle is on the table. The sound of guns is heard faintly in the distance ; directly after there is a knock on the outer door, up L.*

VOICES [*off*]. Hallo there! anyone at home ?
  [*The knocking and shouting is repeated louder. Then enter* JOSEPH ; *he closes bedroom door behind him and goes hurriedly to the outer door where the noise still grows louder.*

[1] Applications regarding amateur performances of this play should be addressed to Messrs Samuel French, Ltd., 26 Southampton Street, Strand, London, W.C.2, or 25 West 45th Street, New York.

JOSEPH [*unfastening door*]. *Pas tant de bruit, messieurs. Silence, s'il vous plaît.*

> [*He throws open door, showing three men standing outside it, one a soldier in an English infantry regiment, the second an Australian, and the third an Indian trooper.*

WHITTAKER [*the Englishman, coming in*]. *Bon soir, monsieur. Pouvons-nous entrer? Compris anglais?*

JOSEPH [*C., behind table*]. *Un peu*—a leetle. *Parlez doucement, s'il vous plaît.*

> [DAOUD *comes down L., opposite fire and stands looking at it.* MURDOCH *comes down L. also.*

WHITTAKER. Speak gently?

JOSEPH. Yes. My wife—— [*Points to room R.*]

WHITTAKER. She's asleep?

JOSEPH. *Non*—not asleep. *Malade.*

WHITTAKER. *Malade.* [*To the others*] His wife's ill.

> [DAOUD *crosses to fire, kneels down and warms hands. He pays no attention to their talk, which he does not understand.*

Je suis bien fâché. Très malade?

JOSEPH. *Elle vient de me donner un fils.*

WHITTAKER. What's that? Say it slowly.

JOSEPH. *Un fils. Un bébé.*

WHITTAKER. Oh—a baby!

MURDOCH [*the Australian*]. What's that? His wife just had a baby?

JOSEPH [*nodding*]. Yes, yes.

MURDOCH. Then he won't want to put us up for the night?

WHITTAKER. No, I suppose not.

JOSEPH. What is you want?

WHITTAKER. Well—*eh bien*— the fact is we've missed the road.

THE CHILD IN FLANDERS

JOSEPH [*puzzled*]. Road?

WHITTAKER. *Nous avons—perdu—la rue.*

JOSEPH. Ah——

WHITTAKER. *À Arras. Nous retournons tranchées—compris tranchées?—ne pouvons pas trouver la rue dans la nuit.*

MURDOCH. Tell him we can't find the way in the dark.

WHITTAKER. That's just what I've been telling him.

MURDOCH. Well, what does he say?

WHITTAKER. He hasn't said anything yet.

MURDOCH. Well, talk to him till he does. Ask him if he hasn't got a barn we can sleep in.

WHITTAKER. Blimy if I know what's the French for barn.

MURDOCH. Well, stable then.

WHITTAKER. *Pouvons-nous dormir—avec les chevaux?*

JOSEPH. *Je n'ai pas de chevaux, monsieur.*

WHITTAKER. He hasn't got any horses, so I suppose he hasn't got any stable.

JOSEPH. No—no stable. Only my small 'ouse.

MURDOCH. I suppose you couldn't let us sleep in your small house till five to-morrow morning?

JOSEPH [*puzzled*]. Five?

WHITTAKER. *A cinq heures demain.*

JOSEPH [*doubtfully*]. *Jusqu'à cinq heures demain matin?*

MURDOCH. It's snowing.

WHITTAKER. *Neige*, you know—*compris neige?* [*Points to* DAOUD, *the Indian, who is warming his hands at the fire.*] *Il est froid.*

JOSEPH. *J'crois bien, le pauvre garç . . . mais ma femme!*

MURDOCH. We'll lie on the floor and be as quiet as mice.

JOSEPH. *Qu'est-ce qu'il dit?*

WHITTAKER. *Il dit—nous serez tranquilles—comme petits souris.*

MURDOCH [*showing money*]. And we're quite willing to pay.

JOSEPH. *Non, non—c'est à cause de ma femme.*

MURDOCH. Well, perhaps we'd better try somewhere else. Ask him if he knows of anywhere ?

WHITTAKER. *Vous savez une autre maison ?*

JOSEPH. *Non*—my small 'ouse alone.

[*The soldiers look at each other disconsolately.*

MURDOCH [*going*]. Well, I suppose there's nothing for it.

WHITTAKER [*whistles*]. Come along, Johnny. [*To* DAOUD *who rises from fire.*]

JOSEPH. *Attendez.* Very quiet ?

WHITTAKER.⎫
MURDOCH. ⎬ Very.

JOSEPH. Not drink ?

MURDOCH. No chance of that, old son, unless you stand treat.

JOSEPH. *Hein ?*

WHITTAKER. *Non, non—pas de boire.* [*Shakes his head vigorously.*]

JOSEPH. *Eh bien, couchez-vous auprès du feu.*

WHITTAKER. Eh ?

JOSEPH. Sleep—by—fire.

MURDOCH. Thanks, mate—do the same for you if ever I get the chance. [*To* DAOUD] He says we can stay, Johnny. [*Crosses to R. near fire—above it.*]

DAOUD. That—is—good. [*He turns to fire again.*]

WHITTAKER. And don't you be afraid we shall disturb the missus. She shan't hear a sound. *Pas le plus petit bruit.* [*Moves to L.* JOSEPH *is still behind the table.*]

JOSEPH. *C'est bien.* [*He brings plates from cupboard, or side-table.*] Some bread—cheese. [*Points to pot on hearth.*] 'Ot water—for tea.

MURDOCH. Thanks, old son—and the compliments of the season.

JOSEPH. Season ?

WHITTAKER. *Compliments du saison*—Christmas. *Noel— compris Noel ?*

JOSEPH. *Oui, c'est la veille de Noel.* . . . Good night.

ALL. Good night.

> [*Exit* JOSEPH *into room* R. *The soldiers remove packs and group themselves round the fire, making tea. They can take time about removing packs and getting out mugs.* WHITTAKER *does not speak until he has put pack down* L. *and handed his mug to* MURDOCH (*who, with* DAOUD, *is watching the water boil*) *and sat down* R. *of table.* DAOUD *is squatting in front of fire, his back to the audience.*

WHITTAKER [*sitting* R. *of table*]. He's got more luck than some.

MURDOCH. Why ?

WHITTAKER. To have his kiddie. I've never seen mine.

MURDOCH. How old ?

WHITTAKER. Getting on for three months. Born the second of October. A girl. The missus is going to send me her photograph. She's called after me—I'm Henry and she's Henrietta. . . . Queer, never having seen your own kid. . . .

> [MURDOCH *leaves fire, goes to table above* WHITTAKER *and cuts bread.*

I sent her a present for her first Christmas—a woolly bonnet with satin strings. Pale blue and trimmed with lace. Bought it at Amiens. . . .

> [*He gazes at the fire ; then* DAOUD, *kneeling beside it, hands him a mug of tea.*

Thanks. . . . Have you got any children at home, Johnny ?

DAOUD. Yes.

> [DAOUD'S *eyes also turn to the fire and for a moment all*

*three are silent, lost in thought until door R. opens
and* JOSEPH GARNIER *comes in carrying his baby
swathed in a shawl.*

MURDOCH. Hullo, what have you got there?

WHITTAKER [*jumping up*]. The baby!

[*They crowd round* JOSEPH, *who looks proudly down at
his son.* WHITTAKER *is on his R., and* MURDOCH
is on his L.

JOSEPH. He come wish you good Christmas.

WHITTAKER. Same to him and many of 'em.

MURDOCH. A boy, eh?

JOSEPH [*nodding*]. *C'est un défenseur.*

MURDOCH. Eh?

JOSEPH. *Un défenseur de la patrie.*

MURDOCH. What's that?

WHITTAKER. Fine kid, I suppose. [*To* GARNIER] Oh yes,
a *défenseur*—one of the finest I've seen.

MURDOCH. He ought to be lucky, born at Christmas.

JOSEPH. Now you see him, I take him to his mother.

WHITTAKER. Wait a minute—must give the little chap
something for luck. [*Feels in pockets.*] Don't seem to
have nothing but my mouth-organ. [*Shows it to* GARNIER.]
Musique—pour bébé. [*He plays refrain of "Swannee River"
on the mouth-organ*—GARNIER *laughs.*] Look how he perks
up. He's a born musician, that's what he is.

MURDOCH. That's why he don't think much of it. He's
wrinkling up his forehead—frowning at you. Thinks he
could do better himself.

WHITTAKER. Garn, he likes it. Look at him wagging that
fist of his—he's trying to clap. . . . There you are, sonny—
for keeps. [*Gives mouth-organ.*]

MURDOCH. Here's my muffler. It's not as new as it was,
but it'll do to wrap him up in.

JOSEPH. *Merci, messieurs.*

WHITTAKER [*coming down to* DAOUD]. You got something, too ?

[DAOUD *nods, gets up and goes to* R. *of* JOSEPH, *and gives a coloured handkerchief—then bends over* BABY, *holding a finger to it.*

WHITTAKER [*peering over* DAOUD's *shoulder*]. Gor-blimy, if he ain't got hold of Johnny's finger—there's a grip for you !

JOSEPH [*going*]. When he big, I tell him.

WHITTAKER. Righto—good luck to him.

[*Exit* JOSEPH GARNIER *and the* BABY. DAOUD *lies down before the fire, making ready for the night.* WHITTAKER *crosses to* L., *moving below table,* MURDOCH *to* R. *moving above it ; then both stand thoughtful till* MURDOCH *begins to whistle absently* "*Good Christian Men, Rejoice.*"

WHITTAKER. They'll be singing that at home to-night.

MURDOCH [*slowly*]. . . . They—will.

WHITTAKER [*after a moment's silence—yawning and indicating* DAOUD *on the floor*]. Perhaps we'd better follow his example.

MURDOCH. Aye. Which plank have you got a fancy for ?

WHITTAKER. Think I shall try the chair for a change. [*Sits* L. *of table.*] Yes, this'll do me all right. . . . Done with the light ? [*Puts feet on table.*]

MURDOCH [*lies on floor, feet towards the fire, fidgets for a moment.—Then, when he has settled himself and laid head on pack*]. Yes.

[WHITTAKER *blows out candle ; room is lit only by red light from fire. There is a silence—then the sound of distant guns—two faint booms, one after the other. When the second has died away there is a soft chorus of angel voices.*

Cradle Song of " The Blessed Virgin."

1st Verse

The Virgin stills the crying
Of Jesus sleepless lying ;
And singing for His pleasure
Thus calls upon her Treasure,
My Darling, do not weep,
My Jesu, sleep.

[*As the chorus swells a little,* WHITTAKER *opens his eyes and moves.*

MURDOCH [*when the sound has died away—sleepily*]. Ain't your chair comfortable ?   Try the floor.

WHITTAKER. . . . I . . . thought I heard . . .

MURDOCH. What ?

WHITTAKER. Some one singing . . .

MURDOCH [*almost asleep*]. You're dreaming. . . .

WHITTAKER [*after listening a moment*]. . . . I suppose I was. . . .

[*There is no answer.   He puts his arms on the table, rests his head on them—sleeps.   Again guns—then, after a moment, the chorus is heard again.*

2nd Verse

O Lamb, my love inviting,
O Star, my soul delighting,
O Flower of mine own bearing,
O Jewel past comparing,
My Darling, do not weep,
My Jesu, sleep.

The curtain comes down on the three soldiers sleeping in the firelight.

THE CHILD IN FLANDERS

THE VISION

Gounod's " Ave Maria " is played twice—*once through before rise of curtain.*

Curtain to rise on opening bars of repeat.

Note. *The " Ave Maria " should be played only,* not *sung.*

There is a prie-dieu up R. C. and a cushion slightly down L. C.

If possible the lights should not be full up till Gabriel *enters, the stage growing brighter as he appears, darker as he goes.*

When the curtain rises the virgin *is bending over the prie-dieu, on which is an open book. She is reading the Scriptures and " pondering all these things in her heart." She turns over a page, looks out musingly, then back to book, then up as if in prayer—all very slowly and with hardly a movement—finally crosses thoughtfully, sits on cushion, takes up work and sews. By the last few bars of the " Ave Maria " she has ceased to sew; the work has dropped to her knees and she gazes dreamily before her.*

Change of music

Gabriel music (Welsh air, " David of the White Rock ") played three times *(orchestra).*

When the music changes to herald the coming of the angel *she turns and looks expectantly towards the back of the stage. When the curtains part and* Gabriel *enters she kneels.*

Gabriel *comes down stage R. and turns with his back to the audience.* mary, *always on her knees and in the same place, has turned towards him as he comes down; she is above him and therefore with her face to the audience.*

While Gabriel *lifts his hands in blessing the following words are chanted off the stage while the Gabriel music is twice repeated :*

" Hail, thou that art highly favoured, the Lord is with Thee; blessed art thou among women.

" Fear not, Mary; for thou hast found favour with God.

" And behold thou shalt conceive in thy womb and bring forth a son and shalt call his name Jesus.

" He shall be great and shall be called the Son of the Highest; and the Lord God shall give unto him the throne of his father David.

" And he shall reign over the house of Jacob for ever; and of his kingdom there shall be no end.

" The Holy Ghost shall come upon thee and the power of the Highest shall overshadow thee; therefore, also, that holy thing which shall be born of thee shall be called the Son of God."

Change of music

Solo off:

" Behold the handmaid of the Lord; be it unto me according to Thy Word."

THE CHILD IN FLANDERS

[GABRIEL *moves slowly to the curtains at the back of the stage, which part before him and fall behind him.*

Orchestra, for Gabriel's Exit.

Exit Gabriel.   On to Magnificat.

Change of music

Magnificat.   Full choir and orchestra.
The choir (unseen) sings exultantly :

" My soul doth magnify the Lord ; and my spirit hath rejoiced in God my Saviour.

" For he hath regarded the lowliness of his handmaiden.

" For behold from henceforth all generations shall call me blessed.

" For he that is mighty hath magnified me ; and holy is his Name.

" And his mercy is on them that fear him ; throughout all generations.

" He hath shewed strength with his arm ; he hath scattered the proud in the imagination of their hearts.

" He hath put down the mighty from their seat ; and hath exalted the humble and meek.

" He hath filled the hungry with good things ; and the rich he hath sent empty away."

[*During the above the* VIRGIN *has risen from her*

249

*knees; her face and gestures shew the ecstasy of
the words—which are her thoughts. During the
singing of the next (last) verse she goes back to the
prie-dieu.*

Diminuendo

" He remembering his mercy hath holpen his servant
Israel; as he promised to our forefathers, Abraham and
his seed, for ever."

*[And the curtain falls upon her musing over the book
as at the opening of the scene. Lights growing dim-
mer if possible. If not, Curtain before last notes.*

Change of music *for interval*

First two verses of carol, " The First Nowell."

Scene Two—The Shepherds (*Front Scene*)

The Scene should be as dark as possible. Blue footlights.

Change of music

Shepherd's music played four times (*orchestra only*).

THE CHILD IN FLANDERS

*Enter from L. *1ST SHEPHERD* on second bar of first repeat,
playing on a pipe. Comes to centre of stage, stops piping,
shivers and rubs his hands together—shades his hands and
looks off to R., then beckons to some one in the distance.
Sits on ground a little to L. of centre of stage.*

*Enter from R. *2ND SHEPHERD*. He blows on his fingers, beats
his hands on his sides, then sits (C.) beside the *1ST SHEP-
HERD*. The *1ST SHEPHERD* hands him a gourd—he drinks
from it and gives it back.*

*Enter from R. *3RD SHEPHERD*. He sits below *2ND SHEPHERD*
with his back to audience. Signs that he wants the gourd.
The *1ST SHEPHERD* hands it to him. He drinks until the
music stops, tipping back his head. The *1ST SHEPHERD*
holds out his hand, as if anxious to get the gourd back.*

*After the last note of the Pipe Music, the *3RD SHEPHERD*
hands back the gourd.*

Change of music

"Alleluia"—*choir*—twice. *First time ppp.—then
a little louder.*

*The *1ST SHEPHERD* has just taken the gourd when the Angel*

251

Choir is heard singing " Alleluia " very faintly and distantly. The SHEPHERDS *lift their heads and listen.*

As the " Alleluia " is repeated the SHEPHERDS *rise and look about them—bewildered and moving slowly. The* 3RD SHEPHERD *rises first and goes down to extreme R.—the* 2ND SHEPHERD *follows and stands near him ; the* 1ST *goes down to extreme L.*

Change of music

Gabriel, "David of the White Rock"—once (orchestra). GABRIEL *enters end of first bar.*

When the music announcing GABRIEL *is played they are all, with their backs to the audience, looking towards the curtains through which he is about to enter.*

The curtains part slightly to admit GABRIEL, *who stands in the centre of the stage with uplifted hand. The* 1ST *and* 3RD SHEPHERDS *fall on their knees ; the* 2ND SHEPHERD, *too bewildered to move, does not kneel till the words " Fear not."*

The following is chanted off the stage :

" Fear not ; for behold I bring you good tidings of great joy which shall be for all people.

" For unto you is born this day in the City of David a Saviour which is Christ the Lord.

" And this shall be a sign unto you ; Ye shall find the babe wrapped in swaddling clothes lying in a manger."

Coda of " David of the White Rock."

[GABRIEL *turns to the curtains, which draw back before him disclosing the first Manger Scene.*

THE CHILD IN FLANDERS

First Manger Scene (*Full Set*)

The lights are full up as curtain is drawn back.

The VIRGIN, *with the* CHILD *in her arms, is seated on a raised platform—a step or steps leading to it—at the back. On her L. and a little behind her is* ST JOSEPH, *looking down on the* CHILD. *On her R., below the platform, is an* ANGEL, *his hands joined in adoration. The* SHEPHERDS *remain kneeling, having been brought into the scene by the drawing back of the Curtain.*

Coda, " David of the White Rock."

GABRIEL *takes his place L. of the* VIRGIN, *opposite the other* ANGEL, *and stands in the same attitude of adoration.*

Change of music

Coventry Carol—choir—two verses—pp.
While " Lullay, thou little tiny child " (Coventry Carol—two verses) is being sung there is no movement on the stage.

Change of music

" Seven Joys of Mary " (full) (very cheerful).
While the choir (off) is singing " The Seven Joys of Mary " the movements on the stage are as follows :

The first good joy that Mary had
It was the joy of one,
To see the dear Lord Jesus Christ,
When He was first her son.
When He was first her son, good Lord,
And happy may we be.

GABRIEL *comes down to* 2ND SHEPHERD [*R.*].

2ND SHEPHERD *rises slowly—understands he is to approach the* CHILD—*moves towards Him with awkward reverence. Kneels on step.*

Praise Father, Son, and Holy
    Ghost
To all eternity.

The next good joy that Mary
    had
It was the joy of two,
To see her dear son, Jesus
    Christ,
Making the lame to go.
Making the lame to go, good
    Lord,
And happpy may we be.
Praise Father, Son, and Holy
    Ghost
To all eternity.

2ND SHEPHERD rises, looks round uncertainly, as if asking what next. GABRIEL *indicates platform ;* SHEPHERD *sits on it, at* JOSEPH's *feet,* GABRIEL *returning to his former place and position.*

The next good joy that Mary
    had
It was the joy of three,
To see her dear son, Jesus
    Christ,
Making the blind to see.
Making the blind to see, good
    Lord,
And happy may we be.
Praise Father, Son, and Holy
    Ghost
To all eternity.

2ND ANGEL *comes down to* 1ST SHEPHERD.

1ST SHEPHERD *rises. Approaches* VIRGIN *and kneels —looks in* CHILD's *face, then turns his head to smile at* 3RD SHEPHERD.

The next good joy that Mary
    had
It was the joy of four,

Looks back at CHILD— *then rises.* 2ND ANGEL *indicates platform ;* 1ST SHEP-

To see her dear son, Jesus
 Christ,
Reading the Bible o'er.
Reading the Bible o'er, good
 Lord,
And happy may we be.
Praise Father, Son, and Holy
 Ghost
To all eternity.

HERD *sits on it to R. of*
VIRGIN, *opposite* 2ND SHEP-
HERD. 2ND ANGEL *returns
to his first position.*

 GABRIEL *moves towards*
3RD SHEPHERD.

The next good joy that Mary
 had
It was the joy of five,
To see her dear son, Jesus
 Christ,
Making the dead to live.
Making the dead to live, good
 Lord,
And happy may we be.
Praise Father, Son, and Holy
 Ghost
To all eternity.

 3RD SHEPHERD *approaches,
bends over* CHILD, *as he
kneels, in a friendly familiar
fashion—then sits, back to
audience, just in front of
steps.* GABRIEL *returns to
first position.*

The next good joy that Mary
 had
It was the joy of six,
To see her dear son, Jesus
 Christ,
Upon the crucifix.
Upon the crucifix, good Lord,
And happy may we be.
Praise Father, Son, and Holy
 Ghost
To all eternity.

 *This must be sung with
great cheerfulness, so choir
must slur words !*
 *During this verse (which
is very loud and cheerful)*
3RD SHEPHERD *snaps his
fingers in time to the tune.*
1ST SHEPHERD, *on one knee,
is playing his pipe, and* 2ND
SHEPHERD *claps his hands—
as if to amuse the* BABE.

The next good joy that Mary
   had
It was the joy of seven,
To see her dear son, Jesus
   Christ,
Ascending into heaven.
Ascending into heaven, good
   Lord,
And happy may we be.
Praise Father, Son, and Holy
   Ghost
To all eternity.

SHEPHERDS *continue piping, clapping and snapping fingers till fall of curtain— while singing grows fainter. Lights down if possible—to blackness.*

Curtain before music has died away.

KINGS' SCENE (*Front Scene*)

Change of music

Choir for short interval—two verses of "First Nowell," beginning "And by the light of that same star," and "Then entered in those wise men three."

Change of music

King's music, "Solemn Melody" (Walford Davies).

Enter L. the 1ST KING, *a very old man, leaning on his little page—who carries casket. They cross the stage slowly, halting for a moment in the centre and then moving on to extreme R. and standing there.*

Enter L. the 2ND KING—*the Warrior, the man in the prime of life (Eastern, dark-skinned). He goes towards the* OLD KING *and the two (when* 2ND KING *has halted) salute each other by raising their right arms slowly till they are straight above their heads. They drop them slowly; then*

THE CHILD IN FLANDERS

2ND KING *moves to extreme L. of stage and stands with arms folded.*

Enter L. the 3RD KING—*the youth. He crosses first to* OLD KING *and they salute each other—as before. Then turns to* 2ND KING—*they also salute.* 3RD KING *then moves towards* 2ND KING *and stands near him. They remain motionless to the end of their music and also while the following solo is chanted off :*

Change of music

Solo (male voice), " Where is He born."
    " Where is He born, the King of the Jews ; for we have seen His star in the East and are come to worship Him."

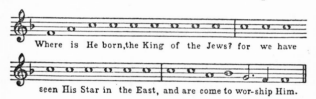

Change of music

"Alleluia," choir (once only).
The Angel Choir sings "Alleluia," and the KINGS *raise their heads to listen.*

Change of music

" David of the White Rock," orchestra—once.

When the Gabriel music begins all turn towards the curtains, awaiting him. As the curtains part and GABRIEL *enters the three* KINGS *sink on their knees. The* BOY *remains standing for a moment, gazing at* GABRIEL *; then realizing that the others are kneeling, he also falls on his knees.*

257

The following words are chanted off :

" I am Gabriel that stands in the presence of God ; and am sent to speak unto ye, and to show ye these glad tidings."

Coda, " David of the White Rock."

> [GABRIEL *turns to curtains, which part before him, showing second Manger Scene.*

SECOND MANGER SCENE (*Full Set*)

Lights full up.

The VIRGIN *and* ST JOSEPH *as before—on platform, with* 2ND SHEPHERD *sitting at* ST JOSEPH'S *feet and* 1ST *and* 3RD SHEPHERDS *sitting on* VIRGIN'S *right—all on platform.* 2ND ANGEL *in same position and attitude.*

Coda, " David of the White Rock."

GABRIEL *goes up and stands opposite* 2ND ANGEL.—*as before.*

Change of music

" Sleep, Holy Babe," choir—one verse.
During the singing of " Sleep, Holy Babe," no one on the stage moves.

Change of music

" O come, all ye faithful." Sung by choir and orchestra.
During " O come, all ye faithful," the action is as follows :

O come, all ye faithful,	GABRIEL *comes down to-*
Joyful and triumphant,	*wards* OLD KING, *who rises*
O come ye, O come ye to	*and totters slowly to steps*
Bethlehem ;	*—leaning on* BOY. *Kneels,*
Come and behold Him	*bows head, then takes cas-*
Born the King of Angels ;	*ket from* BOY — *standing*

258

O come let us adore Him,
O come let us adore Him,
O come let us adore Him,
Christ the Lord.

REPEAT from " Come and behold Him."

(*Note for conductor.* This verse may have to be taken slowly—at any rate the repeat —to time it with the movements of a very old man.)

God of God,
Light of Light,
Lo, He abhors not the Virgin's
  womb ;
Very God,
Begotten, not created ;
O come let us adore Him, etc.

REPEAT from " Very God," etc.

Choir and orchestra.
Sing, choirs of angels,
Sing in exultation,

beside him—lays it on step. Raises hands in adoration.

At repeat rises, moves backward, leaning on BOY, *to original place (down* R.). *Kneels.* BOY *stands, watching the others with interest.*
(*Note. When* OLD KING *reaches steps,* GABRIEL *returns to his place.*)

2ND ANGEL *comes down to* 2ND KING, *who rises, follows him to* C., *makes deep reverence, goes to steps, kneels, offers casket, holding it high above head before placing on step.* 2ND ANGEL *goes back to place.* KING *kneels till end of verse.*

2ND KING *rises, backs, stops for deep reverence— more than one if needed to fill out music—kneels in former place.*

2ND ANGEL *comes down to* 3RD KING. *As he does so,* GABRIEL *crosses over and takes place* 2ND ANGEL *has*

Sing, all ye citizens of heaven
    above ;
Glory to God
In the highest ;
O come let us adore Him, etc.

left. As YOUNG KING *goes up to steps* 2ND ANGEL *takes place* GABRIEL *has left.* YOUNG KING *offers his crown, holding it above his head as he kneels.*

REPEAT from " Glory to God," etc.

Rises and returns on repeat. Kneels.

FOURTH VERSE : Melody on orchestra only. No choir. No REPEAT. Played quietly but with dignity.

GABRIEL *comes forward (from* R.), *holding the Australian's muffler. Offers it to* BABE, *the* VIRGIN *smiling as he places it round Him. Goes back to his first place, L. of platform (by* 2ND ANGEL).

FIFTH VERSE : Melody on orchestra only. No choir.

During the last half slower and softer—at the end, when the ANGEL is playing, very soft ; the idea being that the hosts of heaven cease their harping, that the Lord may hear the soldier's mouth-organ.

2ND ANGEL *comes forward (from* L.) *and offers Indian's handkerchief. Same business. Then mounts platform,* R. *of* VIRGIN—(*Note.* SHEPHERDS *must make room for him)—and over her shoulder holds out mouth-organ showing it to* BABE. *At last line of melody (" Christ the Lord ") has mouth-organ at his lips, bending over and playing it.*

THE CHILD IN FLANDERS

VIRGIN *rises—the muffler and handkerchief still wrapped round the* CHILD *as she holds Him for adoration.* BOY *and* SHEPHERDS *also kneel.* JOSEPH *comes down below platform, stands with hands lifted towards* BABE. 2ND ANGEL *comes down from platform, stands opposite* GABRIEL. *All except* JOSEPH *have their hands joined in gesture of adoration.*

REPEAT. " Glory to God
   In the highest,
   O come let us adore
   Him," etc.
 Full choir and orchestra fff.

Yea, Lord we greet Thee,
Born this happy morning ;
Sing, all ye citizens of heaven
 above.
Word of the Father,
Now in flesh appearing ;
O come let us adore Him,
O come let us adore Him,
O come let us adore Him,
Christ the Lord.

No movement during this verse—which begins loud and dies gradually away. If possible, light should grow fainter with the music, finishing in complete darkness as the vision fades. The curtain should come down slowly before the end of the verse.

When the music has quite died away guns are heard faintly in the distance.

CURTAIN

THE EPILOGUE

Music for interval must end with " Trail that leads to Home,"
just as in overture. Curtain rising on Epilogue on last bars
of repeat.

When the curtain rises, the room is in darkness except for
faint glow from fire by which the soldiers are seen lying
asleep—as when curtain fell on Prologue. When music
has died away, there is a distant gun ; then enter JOSEPH
GARNIER *from R.*

JOSEPH [*going to* WHITTAKER]. *Allons—cinq heures.* [*Shakes*
him. WHITTAKER *awakes with a start and stares about him as*
if dazed.]

WHITTAKER. Eh—what is it ?

JOSEPH. *Cinq heures—temps de partir.* [*He strikes match*
and lights candle on table.]

WHITTAKER [*stares a moment at light, then starts up*]. Here,
you two—get up. [*He shakes and rouses the others.*]

MURDOCH [*staring about him as* WHITTAKER *did before*]. Eh
—what ?

WHITTAKER. It's just on five—get a move on.

MURDOCH [*absently*]. Just on five. . . .

[*While* WHITTAKER *wakes the others,* JOSEPH *puts bread,*
etc., in cupboard.

WHITTAKER. Yes, wake up. [*To* DAOUD] You too,
Johnny—show a leg.

MURDOCH [*rousing himself; to* JOSEPH]. Which way—
Arras ?

WHITTAKER. *Route Arras—compris?*

JOSEPH. *Je vous mettrai sur la route.*

MURDOCH. Eh ?

WHITTAKER. Says he'll put us on the road. *Merci,*
monsieur.

MURDOCH. *Oui, merci beaucoup.*

JOSEPH. *Je vais allumer ma lanterne.*

WHITTAKER. He's going to fetch his lantern. [*As* JOSEPH *is going R.*] Here—*ils sont bon ?*

JOSEPH [*puzzled*]. *Plaît-il ?*

WHITTAKER. *Petit enfant—bébé—sont bon ?*

JOSEPH. *Ah, oui, oui—il va très bien. Lui et sa mère, ils ont passé une bonne nuit.*

WHITTAKER. *C'est une bonne chose.*

JOSEPH. *Je reviendrai tout à l'heure.* [*Exit* JOSEPH *R.*

MURDOCH. What does he say ?

WHITTAKER. He's coming back directly with the lantern—and he says the kid and the missus are doing fine.

MURDOCH. I'm glad of that. . . . Sleep well, Johnny ?

DAOUD. Very well. . . . I have good dream.

MURDOCH. Did you ? . . . So did I.

DAOUD. Very—good—dream.

WHITTAKER. . . . So did I.

[*They make ready to start—silent and thoughtful.*

[*The Angel Chorus is heard very softly, like an echo.*

Music—Choir

Cradle Song of " The Blessed Virgin "—one verse—ppp.

[*The soldiers do not listen or appear to hear it—but one by one they cease to move—remaining silent and dreaming till after music ends. First* DAOUD—*kneeling, adjusting puttee. By end of first two lines he is motionless, gazing dreamily before him. Next* WHITTAKER, *who is fastening boot, with foot on chair L. of table. Then* MURDOCH, *who, having hoisted on his pack, also stands motionless, R. of chair R. of table. He does not speak till well after the music has died away.*

263

MURDOCH. Queer. . . .

WHITTAKER. What?

MURDOCH. That we should have given the kid those presents.

WHITTAKER [*suddenly interested*]. What makes you say it's queer?

MURDOCH [*awkwardly*]. Oh . . . I don't know. [*He turns away and begins to whistle—unconsciously—" Oh come, all ye faithful."*]

[DAOUD *hearing the tune turns and listens intently.*

WHITTAKER [*notices* DAOUD'S *intentness—recognizes tune in his turn*]. Where did you get that tune from?

MURDOCH [*taken aback*]. That tune . . . [*hesitates*]. Oh, I must have heard it at Christmas, some time. . . . It's a Christmas tune.

WHITTAKER. Yes . . . it's a Christmas tune. . . .

MURDOCH. . . . I . . . seem to have been dreaming about it.

WHITTAKER. . . . Have you?

[*There is a little silence. They look at each other questioningly. Then enter* JOSEPH, *with lantern.*

JOSEPH. *Allons—je vais vous accompagner jusqu'à la grande route.*

MURDOCH [*signing towards bedroom*]. Ask him if he's sure it's all right to leave 'em. I shouldn't like——

JOSEPH [*understanding*]. Yes, all right. They sleep—see.

[*He stands beside door R., looking into inner room, and signs to the three soldiers to approach.*

La mère et le fils—mother and child.

[*He looks proudly through doorway while the soldiers come near him, one by one.* MURDOCH *goes first; as he stands by* JOSEPH, *looking through doorway, his face changes, he takes off his hat slowly, then creeps on tiptoe to door L., waits there.* DAOUD *follows—same business, but instead of removing hat he salutes reverently ; follows* MURDOCH. *When* WHITTAKER'S *turn comes, he has just lit cigarette at candle on table. As* WHITTAKER *puts down candle after lighting cigarette he blows it out. The action will not be noticed and can be done back to audience. It is important as otherwise the lighted candle will spoil the effect of the darkened room at the end. He goes up indifferently to look in his turn ; then, as light from doorway falls on his face, slowly removes cigarette, slowly takes off hat— stands gazing through door—then]*

WHITTAKER [*turning—huskily*]. Come along, boys.

[*All four go out,* JOSEPH *carrying lantern. With removal of lantern the stage is dark except for a stream of light from the open door R.*

[*Two distant guns are heard. Then, very faintly, the Angel Choir sings "Alleluia."*

Music

Choir, "Alleluia." Once, pp.

[*When it has died away, men's voices sing the chorus of " The Trail that leads to Home," growing fainter with the distance.*

[*Chorus, "The Trail that leads to Home" (male voices), once, beginning p. and diminuendo.*

[*As their voices die away with the last notes, the curtain comes down.*

SEQUENCE OF MUSICAL NUMBERS

OVERTURE :
O Little Town of Bethlehem
Solemn Melody
The Trail that leads to Home

PROLOGUE :
Cradle Song of "The Blessed Virgin"

TABLEAU 1 :
Ave Maria
David of the White Rock
Behold the Handmaid (in text)
Magnificat

TABLEAU 2 :
The First Nowell
Shepherd's Pipe (in text)
Alleluia (in text)
David of the White Rock

TABLEAU 3 :
David of the White Rock—coda
Coventry Carol
Seven Joys of Mary

TABLEAU 4 :
Solemn Melody
Recitative (in text)
Alleluia (in text)
David of the White Rock

TABLEAU 5 :
David of the White Rock—coda
Sleep, Holy Babe
O come, all ye faithful

EPILOGUE :
The Trail that leads to Home
Cradle Song of "The Blessed Virgin"
Alleluia (in text)
The Trail that leads to Home

MUSIC REQUIRED FOR "THE CHILD IN FLANDERS"

1. Carol, *O Little Town of Bethlehem*, Walford Davies. Novello.

2. *Solemn Melody*, Walford Davies. Novello.

3. Song, *The Trail that leads to Home*, Mackenzie. West and Co.

4. *Cradle Song of "The Blessed Virgin."* Novello's Christmas Carols, No. 33

5. Gounod's *Ave Maria* (*Méditation sur le premier Prélude de J. S. Bach*). Schott and Co.

6. *David of the White Rock* (Welsh air). Novello.

7. *Magnificat in F*, Rathbone (omitting Doxology). Novello.

8. *The First Nowell.* Novello's Christmas Carols, No. 6.

9. *Coventry Carol.* Novello's Christmas Carols, No. 6.

10. *The Seven Joys of Mary.* Novello's Christmas Carols, No. 12

11. *Sleep, Holy Babe.* Novello's Christmas Carols, No. 9.

12. Hymn, *O come, all ye faithful.*

EXERCISES

RIDERS TO THE SEA

1. Explain the difference between (*a*) the theme, (*b*) the story, of this play.

2. Suggest any poems, novels, or pictures which deal with the same theme.

3. Compare the philosophy (or attitude to life) of Maurya with that of Mary Stewart in " Campbell of Kilmhor." (The final speeches should be studied with particular care.)

4. What is the outstanding difference between a great tragedy and a Grand Guignol horror ?

5. Say why " Riders to the Sea " is considered great and not merely clever.

6. Mr Frank Vernon asserts that " Riders to the Sea " is a local play which is universal. Discuss the significance of this remark.

7. Read Synge's other plays.

WATERLOO

1. Suggest why modern dramatists usually avoid soliloquy. When do you think it may be permissible ?

2. Rewrite the opening scene of " Waterloo " in the form of a dialogue between Norah and Sergeant McDonald.

3. What are the main ideas that obsess the mind of Corporal Brewster ? What is the dramatist's reason for making the old man repeat himself so often ?

4. Say whether you consider this play to be comedy or tragedy. Give reasons for your opinion.

5. Study the description of the death of Colonel Newcome

269

in *The Newcomes*, by Thackeray, or of Ase, in *Peer Gynt*, by Ibsen.

6. Read "The Great Shadow" by Sir Arthur Conan Doyle, and the Waterloo chapters of *Les Misérables* (Victor Hugo).

IT'S THE POOR THAT 'ELPS THE POOR

1. Summarize the story as briefly as possible.

2. Describe the characteristics of the women in this play.

3. Why has Harold Chapin introduced over a dozen characters in this one-act play? By what means has he made each one stand out distinctly? By what devices has he made the principal figures most emphatic?

4. Do you consider that humour contributes to or detracts from the sense of tragedy? Compare this play with the two which precede it.

5. Write a description of the room as a novelist would probably do it.

6. What is irony? Give examples from any books or plays you know.

7. Mention any other plays which have ironical titles.

A MARRIAGE HAS BEEN ARRANGED

1. In this play there are two characters only, whereas in the preceding one there are thirteen. Make any intelligent comment on this fact.

2. There is no description of the characters in this play. Describe them as you imagine them from their conversation.

3. Contrast this play with " It's the Poor that 'Elps the Poor."

4. Why did Lady Aline accept Crockstead's final offer of marriage? Did this ending come as a surprise or were you prepared for it?

5. Discuss the effect of waltz-music throughout the conversation and explain the dramatic significance of the change to " God Save the King " at the end.

6. Write an essay on either (*a*) " The Importance of being Candid," or (*b*) " Irony in Comedy and in Tragedy."

EXERCISES

LONESOME-LIKE

1. What feeling is conjured up by the title of this play? Can it be paraphrased without losing its effect?

2. Give an account of the character of Sam Horrocks, and compare him with any other character in fiction of whom he may remind you.

3. What is Mr Brighouse's purpose in introducing the curate?

4. What sidelights does "Lonesome-like" throw on the life of the working classes in Lancashire?

5. "A Marriage has been Arranged" deals with Society people, and "Lonesome-like" deals with the mill-hands of Lancashire. Show how the dramatists discover the same fundamentals in the two classes.

6. Write an article on "Strong-minded Women" suitable for a woman's magazine.

7. Discuss the appropriateness of the concluding scene.

THE RISING OF THE MOON

1. What is (*a*) the moment of highest comedy, (*b*) the moment of greatest suspense, in this play? Which do you think the dramatist conceived first?

2. Why does the Sergeant forfeit the reward and neglect his duty? Imagine that he argues the matter over with himself afterward, and say what he would be likely to bring forward in self-defence.

3. Compare this play with "Riders to the Sea" (*a*) in the language spoken by the characters, (*b*) in the action.

4. It has been said of Lady Gregory: "Her craftsmanship is delectable; it is almost too trustworthy." Can you illustrate the meaning of this remark from "The Rising of the Moon"?

5. What is there in this comedy which strikes you as distinctively Irish?

6. Draw a silhouette of the scene where the Sergeant and the Ragged Man sit on the barrel.

THE KING'S WAISTCOAT

1. Describe the character of Lord Francis Webling as it is revealed during the course of the play.

2. Contrast Felicity with Lady Susan Harcourt.

3. What words or incidents of the play remind you that it deals with the seventeenth century?

4. Make any intelligent comment on the final scene.

5. Do you consider that Miss Olive Conway has been just to the two types—Royalist and Puritan? Or do her sympathies tend to favour one party at the expense of the other?

6. Read *Woodstock*, *Peveril of the Peak*, and any other books which describe Stuart and Cromwellian times.

THE DEAR DEPARTED

1. What, in your opinion, is the supreme moment of this play? What circumstances prepared the way for the 'surprise,' and for what reason is the interest still maintained?

2. Say whether the omission of Victoria would strengthen or weaken the story.

3. Compare this Lancashire comedy with "Lonesome-like." What quality appears in the latter which is missing in the former?

4. Do you consider that Stanley Houghton thinks primarily of plot or of human character? Apply the same test to the authors of "Waterloo," "The Rising of the Moon," "Riders to the Sea," and "Lonesome-like."

5. Read "Master of the House," by Stanley Houghton, and show how one play is almost a converse of the other.

6. Draw up a cast of living actors and actresses whom you would like to see perform this play, or, if this is too difficult, suggest a cast from your own form or class.